Mormons, Musical Theater, and Belonging in America

MUSIC IN AMERICAN LIFE

A list of books in the series appears at the end of this book.

Mormons, Musical Theater, and Belonging in America

JAKE JOHNSON

UNIVERSITY OF
ILLINOIS PRESS
Urbana, Chicago, and Springfield

Publication of this book was supported by a grant from the AMS 75 PAYS Endowment of the American Musicological Society, funded in part by the National Endowment for the Humanities and the Andrew W. Mellon Foundation.

Saturday's Warrior
Book and Lyrics by Doug Stewart
Music and Arrangements by Lex De Azevedo
© 1974 by Doug Stewart and Lex De Azevedo
Used by permission

Life More Sweet than Bitter
Book and Lyrics by Pat Davis
Music and Arrangements by K. Newell Dayley
Suggested by Maurice Warshaw's Autobiography "Life—More Sweet Than Bitter"
© 1977 by Pat Davis and K. Newell Dayley
Used by permission

All published rehearsal materials and live and other performance rights to the above listed musicals are licensed through:
Zion Theatricals
P.O. Box 536
Newport, ME 04953
801–550–7741
www.ziontheatricals.com
editor@ziontheatricals.com

Promised Valley
Book and Lyrics by Arnold Sundgaard
Music and Arrangements by Crawford Gates
www.crawfordgates.com
Used by permission.

Portions of chapter 6 and epilogue were previously published in "Mormons, Musical Theater, and the Public Arena of Doubt," *Dialogue: A Journal of Mormon Thought* 48, no. 2 (Winter 2015).

© 2019 by the Board of Trustees
of the University of Illinois
All rights reserved
1 2 3 4 5 C P 5 4 3 2 1
♾ This book is printed on acid-free paper.
Printed and bound in Great Britain by
Marston Book Services Ltd, Oxfordshire

Library of Congress Cataloging-in-Publication Data
Names: Johnson, Jake, 1984– author.
Title: Mormons, musical theater, and belonging in America / Jake Johnson.
Description: Urbana: University of Illinois Press, [2019] | Series: Music in American life | Includes bibliographical references and index.
Identifiers: LCCN 2018059624 (print) | LCCN 2019004868 (ebook) | ISBN 9780252051364 (ebook) | ISBN 9780252042515 | ISBN 9780252042515 (cloth : alk. paper) | ISBN 9780252084331 (pbk. :alk. paper)
Subjects: LCSH: Musicals—United States—History and criticism. | Mormons—United States—History. | Musicals—Religious aspects—Mormon Church.
Classification: LCC ML2054 (ebook) | LCC ML2054 .J65 2019 (print) | DDC 782.1/40882893—dc23
LC record available at https://lccn.loc.gov/2018059624

For BrieAnn

Contents

Acknowledgments   ix

Prologue   1

Introduction: Vicarious Voices   9

1   "Come, Listen to a Prophet's Voice, and Hear the Word of God":
The Voice and Mormon Theatricality   32

2   *Promised Valley*, Integration, and the Singing Voice   55

3   Exoticized Voices, Racialized Bodies:
Lineage and Whiteness on Stage   83

4   "I've Heard That Voice Before": Reprising the Voice
in Sacred Time   113

5   Voice Interrupted: *Book of Mormon* and the Failed Message
of Correlated Mormonism   142

Epilogue   169

Notes   171

Bibliography   187

Index   195

Acknowledgments

The acknowledgements page admits that a single book speaks on behalf of many, many people. Much of this research was funded by a Mellon Fellowship of Distinction at UCLA and research and travel grants by UCLA's Herb Alpert School of Music. I owe an enormous debt of gratitude to the staff in UCLA's Musicology Department, especially Barbara Van Nostrand, Jessica Gonzalez, and Michele Yamamoto, for helping keep track of all the bureaucratic particulars during my time as a graduate student. This project also took shape at conferences supported in part by Oklahoma City University's Faculty Scholarship Committee and the Lowell Milken Fund for American Jewish Music. For their help in keeping me organized and my research trips expedient, I want to extend a big thanks to the staff at the Library of Congress, at BYU's L. Tom Perry Special Collections, and at the Church History Archives in Salt Lake City.

It is for me a great honor to have my work associated with the Music in American Life series at the University of Illinois Press. Laurie Matheson was a keen supporter of this project from its inception and a voice of encouragement and patience throughout. She also found excellent reviewers and readers at crucial moments of the manuscript's development. Michael Hicks at Brigham Young University gave sensible advice for this project when I wanted to hear it the least—and gave validation and suggestions for improving this manuscript when I needed to hear it the most. Other anonymous reviewers over the years helped me refine the scope of my argument and directed my attention to avenues I had not considered before. This work bears their fingerprints and is all the better for them.

I was fortunate to have many opportunities to share parts of this research as the project unfolded. Members of the Musical Theatre Forum provided

X · ACKNOWLEDGMENTS

encouragement and validation for the project at a crucial stage in its development. For their input then and now, I want to thank Raymond Knapp, Jeff Magee, Carol Oja, Arianne Johnson Quinn, David Savran, Jessica Sternfeld, Dominic Symonds, Stacy Wolf, and Elizabeth Wollman. As this work was presented in various formats and during several conferences, I was lucky to have many excellent interlocutors. They are too many to name here, but I want especially to acknowledge help from Sam Baltimore, Judah Cohen, Elizabeth Titrington Craft, Zev Feldman, Bryan Gilliam, Daniel Goldmark, Lily Hirsch, Josh Kun, Peter McMurray, Tiffany Naiman, Arreanna Rostosky, Mark Slobin, Holley Replogle-Wong, Morgan Woolsey, and Schuyler Whelden.

In one of the more fortuitous opportunities of my career, I was able to receive doctoral training with faculty at both the University of Chicago and the University of California, Los Angeles. At Chicago I want to thank Phil Bohlman, Berthold Hoeckner, and Larry Zbikowski for their guidance and friendship over the years. At UCLA, this project quickly gained ground and would not have been possible without the generosity and encouragement of my faculty mentors Nina Sun Eidsheim, Bob Fink, Mark Kligman, Mitchell Morris, Shana Redmond, and Jessica Schwartz, as well as the many Westwood conversations with my dear cohort members Patrick Bonczyk, Pheaross Graham, Kacie Morgan, and Helen Rowe. Fiona Givens affirmed the necessity of this project when I was still unsure, and Patrick Q. Mason willingly and enthusiastically brought a unique and necessary perspective to this project. I thank him for his patience and understanding as I sorted through Mormon history and practice. Of course, I could not have picked a better human and scholar to guide this project than Raymond Knapp. His benevolent scholarly shadow will cast itself broadly over my life, though not as widely as will his kind spirit.

Living a life of music and writing about religion can both be fraught endeavors, and my family deserves far more than just recognition for supporting me through all the ups and downs. Our first piano was a loaner from my grandmother, and it's where I started first exploring music. My parents, Vaughn and Tracey Johnson, and my brother, Parker Johnson, patiently plugged their ears and turned on captions for television programs while I nurtured a someday career at that piano. They also saw me through religious transitions and fiercely backed my decisions even when they might not have understood them. I hope this book bears fruit for their patience with my leading a restless life.

Finally, I want to thank my daughters Cora and Magnolia for their insistence that no amount of work is worth sacrificing our time together, and my wife BrieAnn Lund Johnson, who has traversed great distances and ideologies with me for a long, long time. This one's for you.

Mormons,
Musical Theater,
and
Belonging in America

Prologue

Whenever people found out I was writing a book on Mormons and musicals, the typical response was a skeptical, "Well, I know *one*." To be fair, the Broadway hit *Book of Mormon* is nearly unavoidable and has really upped the ante in terms of Mormon representation in popular culture. Creators Trey Parker and Matt Stone brought a queer version of Mormonism to the stage in 2011 and largely, I think, showed Mormons a version of themselves they found unbelievable yet showed non-Mormons a version of Mormonism that instinctively felt true and real. Where you fall within these two camps probably has less to do with the kind of Mormon history you know and more to do with how much you are aware of just how entwined Mormon ideologies and musical theater really are. Mormons and musicals (and Mormons *as* musicals) just seem to make sense together. For better or worse, the Broadway version of Mormonism is sticking well. I'll let you guess what comes up first when you Google the words "Book of Mormon."

In truth, though, the hit musical overshadows the fact that real Mormons actually have a lot to do with musicals, and musicals with Mormons—from the classic film musical *Saturday's Warrior* to the evening performances at the Church-owned Polynesian Cultural Center to the enormous outdoor music drama at the Hill Cumorah Pageant, Mormons rely on musical theater's aesthetic not only for wholesome entertainment but also for theological reasons. *Book of Mormon* may have brought Mormonism into a heightened discussion in the new millennium, but Mormonism has had a long relationship with musical theater, and audiences have long perceived a relationship between the conventions of the musical stage and the manner in which Mormons conduct themselves.

2 · PROLOGUE

My interest in Mormons and musicals was born of my conversion to Mormonism on the day after my nineteenth birthday. Mormonism was not completely new to me, even at that age; I was raised within a more progressive faction of Mormonism's Restoration movement, a church known at the time as the Reorganized Church of Jesus Christ of Latter Day Saints (or RLDS, now Community of Christ), so many of the distinguishing aspects of Mormon doctrine were familiar to me. In quick order, my wife and I were immersed within Mormon culture—the casseroled meals, ironed white shirts and tie, youth dances, temple trips, and, of course, musical dramas. While all new and peculiar experiences for me, the latter I was the least prepared to understand. My RLDS church congregation had no strong cultural ties with theater, which perhaps made my introduction to Mormon musical theater practices that much more of a shock. I started taking note of how often musical dramas took place at Mormon events and soon saw musical theater happening not just overtly (as in road shows or discussions of *Saturday's Warrior* from the pulpit [see chapter 4]), but also in ways less noticeable yet fundamental to how Mormons think, organize themselves, and even sound.

I eventually left Mormonism but, as the saying goes, Mormonism has not left me. Even positioned on the outside of the faith—and maybe precisely because of my fringe status—I continued my fascination with the religion and its practices and found ways to appreciate Mormon culture and history as an outsider looking in. Slowly, pockets of ideas that would ultimately be sewn together in this book started forming. While this book is not an ethnography in any technical or even methodological sense, I did approach the topic and my Mormon subjects as an ethnographic endeavor. Many ideas fleshed out in these pages have been sourced over several years from conversations with countless individuals associated with Mormonism to one degree or another, often in casual or informal settings like between church services, during dinners, or on car rides.

I hope to honor those contributions, even as I undoubtedly will raise flags of suspicion for some as a potentially anti-Mormon voice. My intentions are only to understand Mormonism better through the prism of musical theater, though I anticipate pushback with some of the conclusions I draw in this book about that relationship. Mormons are very proud of the place their religion holds in American history, and much of that hubris is in no small way connected to their perceived victimhood in that history. Theirs is a narrative of beating herculean odds in the race to leave, and then successfully rejoin, American society. To shine a light on dark corners of that narrative is not always a welcome gesture, particularly for an organization that firmly maintains its version of that history (see chapters 4 and 5).

The larger story of Mormonism that I prefer, however, is not unidirectional or predictable, and its followers have not always been members of a religion bound to tradition or political conservatism. Many tenets of today's progressive wing of American politics were embroiled within Mormon ideology as early as 1830, including a proto-socialist economy, a female deity, a plant-based health code, and an acceptance (even promotion) of non-normative family units. In my journey in, through, and out of Mormonism, I have grown to appreciate the radical concepts that once animated Church leaders even as Mormonism's most radical branches have today been cut down considerably. I also have come to accept that Mormonism is not alone in representing how strong the pull of conservatism can be, even on the most brazenly individualistic value systems. As a musicologist, I take note of how deeply enmeshed within that value system is the role of voice in the developing Mormon theological worldview. And it begins, as does this story, with the vocal performances of Mormonism's founder, Joseph Smith.[1]

Sounding a New World

In 1838 Joseph led a small group of Mormon men on an exploration of Daviess County, Missouri. The county had been renamed only two years before in honor of Major Joseph Hamilton Daveiss, who was killed in 1811 at the Battle of Tippecanoe. Daveiss had unsuccessfully prosecuted vice president Aaron Burr, though his military honors carried his namesake into a legacy with an unfortunate (and apparently systemic) typographical error. Three other American counties were named after Daveiss—in Indiana, Illinois, and his home state of Kentucky—yet all three are misspelled. Daviess County, Missouri, however, was the youngest of these frontier spaces; in the early nineteenth century, western Missouri marked the figurative end of modern civilization and the beginning of a seemingly endless stretch of wilderness, Indian settlements, and untapped potential.

The ferry guiding Joseph and his companions up the Grand River docked on the bank. Someone from the party noticed atop a high bluff what appeared to be rocky ruins, perhaps of an ancient altar, and directed Joseph toward it. This moment of contact with a presumed ancient relic brought the surrounding wilds into focus, like Wallace Stevens's anecdotal jar on the hill. With a broad glance over the unceasing prairie before him, and preceded by a dramatic silence, Joseph sounded a magisterial transformation of the ordinary into the sacred: "This is the valley of God in which Adam blessed his children, and upon this very altar Adam himself offered up sacrifices to Jehovah," he pronounced. "We will lay out a city which shall be called

Adam-ondi-Ahman. Here Adam, the Ancient of Days, shall come to visit his people."[2] Brigham Young, who would succeed Joseph as the second president and prophet of the Mormons—or Saints, as they called themselves—later recounted Joseph's revelation that

> the garden of Eden was in Jackson Co Missouri, & when Adam was driven out of the garden of Eden He went about 40 miles to the Place which we Named Adam Ondi Ahman, & there built an Altar of Stone & offered Sacrifize. That Altar remains to this day. I saw it as Adam left it as did many others, & through all the revolutions of the world that Altar had not been disturbed.[3]

Other witnesses add that "about half a mile or between a quarter and a half of a mile" away from that spot, the party discovered a slightly elevated knoll "which was thickly dotted with cobble stones." As Oliver B. Huntington recorded his secondhand account in 1895, "'Here,' the Prophet and Seer said, 'Adam built a tower, from the top of which he could see all the surrounding country, and this knoll is formed of its remains.'" Huntington continues with this testimony: "I want my friends, and in fact all people, to understand that Joseph Smith could see events that transpired and people who lived hundreds or thousands of years ago as if they were then before his eyes."[4]

What Joseph *saw* that afternoon was less transformative than what he *spoke*. Joseph's pronouncement modulated the mundane prairie surrounding him and his followers into a mythical and sacred landscape. In his discourse, he effectively rewrote the first seven chapters of the book of Genesis and placed the American continent as central to the foundations of humanity. Joseph's friend and prophetic successor Brigham Young most explicitly connected the dots of Joseph's declaration with its current geopolitical identity: "In the beginning, after this earth was prepared for man, the Lord commenced his work upon what is now called the American continent, where the Garden of Eden was made. In the days of Noah, in the days of the Boating of the ark, he took the people to another part of the earth. . . . There the human race, in its second start on earth," Young concludes, "began to multiply and fill the earth."[5]

A North American Eden had been a well-trodden topic dating back to the earliest Puritan settlers, but largely figuratively so. By the nineteenth century, matters had become much more explicit. Many of Joseph's literary contemporaries, including Nathaniel Hawthorne and Herman Melville, found within Adam a purity and fierce independence, fitting qualities of a new American hero. Twentieth-century observations of this American myth have been attested by the likes of Leo Marx, Henry Nash Smith, and R. W. B.

Lewis. "It is not surprising," Lewis remarks, "in a Bible-reading generation, that the new hero (in praise or disapproval) was most easily identified with Adam before the Fall."

> Adam was the first, the archetypal, man. His moral position was prior to experience, and in his very newness he was fundamentally innocent. The world and history lay all before him. And he was the type of creator, the poet par excellence, creating language itself by naming the elements of the scene about him. All this and more were contained in the image of the American as Adam.[6]

Like Joseph standing on the precipice of a vast grassland and speaking for the space a sacred name, Lewis's "American Adam" likewise distinguished himself characteristically as a creator whose naming of his surrounding world was a "heroic embodiment of a new set of ideal human attributes."[7] As much as Melville's characters and Hawthorne's sentiment explore figuratively the Adamic hero, Joseph's religion took the argument to its extreme by declaring the land those writers and characters trod upon as ancient and exceptional, the place of original human–Divine interaction. Even more, with Joseph's revelation the Mormon faith, which by 1838 was only eight years old, now had a (literal) foundation upon which to build new cities, new prospects—indeed, a new American religion. As in Hawthorne's short story "Earth's Holocaust," where a community gathers on the edge of civilization to burn all the traps and artifacts of the Old World in order to start anew; or in *The House of Seven Gables*, where Holgrave argues against permanent public buildings, suggesting rather that they should be built to crumble "as a hint to people to examine and reform the institutions which they symbolize";[8] Joseph too, with a gestural gaze, sweeps away the past by claiming a new kingdom to be built upon the ruinous conceptions of past generations. He was also attuned to the peculiarities of ancient speech; years earlier, when Joseph first met Brigham Young, Joseph declared that Young spoke with the language of Adam.[9] To the young prophet, voice was a powerful tool, one that could reveal ancient sounds or reshape the frontier with a single word.

This moment conveniently marks the confluence of America and, as Harold Bloom argues, *the* American religion: Mormonism. Nineteenth-century Mormonism, however, was not an entirely comfortable belief system to inhabit. Six years after his initial exploration into Daviess County, Joseph Smith was killed in a room above an Illinois jailhouse. In many ways, his murder was the rupture of an increasingly tense relationship Mormons maintained with their non-Mormon neighbors in Missouri, Illinois, and Ohio. Unpopular religious practices, self-righteous pronouncements, a penchant for rapid

6 · PROLOGUE

conversions, and, perhaps most important, the ongoing threat of a political bloc made Mormons a difficult bunch to tolerate, particularly on the wilds of frontier America.

For Mormons, life in the wilderness was both a necessity and a divine challenge. As members faced harassment from surrounding communities, Joseph spread the membership around various settlements—first in Ohio, then westward into Missouri, and eventually to Illinois, where Mormons built the city of Nauvoo, which at that time was the second-largest city in the state. On the other hand, Mormons understood the "barren wilderness" of middle America to be a place traced with divinity and, therefore, a place—precisely because of its difficulties—able to wear the faithful smooth, like a "huge, rough stone rolling down from a high mountain."[10] "Life in a garden is relaxed, quiet, and sweet," writes Leo Marx in *The Machine in the Garden*, "but survival in a howling desert demands action, the unceasing manipulation and mastery of the forces of nature, including, of course, human nature. Colonies established in the desert require aggressive, intellectual, controlled, and well-disciplined people. It is hardly surprising that the New England Puritans favored the hideous wilderness image of the American landscape."[11] As Mormons would soon discover, life in the desert would take on entirely new meaning after the death of their beloved Prophet.

Despite, or perhaps in spite of, Mormonism's at-times-tenuous presence in America, it occupies a distinct place in American cultural history. Mormonism emerged at a transitional period in the American conscience. Joseph claimed that in 1820, when he was fourteen years old, he was visited by heavenly beings—depending on the version he told, these beings were either an angel, Jesus Christ, or, in what is now the canonical version of his "First Vision," both God and Jesus Christ—and was told that all other religions were incorrect and that he should not join any of them. Later, he was visited by an angel named Moroni (mō-RŌ-nī—the gilded figure with trumpet to his lips famously perched atop almost every Mormon temple), who directed Joseph to a hill near his home in Palmyra, New York, where an ancient record was buried. Joseph later translated this ancient document, which purportedly was written on plates of brass, and published it as The Book of Mormon. The story mostly entails a single Jewish family who fled Jerusalem shortly before its destruction and, by the direction of God, sailed across the sea to what is now the American continent. Eventually, a schism materialized within the family, and two warring tribes—the Nephites and Lamanites—battled one another over the course of several centuries, resulting ultimately in the complete and bloody destruction of the Nephites. Joseph claimed that the Lamanites continued to live upon the American continent, and that modern-day Indians were Lamanite descendants and, therefore, among the Lost Tribes of Israel.

The Book of Mormon tells of a corrupt urban center and the beckoning of new life and escape within nature, and as such it fits nicely within other nineteenth-century American literary themes that prescribe nature as a cure for the hardships of urban living. Journalist Avi Steinberg even goes so far to claim that "American literature got serious at Hill Cumorah," the place where Joseph discovered the ancient plates.[12] Certainly The Book of Mormon emerges during a time when Joseph's contemporaries were contemplating similar themes. As Leo Marx has pointed out, nineteenth-century American writers were haunted by the visage of industrialization impinging upon the natural world. Henry David Thoreau's residency near Walden Pond made a claim for modern man's need to escape industrial city centers for nature's respite; even then, the sound of a distant train whistle mocked his whole project. Nature both enticed and taunted, representing an unreachable relief from an inescapable modern world. The chilling scene in Melville's *Moby Dick*, when the exploration inside a dead and bloated beached whale suddenly shifts to the interior of a mill, perhaps most clearly demonstrates the complexities of modern life that nineteenth-century Americans like Joseph needed to negotiate.

Mormons, Musical Theater, and Belonging in America takes these and other American themes in Mormonism as points of departure in examining how and why Mormons have so closely adopted as theological tenets the vocal and theatrical traditions of American musical theater. By drawing attention to the vocal and listening practices of Mormons over almost two hundred years of religious practice, I am suggesting that a sensorial methodology can amplify how aural traditions can and do affect the historical narrative. I echo historian Mark M. Smith's conviction that underestimating or ignoring altogether the aurality of historical agents "contributes to our deafness by denying us an understanding of how political sounds were shaped by, and in turn influenced, cultural whispers, economic booms, and social screams."[13] The story of Mormons and musical theater addresses a central concern in my research, which is how new ways of *sounding* create opportunities for other ways of *living*. Thus, throughout this book, I look at the way in which American ideologies of sounding were absorbed into Mormonism, first in the primacy of the voice in Mormon theology and the unusually rich performative traditions Mormonism promotes, and second with the elevation of both the voice and the theater as sites of cultural negotiation, culminating in the tradition of musical theater as a unique expressive tool of Mormon culture. I argue that the histories of Mormonism and American musical theater should be seen as ideologically entwined, and that a distinctively American quality of vocality has emerged from the junction of these two iconic American traditions.

Introduction

Vicarious Voices

vicarious, *adj*:
1. That takes or supplies the place of another thing or person; substituted instead of the proper thing or person.
2. Of punishment, etc.: Endured or suffered by one person in place of another; accomplished or attained by the substitution of some other person, etc., for the actual offender.
3. Of power, authority, etc.: Exercised by one person, or body of persons, as the representative or deputy of another.
4. Performed or achieved by means of another, or by one person, etc., on behalf of another.

Vicarious experiences that confirm truth while entertaining an audience are likely to be good theatre.

> —*Theatre Manual*, 1980

As Mark Twain reportedly once said, "Only kings, presidents, editors, and people with tapeworms have the right to use the editorial 'we.'"[1] The line is humorous because Twain's exceptions to what is commonly referred to as the "editorial we" point to the often-absurd faith we place in voices spoken on behalf of others. Vocal vicariousness is also a phenomenological conundrum the ears must sort out for us. Those who speak with the "editorial we" produce a sound undeniably their own that is nonetheless assumed to be heard as not belonging to them, or at least not belonging exclusively to them. I call this sonic surrogacy the *vicarious voice*. To speak on behalf of another is to perform a vicarious voice, a theatrical posture that requires listeners to hear within the sound of a speaker the message of a voice unspoken. This ventriloquizing phenomenon happens regularly: attorneys speaking on behalf

10 · INTRODUCTION

of clients, actors speaking as proxy for the character, and even machines broadcasting a person's voice are just a few examples of the vicarious voice, its performative nature, and its functions in the modern world.

To be sure, people everywhere speak for and over one another numerous times a day, whether legally, ceremonially, figuratively, or literally. Parents, caretakers, physicians, women who are pregnant, translators, Wall Street investors, CEOs, kings, and editors, as well as technological tools like phonographs, tape decks, iPods, and YouTube videos, all speak on behalf of another, promiscuously intermingling one voice with the preemptive desires of an (often) unseen, noncommunicative other. The practice can be quite useful. Vocal vicariousness ensures that transactions, final wishes, or shared interests are kept; in this way, vicariousness is essential to a modern way of life. Furthermore, as the frequent misattribution of Twain's phrase attests, the vicarious voice allows someone to be present when unpresentable, awake when asleep, and even to be alive when dead; its messengers arrive like Hermes on winged heels to deliver words otherwise left unheard. Truly, speaking for someone else makes the impossible possible.

Yet Twain's humor defends against a phenomenon problematic in spite of its usefulness. Speaking for another person has sometimes been a source of trouble since there always remains the possibility that the messenger is being untruthful and that the voice heard is not really communicating what it says it is. Listeners must contextualize the vicarious message and understand that the voice heard is not the *actual* voice of the unseen but is instead a voice conveying something essential about a voice they cannot hear. This requires a listening technique where listeners must separate the vocal sound from the body it comes from in order to understand the message as vicariously delivered.

The voice tells us a lot about someone's identity, or we at least ascribe an identity based on the voices we hear. We are easily bamboozled when voices don't match the bodies to which we imagine they should belong. Ventriloquists, for example, fool audiences with thrown voices that seem to come from illogical places. The line between what the actor speaks and what the character says is a tautological puzzle, often leading listeners to disbelieve that the people behind the camera or on the stage do not in some way share the same qualities as the characters they inhabit. Joe Cocker sang with a voice coded as black, and men singing falsetto are described as sounding like women. Today, machines designed to speak more and more like humans give voice to new anxieties about the limits of humanity and echo old questions about what makes us human in the first place.

The practice of speaking on behalf of another person, therefore, is common and in some cases indispensable to a certain way of life; it is the unspoken that goes spoken, and we rarely think twice about it. Yet to speak or listen vicariously carries sometimes-metaphysical implications of authority and authenticity that are fundamental to most social convictions. In religious communities, perhaps more so than in others, the practice of a vicarious voice can be crucial. The question "Who speaks for God?" has been a particularly volatile and lingering one. In religious terms, the vicarious voice describes the sensual experience of hearing God's voice emanating from a body either unseen or clearly not his own, as well as speaking the voice of God as a sonic qualifier of one's religious authority. Pastors and popes, prophets and TV evangelists, grandmothers and infants, martyrs and revolutionaries, the sane and the institutionalized—all have claimed or been claimed to speak for God. These voices are of comfort to the believing and the bane of the deceived, but in no way can religion escape the puzzle of God's vicarious voice. To be religious, especially in a secular age, is to have come to terms with the inevitability of sonic mediation and vicariousness.

According to a standard biblical interpretation of creation, for example, voicing and vocal sound animate and emanate from the heavens, produced by an unseen Creator: "And God said, Let there be light: and there was light."[2] If humans were able to be present at the beginnings of the universe, this resounding voice would lack a visual referent. The voice would be heard, its sound waves felt in the body, but it could not be traced back to a speaking body. A voice, in other words, would speak form into the universe yet itself carry no form whatsoever. Mladen Dolar called this the *acousmatic voice*—a voice which we cannot locate.

Voice scholars in several disciplines, including and especially musicologist Nina Eidsheim, have recently been building from Dolar's terminology a framework of identification that listeners must use to judge incoming messages (Who is speaking, and how can I know for sure?)—what some have called the "acousmatic question."[3] The always-present acousmatic question brings into question the identity of any speaker as well as our own motives and the practices of listening we use to identify voices as familiar, unfamiliar, trusted, or dangerous. As Anne Carson reminds us, "It is in large part according to the sounds people make that we judge them sane or insane, male or female, good, evil, trustworthy, depressive, marriageable, moribund, likely or unlikely to make war on us, little better than animals, inspired by God."[4]

I recognize the truth of Carson's observation, but also want to build from the work of Eidsheim and others to question the guiding assumption of such a statement—I want to know under what conditions the sounds people make are made and in what ways listeners have been conditioned to hear those sounds as qualifiers of another person's identity or disposition, particularly

INTRODUCTION

when the divine is invoked. If a voice cannot be located—or if the message is being voiced by a proxy body—then what proof do listeners have that what they are listening to is in fact the voice of God? This is the crucial question on which all prophetic religion hangs in the balance.

A Theology of Voice

Mormon theology offers a different perspective on this vocal dilemma, for two principal reasons. First, Mormon cosmology dictates that God is not an amorphous spirit but instead has a body of flesh. Mormon convention traces this revelation back to 1820, when the fourteen-year-old Joseph Smith found a quiet place in a grove of trees near his home to pray about which church he should join. In an answer to his prayer, Joseph later claimed he saw both God and Jesus Christ in the flesh, and God spoke to Joseph with a mouth like a human's. In his personal history, Joseph recounted the experience.

> After I had retired to the place where I had previously designed to go, having looked around me, and finding myself alone, I kneeled down and began to offer up the desires of my heart to God. I had scarcely done so, when immediately I was seized upon by some power which entirely overcame me, and had such astonishing influence over me as to bind my tongue so that I could not speak. Thick darkness gathered around me, and it seemed to me for a time as if I were doomed to sudden destruction.
>
> But, exerting all my powers to call upon God to deliver me out of the power of this enemy which had seized upon me, and at the very moment when I was ready to sink into despair and abandon myself to destruction—not to an imaginary ruin, but to the power of some actual being from the unseen world, who had such marvelous power as I had never before felt in any being—just at this moment of great alarm, I saw a pillar of light exactly over my head, above the brightness of the sun, which descended gradually until it fell upon me.
>
> It no sooner appeared than I found myself delivered from the enemy which held me bound. When the light rested upon me I saw two Personages, whose brightness and glory defy all description, standing above me in the air. One of them spake unto me, calling me by name and said, pointing to the other—*This is My Beloved Son. Hear Him!*[5]

Ironically, the storied First Vision depends less on *seeing* than on the practice of *speaking and hearing*. God's words, "This is My Beloved Son. Hear Him!" grant authority to Jesus to speak on His behalf, just as in times of old (the gospel of Luke records that the disciples Peter, James, and John heard the same words during Jesus's transfiguration on the mount). Joseph's experience in the woods was another confirmation that God chooses to delegate His voice to others, both divine and human. This gives the power of vicariousness a divine mandate.

God's predilection for vicarious voices is a curious quality of an omnipresent being. We know from experience that oral communication is notoriously fickle. Even children understand that the point of the "telephone game" is to show that the corruption of a message is humorously proved inevitable the more sets of ears and tongues are involved. Nonetheless, it seems that God is happy to leave to chance that the message heard will still be the one He delivered. Or maybe God is invested (bound, even) in letting humans decipher His intent using whatever ways they know. Regardless, despite the implications of Joseph's teachings—that the God Mormons pray to has a body of flesh, a mouth from which a voice materially emanates, which behaves in all ways like a human voice does, with reverberations that penetrate the air with the same force and majesty as that of a human, and whose material presence vibrates the eardrums of normal human beings—God chooses more often than not to let His voice be heard vicariously through the lungs and lips of His prophets.

There is also a great vocal symmetry in this scene. God's speaking acts as a dramatic counterweight to Joseph's inability to speak during the experience, which may be explained in a number of ways. Joseph's tongue-tiedness at first seems to him the result of a demonic power, and not for a didactic purpose by God, as other biblical stories of tied tongues suggest. Most typically, biblical stories relate instances of divinely administered muteness, often in order to draw attention to some transformation of character. An angel placed hot coals on the lips of the prophet Isaiah in order to purge his sins and, presumably, to discipline his speech to fit that of a prophet. Babel, while cacophonous with voices, represents a place where everyone was symbolically rendered dumb in that their voices lacked any meaning. While John the Baptist was in his mother's womb, his father Zacharias was struck dumb. In The Book of Mormon, a young man named Alma has a conversion experience similar to that of Saul on the road to Damascus, except that Alma loses both his ability to speak and to see for a span of several days.

Nineteenth-century believers, on the other hand, were anything but tongue-tied. "God was hardly falling silent," writes Leigh Eric Schmidt of the early nineteenth century. "Instead, with the crumbling of established authorities, God had more prophets, tongues, and oracles than ever before."[6]

14 · INTRODUCTION

Enlightenment thinking in the early half of the nineteenth century had forged for many people an uneasy relationship with the material and supernatural world. As a result, people continued to report visions and direct communion with heavenly beings, deceased ancestors, and spirits as they had for centuries, but now, fueled by an authoritarian skepticism marred by miseducation and gullibility, those supernatural experiences had greater import as signs of Jesus's impending return to earth.

In this intense climate, nineteenth-century spiritualist traditions flourished. Joseph spent his formative years in what was called the "burnt-over district" of central and western New York, so named for the tremendous outpouring of spiritualist practice there during the Second Great Awakening. He received direct instruction by God and Jesus Christ, as well as by Moses, John the Baptist, the disciples Peter, James, and John, Elijah, and numerous angels. But he wasn't the only one hearing voices. Swedenborgians, Shakers, Adventists, and many other revivalist traditions sprouted up during this same time and roughly in the same region of America, and their followers were likewise reporting similar experiences with a speaking God.

With so many claiming to speak on behalf of God, new anxieties emerged for those within earshot. As with any vocal vicariousness, listeners must ask of the voice, Who is speaking? and How can I know this for certain? Vocal vicariousness is a tautological puzzle, compounded in spiritualism by the almost-never-seen body of a speaking God. In a fundamentally duplicitous act, the vicarious speaker maintains believability by keeping his distance as messenger but must also be careful to not be too distanced or else the message may fail. When a human delivers a message from God, that vicariousness comes in the form of revelation, which fundamentally is haunted by the question, Is God speaking through this person, or is this person speaking through the idea of God? For nineteenth-century believers, the stakes for these vicarious voices could not have been any higher—with new information from God daily, a person's position relative to heaven and hell was kept in balance by her ability to discern God's many vocal proxies. "Thus," Schmidt writes, "the modern predicament actually became as much one of God's loquacity as God's hush."[7]

Second, and perhaps most crucial, Mormonism's loquacious God stands apart from others in His delegation of vocalic power. A revelation given to Joseph in 1831 suggests the power of the spoken word is implicit and not a condition of the voice carrying the message. On the contrary, no discernment is given for when the voice heard comes from God and when it comes from someone or somewhere else. The revelation is recorded as follows: "What I the Lord have spoken, I have spoken, and I excuse not myself; and though the heavens and the earth pass away, my word shall not pass away, but shall all be fulfilled, *whether by mine own voice or by the voice of my servants, it is the same.*"[8]

On the surface, this passage seems to grant God's voice to all those He authorizes (his "servants"). God seems to be offering an authoritative position vis-à-vis His vocalic power to whomever is willing to obey Him. The hierarchical premise behind God's voice in itself is not wholly new; Don Ihde writes that the liturgist "bespeaks tradition and the voices of the gods. They sound in his voice."[9] Likewise, Adriana Cavarero writes rather pointedly that "speech, according to the ritual formula 'word of God,' is what God becomes through the prophets who lend him their mouths."[10] One consequence of a loquacious God is that, if everyone is speaking for God, then in fact no one is speaking for God. Joseph quickly realized this whenever followers began to express communications or experiences with the divine that were contradictory to what he had taught or received himself. A hierarchical schema was established that made it clear that only one person on earth at a time could speak on behalf of God, and at that moment that person was Joseph Smith, the Mormon prophet. Therefore, voice is not just one aspect of determining godly appointment or divine mandate—it is the *principal* means of understanding another person's righteousness and devotion to religious values. For this reason, I describe Mormonism as a *theology of voice*.

Today, the "voice of my servants" is taken to mean the prophets and apostles who constitute the hierarchy of the Mormon Church. In other words, God comes into being the moment a *particular* man voices Him. God's revelation to Joseph therefore not only gives unilateral power for divinely elected men to speak on behalf of God by literally voicing God, but it also suggests a listening technique required to hear God's voice whenever a prophet opens his mouth. A popular Mormon hymn sums this up tidily: "Come, listen to a prophet's voice, /And hear the word of God." Furthermore, ethnomusicologist Peter McMurray has recently argued that the God in The Book of Mormon sometimes will "take verbal cues from prophets, reciting or re-uttering those prophets' words himself," which suggests The Book of Mormon–style interactions with God closely resemble Bakhtin's notion of dialogism, and that, curiously, God is as much a mimic of His servants as His servants are of Him.[11] At any rate, in Mormonism God permits—even commands—a practice of vocal vicariousness wherein speakers may speak for God, God may speak for them, and listeners attune ears to God's voice, even when the body of God is nowhere to be seen.

16 · INTRODUCTION

The same question of plausibility that besets all practices of vocal vicariousness is no less a condition with God's voice. If one man has the power to speak on behalf of God (or inversely, that God has the limited power to speak through only one man), but that man says thousands of words a day that seem unrelated to anything prophetic, how does the listener decipher between words spoken *by* a man and those spoken by God *through* that man? Religious communities often differ in how they square that circle. Charismatic Christians, for example, maintain that the Holy Spirit speaks through humans during moments of ecstasy (what Durkheim calls "collective effervescence"). Mormons do not believe it is possible for the prophet to lead them astray—otherwise, the entire plan of redemption would be frustrated—but that doesn't mean they hold their leaders to be infallible. To preserve this paradox, Mormons have constructed a very loose structure— on which they almost always disagree—for determining when a prophet is speaking for God and when he is not. Similar to the papal privilege of speaking *ex cathedra* (literally, "from the chair"), where the infallibility and authority of the pope's decree is bound by the nature of the religious office he holds, Mormons believe that when the prophet speaks "as a prophet," it is in fact the word and voice of God. Therefore, when a prophet speaks a certain way—and says things that seem more or less in line with what has been stated by previous prophets and sustained by particular scriptures, and in a manner understood to be prophetic—he is in effect speaking "as a prophet." There are no hard and fast rules here for when the prophet speaks as a man and when he speaks on behalf of God. The scriptural verse "by their fruits shall ye know them" seems as much a guiding principle as anything else.[12]

With divine revelation, of course, we are dealing with something understood as patently different from normal communication between two people. Still, independent of the nature of divine pronouncement from God's lips to the prophet's ear, that prophet must nonetheless communicate the message as one human to another human. It is this second message that raises issues of credibility and cleaves a division between reason and revelation famously argued in Immanuel Kant's *Critique of Pure Reason*. To place an even finer point, George Steiner's statement that "any model of communication is at the same time a model of trans-lation, of a vertical or horizontal transfer of significance" haunts any belief that revelation once communicated outward retains all (or any) of its original meaning.[13]

In *Revelation in Religious Belief*, philosopher George Mavrodes proposes a different communicative model. He entertains the objection that just because God may reveal a piece of information to someone doesn't preclude the fact that the same information, once communicated by the receiver to another person, becomes a different kind of communication altogether. To put it another way, he has faith that a message from God can be delivered vicariously from one human to another.

> Assume that God has revealed a certain proposition, p. And now someone makes the claim (a true claim, given our assumption) that God revealed p. That claim is also a proposition—call it q—and it is a proposition distinct from p. It is a proposition about p, perhaps about how p came into human intellectual life, or about how someone came to know that p, or something of the sort. And the objector goes on to assert that it is not possible that a proposition such as q should ever be proved as a piece of natural knowledge. If q—the claim that p was revealed—is to be known at all, then q must itself be revealed just as p was.[14]

Mavrodes maintains that just because proposition q cannot be proved or known the same way that proposition p was made known does not mean that both propositions are untrue. He also doesn't rule out the possibility that proposition q could be "acquired as natural knowledge" (for example, a medical researcher proving the healing powers of a certain herbal concoction professed by mystics for centuries). Instead, Mavrodes counters Kant's judgment that the relationship between reason and revelation is cleaved by arguing that "there appear to be cases (or, again, possible cases) of religious belief or knowledge that depend both on revelation and on reason, and in which neither element is dispensable."[15]

While Mavrodes is skeptical that people can hear God's voice in a literal sense, he does suggest that God may communicate with humans through one of three ways: the *causation model,* wherein God inserts ideas into the mind of a human, perhaps unbeknownst to the human; the *manifestation model,* as when heavenly beings appear or make themselves visible (and possibly audible) to humans; and the *communication model,* which is perhaps the most understood and expected mode of revelation wherein God communicates to humans in some fashion.

Applying Mavrodes's taxonomy to Mormonism, we might say that God speaks to Mormons atypically through the manifestation model (for example, Joseph's First Vision) and typically through the communication model via prophetic teachings. We might also say that Mormon prophets likewise speak through the communication model when they speak on behalf of and with the voice of God. The revelatory paradox Mavrodes describes above, with the whole notion of revelation being built upon a series of unverifiable

18 · INTRODUCTION

propositions that nonetheless aren't in themselves proof of faulty reason, isn't a paradox at all in Mormonism. On the contrary, Mormonism extended the communication model indefinitely when God insisted that prophets could and would speak on His behalf. The message spoken by God and the message that "God has spoken" may conventionally be understood as separate propositions. In Mormonism, however, they are one and the same.

Mormons and Musicals

At heart, this is a story about how Mormons came to be associated with the American musical and what that association demonstrates about vocal vicariousness. This book takes as its premise that the story of Mormon acculturation and identity may be understood anew by looking at Mormonism askance—by "hanging up looking glasses at odd corners," to use Virginia Woolf's phrase—through the lens of musical theater.[16] This project is thus a reimagining, equally, of Mormon history and of the history of the American musical, how these reimagined histories speak, and what they speak to. I draw upon theories and principles of the burgeoning field of voice studies to thread together what may at times seem unruly disciplinary partners. The seemingly strange combination of disciplinary methods and theories required to tell this story are a testament to the seriously knotted and entangled histories that make up the cultural fabric of both Mormonism and American musical theater.

It seems to me that parsing the phenomenological aspects of the vicarious voice is the best way to come to understand the Mormon fascination with American musical theater. I focus on Mormons here both for the pervasiveness of the religion as well as its peculiarity, though certainly other religious movements have maintained some relationship with musical theater. Henry Bial's *Playing God: The Bible on the Broadway Stage* and Ian Bradley's *You've Got to Have a Dream: The Message of the Musical* are but two scholarly considerations of the link between Broadway and religion.[17] Outside Broadway, however, religious people have used musicals in creative ways to help make sense of themselves. Growing up in the Bible Belt of the American Midwest, for example, I was surrounded by Christian denominations of all stripes, almost all of which frequently performed both secular- and sacred-themed musicals within the church building. Clearly, some identity work among religious people gets established through the musical genre, and probably to multiple degrees and purposes. Mormonism is thus not exceptional for its religious association with musical theater, but I argue it is exemplary. The proximity of Mormons to musical theater has been popularly epitomized through satirical productions from the early twentieth century on; even more prominent and interesting, though, are the ways Mormonism has crafted an American identity *through* and *as* musical theater.

I have experienced firsthand this cultural fascination Mormons have with musicals. I joined the Mormon Church as an adult and over time became aware of a prominent aesthetic for musical theater conventions within Mormonism. This aesthetic is revealed in two ways. First, through the many musicals or musical dramas Church members create and perform for one another—musical pageants, rock musicals, road shows, historical enactments dramatized to music, and so forth. Mormons also have a second, subtler aesthetic connection to musicals, however, that has nonetheless made an association between the genre and the faith an easy one. *Book of Mormon* creators Trey Parker and Matt Stone in an interview with Terri Gross in 2011 explained this association:

> To us there's so many things about Mormonism, even the way [Mormons] present themselves, when you go to Salt Lake City, the temple, when you go to some of their things, they present themselves in a very kind of Disney kind of way.
>
> And we would have this running theme. We would always say when we're working on either the sets or the costumes or whatever, we'd say: No, make it more Rodgers and Hammerstein. Or make it more Disney. Or make it more Mormon. And they're like: Well, which one is it? And we're like: No, it's all the same word for the same thing.[18]

That the word *Mormon* could in 2011 stand in for two such iconic American corporate bodies would likely have amused and frightened most nineteenth-century Americans (many Mormons included). But Parker and Stone aren't being just clever or hyperbolic here. Mormons in the twentieth century clearly saw the messaging within the musicals of Rodgers and Hammerstein as a path toward acceptance and therefore adapted themselves to the conventions they established (see chapter 2). Even more, the Walt Disney Company is arguably covered with a Mormon veneer—Jiminy Cricket's "When You Wish Upon a Star" from *Pinocchio* was penned by Mormon composer Leigh Harline, and the song's first seven notes have since been used by Disney to sonically brand the company, including accompanying the opening logo for Walt Disney Pictures since the 1980s. Beyond any literal associations Mormons might share with Disney or Rodgers and Hammerstein, however, Parker and Stone's words speak also to the larger issue this book addresses. As I argue

20 · INTRODUCTION

throughout, to be Mormon is to be a performer who is self-conscious of his theatricality. Characters in musicals often behave this same way. Indeed, what is known as the camp sensibility—a self-reflexive, overt style of performance characterized, as Susan Sontag put it, by "its love of the unnatural: of artifice and exaggeration"—pervades musicals and Mormon identity alike.[19] Therefore, Mormons, Disney, and Golden Age musicals can be easily imagined as "all the same word for the same thing" because, in action, both Mormons and musicals are campy in this precise way. They appear to speak the same language.

That Mormons speak the same language as musical theater underlines my observation that Mormons practice a theology rooted in voice. In fact, my argument is that Mormonism's fascination with musical theater emerges from two related impulses foundational to Mormon theology: the necessity of performance and the immediacy of vocal mimicry. On the one hand, I argue not only that Mormons find deep theological meaning in theatrical expression, but also that Mormon piety truly depends on repeated acts of theatrics. The Mormon temple ceremony, for example, has been described as "a staged representation of the step-by-step ascent into the presence of the Eternal while we are yet alive."[20] Central to this ceremony is the acting out of a character. Those entering the ceremony for the first time are given a secret name whereby they will be known in heaven. Those who engage the ceremony again are given the name of a deceased person who will experience the didacticism vicariously. The action of the ceremony centers on the creation story, wherein all men pretend as though they are Adam and all women act as though they are Eve. Thus Mormons engaged in temple worship are doubly veiled as both the deceased person whose name they carry and either Adam or Eve, whose actions they follow. Even the language of the theater frames a great deal of Mormon activity. Therefore, faithful Mormons "perform" baptisms for dead ancestors, "play" a role as bishop or Cub Scout den mother, and are criticized by heterodox members for passively treating Church-produced lesson manuals as "scripts." In significant ways, a faithful Mormon is always already a performing Mormon.

On the other hand, Mormons have a unique relationship with the voice, which I understand to be material in effect and essence. I maintain that sound is arguably more the domain of bone and flesh than the air it travels through. The emanating sound waves of my spoken words produce a physiological effect on my body the moment I speak them, just as those traveling waves produce material changes in the ear and instantaneously the mind of whoever hears my voice. Such a position makes voice inseparable from bodies and intimately connected to how those bodies move through and react to the physical world. I consequently examine the Mormon voice as a kind of spiritually infused object, like the posters, relics, and small figurines that Colleen McDannell calls "material Christianity," with the purpose of seeing "how the faithful perpetuate their religion day in and day out."[21]

De-centering Musical Theater

Conversely, musical theater historiography stands to be reimagined when Mormonism is introduced as a serious and important part of musical theater history. Critical studies of the American musical have helpfully considered how religious ideologies shaped the genre's musical style, theatrical conventions, and dramatic content. Religious scholar Ian Bradley argues that the musical "has a significant theological content and spiritual dimension and provides for many people an experience which can genuinely be described as religious as well as entertaining."[22] Bradley's less universalist, but no less provocative, assertion is that Tim Rice and Andrew Lloyd Webber "have arguably done more than most priests and preachers in the last thirty-five years to promote biblical knowledge and theological awareness."[23] Robin Sylvan makes a similar claim about popular music and spirituality when he writes that "for teenagers and young adults especially, the musical subculture to which they belong provides as all-encompassing an orientation to the world as any traditional religion."[24] Others continue: Raymond Knapp writes about religious overtones (and undertones) in *Mary Poppins* (1964), David Stowe looks to the evangelical influence on rock musicals, and Andrea Most's work, as noted, frames the American musical as a space for Jewish assimilation.[25]

Yet for all the richness these and other scholars have offered in their discussions of religious subtext within musical theater, so far not much attention has been given to ways musicals likewise shape religious ideology. Mormons transitioned from a nineteenth-century outlier sect literally on the fringes of the country to become today representative Americans, and they did this in part through an appropriation of musical theater. Musical theater's position as mediator of such a remarkable evolution grants an important and largely neglected perspective to the power of the American musical that the Mormon example helps make clear.

Finally, because most of the musicals discussed in this book are either now forgotten or have only ever had a very small audience, I am making a claim about the assumption within musical theater historiography that the Broadway musical is the primary (if not only) representative of American musical theater. For many people, musical theater and Broadway are one and the same. In contrast to opera, where the Metropolitan Opera House may be a zenith but is still just one of many opera houses where new productions are vetted, New York City is seemingly the only place where musicals can "happen." Times Square teems with tourists who look to a Broadway musical for an authentic New York experience. There are a finite number of theaters in New York City, however, and some of them may be occupied for decades with ongoing runs of megamusicals such as *Phantom of the Opera* (1988–present), *Cats* (1982–2000), or *Les Miserables* (1987–2003, 2014–present). Shows used to close when the local audience ran out. Not so anymore, since the local audience is no longer the target, nor even the lion's share of theatergoers. A hit Broadway musical will stick around for as long as it is generating a profit. And with franchise tours simultaneously crisscrossing the planet (national tours, West End, separate casts in year- or two-year-long runs in cities like Chicago or San Francisco, enormous and costly Southeast Asian cruise ships or resorts, and the like), Broadway producers have little reason to rush their show's moneymaking potential, even if their success is at the expense of the genre's growth and maturity.

Arguably, this situation has been a catalyst for decentering the development of musicals away from Broadway. Because the turnover in theater space is so low and vacancies rare, and because those spaces once vacant are expected to be populated with shows that will earn investors just as much as the previous tenant, few options for newer or daring shows are ever made available. Unsurprisingly, films-turned-musicals such as *Shrek* (2008), elaborate spectacles such as *Spider-Man: Turn Off the Dark* (2011) or *Rocky the Musical* (2012), or, more often, revivals of the now deified "Golden Age" musicals such as *The King and I* (1951) are a safer bet for investors. This has left the genre in something of a silent crisis. On the surface, the industry is doing fine, selling tickets and making money hand over fist. Yet economic constraints of Broadway have crimped the development of the American musical and a slow-creeping stagnation has quietly slipped in.

This is *one* reality of musical theater, but it is not the only one. If the history of the American musical is divorced from its New York locale, different stories surface. The focus on Broadway has simply amplified long-standing realities about musicals in America that render those other narratives invisible. A narrow set of aesthetic ideals and conventions currently define what is typically considered the American musical; shows that either don't feature that narrow band of genre traits or that don't fit within a preferred evolution of those characteristics rarely make their way to Broadway and subsequently are ignored in histories of the musical. To avoid such limited understandings, the history of the American musical might be more accurately and charitably written if it situates Broadway as but one of several regional and local venues where Americans use a wide variety of musical and dramatic conventions to help make sense of their historical place.

Some scholars have attempted to turn attention away from large urban centers as the only sites where theater matters; consequently, their work also frustrates the hierarchy of importance that displaces nonprofessional theatrical productions. For example, in the *Oxford Handbook of the American Musical*, Jennifer Chapman and Chase A. Bringardner explore receptions of amateur theater productions (like those put on by high schools or community organizations) around the country, and also regional variances and interests in region-specific musicals like *Oklahoma!*, *The Music Man*, or *The Best Little Whorehouse in Texas*. Bringardner in particular puts a fine point on the absence of regional concerns in musical theater scholarship when he writes, "Musical theater histories tend toward an unreflecting and often unconscious focus on Broadway, neglecting national tours and alternative centers of musical theater production. Such histories, as well as those that ignore region altogether, underestimate the potential benefits of analyzing a musical and its production history from the perspective of region."[26] Stacy Wolf's research on the local theater scene in Madison, Wisconsin, also attempts to de-center the American musical, insisting that "theatre-going is a profoundly local activity, circumscribed by local figures, local events, and local gossip."[27]

Mostly, though, musical theater scholarship has kept a steady gaze on musicals and New York City. That's not to say that scholars haven't used New York City as an important lens to examine other interpretive cross-sections of the American musical, including socially constructed identities or ideologies. I have already mentioned Andrea Most's (2004; 2013) work on Jewish identity and musical theater, which serves in many ways as a model for this project. By focusing on musicals from the 1920s through the 1950s (roughly corresponding to the second flowering of American operetta through the early years of the American musical's "Golden Age"), she takes a sideways glance at the American musical from the perspective of religious ideology and identity that, in the diasporic trends of New York's Jewish artists and audiences, nonetheless authenticates New York City as the place where musicals matter most.

Raymond Knapp's two-volume history of the American musical contextualizes the musical from two vantage points, those of personal identity

24 · INTRODUCTION

formation and national identity formation. Knapp dedicates a good deal of space in his second volume to the phenomenon of the film musical, which in a sense displaces New York City by its Hollywood credentials and broad production reach into middle America, for instance. Yet the film musical, despite its popularity and importance in building audiences in places far removed from Manhattan, is rarely discussed for its influence on appetites for regional theater or touring companies. Elizabeth Wollman includes with her 2006 study of rock musicals a discussion of the three realms of American musical theater in New York City—Broadway, Off-Broadway, and Off-Off-Broadway—as traditionally studied separately, though they are "in fact interconnected entities."[28] Although her study loosens the grip on Broadway as an economic and aesthetic powerhouse for the entire genre, it still maintains focus on New York City as the default place where musical theater matters most.

These several more recent publications question the American musical as inseparable from New York City yet, though none do so explicitly, nonetheless help further the impression that Broadway is the epitome of musical theater—all other expressions of the genre are either a slow march toward Broadway or else are viewed with suspicion, scrutiny, or are ignored altogether.

This is all to say that this book is framed by the American musical, but it does so primarily by maintaining some distance from Broadway. Rather than painting Broadway, yet again, as the pinnacle of the genre's maturity, and thereby ignoring a tremendous variety of shows performed elsewhere, I foreground musicals largely unknown to the rest of the Broadway community to implicitly argue that, while the Broadway musical has no doubt influenced dramatic traditions elsewhere, it nonetheless does not have the market cornered on what a musical is, how it works, or what it means to audiences.

American Icons

There is something poetic about a union of the quintessential American faith and a genre that seems defiantly American. In fact, both Mormonism and the American musical were formed under similar circumstances and with similar intentions. Mormonism was born in 1830 when Joseph Smith and a small gathering of family and devoted friends met to organize what was then called the Church of Christ in the small township of Fayette, settled among the finger lakes of upstate New York. Joseph published The Book of

Mormon in March 1830, and one month later he gathered in Fayette to officially organize the Church.

The great conviction of Joseph's Mormonism was that "all truth may be circumscribed into one great whole." Truth, in other words, not only stems from the same source but, through the power of God, can also be grafted back to that original wholeness. "If [Mormonism] does not circumscribe every thing that is in heaven and on earth," added Joseph's successor, Brigham Young, "it is not what it purports to be."[29] Joseph believed that remnant truth given by God to Adam and Eve lingered in distilled form throughout the earth, embedded in the variety of human belief systems. Mormonism was to be a great synthesizer of God's word, pulling those loose threads of truth back into a single tapestry of what followers today continue to call the "fullness of the gospel." This is not an incontestable process of cultural absorption, nor is it entirely passive either. As might be imagined, a synthesis of truth from the world's religions carries a great deal of ideologies that cannot be easily reconciled. As a result, Mormonism maintains a steady tension of spiritual and temporal paradoxes. Rather than finding this a liability, Mormons see a paradox of competing truths as a gift, in that a paradox betrays any sense of false comfort and demands a constant turning of one's mind in search of a solution. These paradoxes even define the faith and are what help make Mormonism a theatrically rich religion.

The American musical has roots similar to those of Mormonism, and the intertwining of the two organizations over almost two centuries makes for a rich study of American propriety. As with Mormonism, the American musical is a melding of several dynamic and somewhat distinct strains of musical and theatrical conventions. Operetta, vaudeville, burlesque, and minstrelsy all play a role in the development and codification of the American musical. Operetta dates back to the early nineteenth century and is a genre perhaps best known from the works of Jacques Offenbach in Paris, W. S. Gilbert and Arthur Sullivan in London, and a host of composers centered around Vienna, including especially Johann Strauss II and Franz Lehár. America became crazed with operetta in 1879 with the New York premiere of Gilbert and Sullivan's *Pirates of Penzance*. Operetta subsequently proved its attractiveness as a comedic form and showed its ability to reach audiences far removed from the urban centers of industrial America—parodies of Offenbach's *Barbe-bleue* (1870) make their way into Utah by the late nineteenth century, for example (see chapter 2). Similarly, the exotic and erotic invocations of polygamous Mormonism made for easy shenanigans on American and London stages alike.

Long before Gilbert and Sullivan redirected the development of American musical theater, a distinctive American form of musical theater had already taken root. By 1830, in the same year Joseph Smith organized the Mormon Church, white performer Thomas "Daddy" Rice had codified the white appropriation of black vernacular speech and dance in his minstrel routine Jump Jim Crow. Rice's characterization elevated minstrelsy to a commercial threshold in American popular culture. Like Joseph, Rice and many other white minstrel performers were from cities in upstate New York, such as Rochester, Utica, and Troy. The Jacksonian era had produced men like Joseph and Thomas Rice, men who "sought social order through unquestioned authority and centralized control."[30] Alexander Saxton argues that blackface minstrelsy was similarly a reflection of Jacksonian ideology, writing that "the rise of the first mass party in America and the dominance of the minstrel show as mass entertainment appear to have been interrelated and mutually reinforcing sequences."[31] Minstrelsy largely dissipated in the mid-twentieth century, but its underlying ideology of theatrical self-fashioning, white supremacy, and the promiscuous appropriation of marginalized communities (perhaps most infamously exemplified by the forced relocation of thousands of Native Americans by Jackson's administration) survives as a primary thrust behind both Mormonism and musical comedy today.

Operetta and minstrelsy coalesced with other theatrical traditions during the late nineteenth and early twentieth centuries. The American musical slowly transformed from a mishmash of conventions and styles to the standardized productions Richard Rodgers and Oscar Hammerstein II popularized in the mid-twentieth century. In fact, conventional historical narratives point to the premiere of Rodgers and Hammerstein's *Oklahoma!* in 1943 as when the book musical, or "integrated" musical, was born. *Oklahoma!* signifies the beginning of the principal musical theater convention that songs and dance should contribute to, rather than being ancillary aspects of, the storyline—hence the phrase "integrated musical." By 1943, the Mormon Church, too, was looking for integration, albeit for quite different ends. Chapter 2 presents in greater detail how *Oklahoma!* became not only a codifier of musical theater conventions but also an opportunity for Mormons to gain American acceptance by modeling these newly established conventions of the musical genre. Mormonism and the American musical thus share a historical trajectory that begins with the self-fashioning of Jacksonian ideology and reaches a culmination around World War II. At that point, both the religion and the genre enter a "golden age" against which all subsequent patterns of evolution are compared.

At root, then, musical theater and Mormonism share a common American heritage, a common ideology stemming from Jacksonian democratic principles, and even a common identity as an amalgam of American sensibilities and conventions. More than any geographic mooring to America, it may be the process of synthesizing multiple ideas and putting them to use in a new way that makes Mormonism and musical theater quintessentially American. To put a finer point on the matter, the principle of self-fashioning seems to be underlying all impulses behind Mormonism and musical theater. In addition, while speaking on behalf of others is certainly not exclusively an American sensibility, it may well be that, paradoxically, American forms of democracy depend on the process of speaking vicariously for another person or persons. The Jacksonian era saw large-scale efforts to broaden the realm of voters but did so through mass political parties that speak as a committee rather than through any sense of ventriloquizing the voices of the everyday voter. After all, elected officials by definition speak for and on behalf of a constituency, an ideological gamble that mediates individual voice in the practice of sovereignty.

The Jacksonian ideology certainly pervaded many corners of social and cultural life in the mid-nineteenth century, new religions not excluded. Recall Joseph's revelation that God and God's servants speak with the same voice. This seemingly democratic gesture does not grant just anyone the ability to speak on behalf of God, however, but only an elite class of (male) prophets and apostles. Thus, Mormonism from its earliest moments encapsulates the practice of vocal vicariousness necessary for Jackson's vision of American democratic practices to function. Out of the crucible of the Jackson administration were formed all three components of American life central to this story: American musical theater, American democratic principles of vocality, and the religion that so readily captures American ideologies and practices— Mormonism.

*   *   *

One of the purposes of this study is to track the evolution of musical theater as it pertains to Mormonism. Therefore, this book follows a loose chronology that begins in the nineteenth century and extends to today. My historiographic model for the book is a particular type of pedagogy used in some American medical training, in which information is presented cyclically, and additively, rather than in modules. I call this a spiraling historiographical model. For example, medical students learn some aspects of the heart during a lesson primarily about psychiatry and then build their knowledge of the

28 · INTRODUCTION

heart during another lesson on respiration, and so forth. Thus, information "spirals" upward in complexity or downward in generality according to the primary thrust of the intended lesson. One major benefit to this pedagogical model is that the body is analyzed holistically, emphasizing for students how various physiological strata must be observed as associative rather than restrictive.

Similarly, I construct here a spiraling historiographic model that acknowledges the deeply entwined nature of historical phenomena while also offering readers more straightforward case studies. One effect is that certain characters in the story are only partly fleshed out in each individual chapter but are given a more holistic construction when chapters are read as a group. I frequently return to the three main characters in this story—Mormon prophets Joseph Smith, Brigham Young, and Wilford Woodruff—but under varying historical or theoretical lenses in each viewing, hoping to communicate the shifting identity each man has taken as Mormonism reshaped itself through musical theater to adapt better to a changing American social landscape. That said, this book is not a biographical project, and I do not attempt to make or claim to be making new inroads for understanding these men in their historical moments (though such revelations may indeed come about). Rather, I hope to perform through the spiraling narrative the very manner in which Mormonism has moved through the history of America, along the way adding other rings of complexity to the ongoing construction of historical narratives in Mormon studies, performance studies, musicology, anthropology, and other disciplinary communities, especially those connected with musical theater.

In chapter 1, "'Come, Listen to a Prophet's Voice, and Hear the Word of God': The Voice and Mormon Theatricality," I introduce vocality and theatricality as dual impulses motivating Mormon theology and argue that these two together help explain the Mormon penchant for musical theater. I demonstrate this by using two prominent examples of vocal theatricality in Mormonism: Brigham Young's transfiguration into Joseph Smith in 1844 and the story of Nephi's impersonation of Laban in the opening chapters of The Book of Mormon. I extend my analysis of these two moments in Mormonism to a broader theorization of voice in the Mormon church. As I explain, Mormon scripture designates the voice of the prophets to be literally the same as God's, which sets up the possibility for humans to model God in all things. Thus, through vocal impersonation and theatricality—two key characteristics of musical theater—Mormons can move closer to godliness.

In chapter 2, "'I Sing That We're Going That Way': *Promised Valley*, Integration, and the Singing Voice," I track the development of American operetta in the nineteenth century and offer the first written exploration of anti-Mormon sentiment in this early form of the musical theater genre. I then show how musical theater conventions became codified with *Oklahoma!* in 1943 and explain that the postwar Mormon Church modeled their musical *Promised Valley* (1947) after *Oklahoma!* in order to make the remarkable transition from vilified fringe sect to become what Harold Bloom called "the American religion." The trope of singing permeates *Promised Valley*, and indeed in this musical, to sing means to belong. I examine this theme closely throughout the musical and suggest that *Promised Valley* captures both the Mormon insistence on communal labor (as signified by songs about choir practice, for example) but also the Mormon bargaining of identity in favor of assimilation (where Mormons show their industriousness but also their cultural malleability). I conclude by arguing that *Promised Valley's* insistence on singing as a metaphor for characters to claim a space in the larger community reflects the Mormon Church's ideal of vocality as a means of assimilating into mainstream American consciousness.

In chapter 3, "Exoticized Voices, Racialized Bodies: Lineage and Whiteness on Stage," I suggest that Mormon fascination with *Fiddler on the Roof* (1964) points to the unique relationship between Mormons and Jews. I argue that, with its themes of tradition, cultural adaptation, and religious persecution, *Fiddler* is the most "Mormon" of all musicals. I augment this claim by analyzing the Mormon musical *Life . . . More Sweet than Bitter* (1977) and an original musical performed daily at the Mormon Church–owned Polynesian Cultural Center in Hawaii. *Life . . . More Sweet than Bitter* in many ways constructs a Mormon sequel to *Fiddler on the Roof* in which the main character moves to America, converts from Judaism to Mormonism, and opens a successful chain of grocery stores in Salt Lake City. Likewise, within Mormon cosmology, Polynesians, like Native Americans, are considered to be from the House of Israel, and their performance of musical theater aligns those racialized bodies with Mormon ideals of whiteness. I conclude by arguing these musical dramas express a cultural appropriation of Judaism that reflects the Mormon belief that Jews are Gentiles and Mormons are Jews. In effect, then, Mormons begin using musicals to explain and sustain a complex heritage—a practice Jews also had been doing with musical theater since the nineteenth century.

In chapter 4, "'I've Heard That Voice Before': Reprising the Voice in Sacred Time," I examine vocality in the iconic Mormon rock musical *Saturday's Warrior* (1973), a show that suggests the voice is a stable identifier transcendent of time. *Saturday's Warrior* extends the idea of voice as symbol of community and belonging to include eternal commitments and relationships identifiable principally through the voice—the only material witness to a pre-mortal life forgotten during mortality. Using *Saturday's Warrior* as a lens into Mormon preoccupations with time and memory, I argue that the musical puts pressure on ideals of memory and forgetfulness that have come to characterize Mormonism since 1960. I contextualize *Saturday's Warrior* by detailing the structural changes the Mormon Church underwent in the 1960s and 1970s, particularly the process of Correlation and its streamlining of the faith's theology. I argue this Mormon musical inherently challenged the authority of modern Mormonism by injecting a form of folk doctrine into Mormon culture that continues to inform that culture's views of cosmology. Moreover, I return to the act of vocal modeling and argue that Correlation created an environment of unity and sameness that consequently reshaped how Mormons speak. Under Correlation, the Mormon voice becomes an emblem of exactness and a material demonstration of Mormon mastery and faithfulness.

In chapter 5, "Voice Interrupted: *Book of Mormon* and the Failed Voice of Correlated Mormonism," I explore the role of aurality in contemporary Mormon political life. I look to the place of voice in modern Mormonism and argue that Mormon aurality during Proposition 8 in California led to satirical works of musical theater against the Church, including *Prop 8: The Musical* (2008) and *Book of Mormon: The Musical* (2011). I show how *Book of Mormon*, especially, uses musical theater conventions to recall actual Mormon theatricality. This is done by portraying Mormons as musical theater caricatures, further conflating the religion and its musical-theatrical practice.

Through the musical, gay performers are able to don a Mormon costume and cheery demeanor to perform a particularly queer version of Mormonism, where rigid orthodoxy gives way to empathy and adaptation. I theorize this by building from Levinas's theories of communication ethics, where he argues interruptions, mishearings, and messages lost in translation ultimately create ethical communication models. Inasmuch as correlated Mormonism has standardized the voice of the prophet and made the message of Mormonism streamlined and unwavering, this model of communication makes the voice an extension of hegemonic control. *Book of Mormon*, in spite of its satirical gesturing toward Mormonism, opens up a space where the message of Mormonism can get interrupted, thus loosening the grip of the institution on the message it pronounces. With the voice of Mormonism thus proved interruptible, *Book of Mormon* makes the case for a Mormon theology that succeeds precisely because its message misses the mark, and not for its uniformity in type and delivery.

In a truly spiraling nature, this book ends by arcing back to the beginning and begins by way of conclusion. Such a form seems only fitting for a discussion about a religion that values eternal progression rather than stasis. As such, there is an innate dynamism within Mormonism, characteristically American in one sense of the word, but also characteristically nonreligious (more precisely, non-*Western* religious) in another. Mormons see the end of the world as the beginning of another and yet another—"worlds without end"—which makes it an orphan among other religions in America, especially those with a strong eschatological vision. Still, I hold that Mormonism's non-eschatological values are precisely what give the religion an optimistic character, defiantly American and endemically musical-theater-like.

As Émile Durkheim suggests, there is a reason that religious life remains vibrant and refreshing. As a gesture of vocal vicariousness, I will speak through Durkheim (or is it he speaking through me?) to gesturally give him the last word.

> Before all, it [religion] is a system of ideas with which the individuals represent to themselves the society of which they are members, and the obscure but intimate relations which they have with it. This is its primary function; and though metaphorical and symbolic, this representation is not unfaithful. Quite on the contrary, it translates everything essential in the relations which are to be explained: for it is an eternal truth that outside of us there exists something greater than us, with which we enter into communion.[32]

1

"Come, Listen to a Prophet's Voice, and Hear the Word of God"

The Voice and Mormon Theatricality

And whoso receiveth not my voice is not
acquainted with my voice, and is not of me.
— Doctrine and Covenants 84:52

So then faith cometh by hearing,
and hearing by the word of God.
— Romans 10:17

To speak vicariously is, in the first place, a theatrical gesture. It is a practice of taking on another identity and presenting it in the fashion of your own, as is commonplace in religious traditions like Pentecostalism where glossolalia, or speaking in tongues, is practiced. Speaking in tongues was first recorded in the book of Acts during the effulgence of spiritual awakenings known as Pentecost. Theologically, the first-century Pentecost was the fulfillment of Babel's linguistic estrangement, though vocally they are both instances of large-scale cacophony. Today, tongue speaking, as theologian Harvey Cox understood it, democratizes divine speech by providing people with all levels of linguistic ability, "the sounds by which a stammering soul [can] speak to God."[1] Tongue speaking therefore qualifies as something of a remedy to the disabling narrative typical of divine encounters, as with Moses, Saul, or Joseph Smith.

Not unlike Mormons, evangelicals and charismatic Christians listen in these moments of collective effervescence for a particular quality of voice that signals the appearance of the Holy Spirit. This tongue speaking is understood by practitioners to be patently individualistic, although as others have observed, the degree to which the cacophony of speaking in tongues begins to standardize into a singular, homophonic texture makes evident that at least some degree of social disciplining is at play. Inasmuch as these displays of glossolalia in such communities are normative and seem overtly theatrical, however, reducing to mere theatrics what is considered to be the manifestation of God would misrepresent the work such vocal phenomena are doing for these communities. These vocal theatrics are like enchantments, drawing God to the listener through the conduit of a pious tongue speaker. Both speaking in tongues and speaking on behalf of God, despite their theatrical nature, therefore are understood by practitioners to be an active means of reaching God—bending His ear toward them through extraordinary speech acts rather than listening in quiet meditation for God to speak of His own volition.

In this chapter I look to two examples in Mormon lore—one in the midnineteenth century and the second on the outskirts of ancient Jerusalem—where vocal vicariousness is closely tied with elements of theatricality, and explore how these stories set a standard of vocal theatrics that continues to inform Mormon practice today. This chapter also lays the groundwork for considering Mormonism as a theology of voice and for understanding how, as a genre, musical theater most conveniently allows faithful Mormons to exercise piety in voice and theatricality.

Brigham Young's "Transfiguration"

In August 1844, more than five thousand Mormons gathered in the sweltering heat along the banks of the Mississippi River to decide what until a few months before must have been unthinkable: who should be their next leader. Mormon founder and prophet Joseph Smith was violently murdered in June, along with his brother Hyrum, and because Joseph left no consistent instructions for how to proceed in the event of his death, several individuals now publicly debated how to resolve what would eventually be known as the "succession crisis." Most historical attention is given to a lively debate between two prominent leaders, Sidney Rigdon and Brigham Young. By law, Sidney Rigdon was poised to be Joseph's legal successor. Rigdon had served as counselor to Joseph in the First Presidency—the highest council in the Church—and in the original incorporation document from 1841, Joseph states "I was elected Sole Trustee for said Church to hold my office during life (my successors to be the first Presidency of said Church)."[2] As a former Campbellite preacher, Rigdon had a formal education and possessed great

34 · CHAPTER 1

rhetorical flair. Brigham Young, on the other hand, was one of the twelve apostles appointed by Joseph to lead the Church. Compared to Rigdon, he had a more modest intellect, but Young had been a close companion to Joseph for several years and remained fiercely loyal to Joseph and the Church.

Yet the matter of succession seemed settled once and for all when Young stood to speak to the gathered crowd. Others had spoken before him, either self-nominating or advocating for the leadership of another. Young's argument was stealthier. He argued that no one should lead the Mormons because no single person could fill Joseph's shoes. Rather, Young insisted that all the authority necessary to continue the Church's mission were given by Joseph to the Twelve Apostles—a group of men Young happened to preside over. Under the Twelve's collective leadership, Young argued, the Church could move forward with the work Joseph had begun.

What happened next has been the source of great conflict, amusement, and wonder for 180 years. As Young spoke, some in the audience recalled hearing from Young the voice of Joseph Smith and seeing in him the visage of their slain prophet. For many of those gathered, this was a miraculous event, and a divine confirmation that Young's plan was in harmony with Joseph's intentions.

This "transfiguration," as it has since been known, serves many functions for Mormons today as it did to those Mormons in the mid-nineteenth century. For one, the transfiguration is a neat parallel to the dove-like descent of the Holy Ghost upon Jesus following his baptism in the river Jordan. Like the biblical account, where God's voice confirmed the action and divinity of Jesus through baptism ("Thou art my beloved Son; in thee I am well pleased"), Brigham Young's transfiguration provides a remarkable instance of voice serving as holy confirmation and remains one of the most important testimonies in Mormonism to this day.[3] According to witnesses, even the slightest particulars of Joseph's voice could be accounted for—the idiosyncratic cough he gave before beginning his sermons, the faint whistle in his speech caused by a chipped tooth during an assassination attempt in 1832.[4] So while Young did appear to take on the physical characteristics of Joseph in those moments, what seems most prevalent in the historical record is the fact of voice.

That sound plays such a crucial role here isn't all that surprising. Hearing has a more persistent and haunting quality than our much more trusted, albeit frequently overindulged, sense of sight. Stephen Connor has made the argument that auditory "hallucinations" are much stickier, more apt to linger, and often nearly impossible to forget when compared with things seen. He writes, "Because a voice is an event in time, something that happens to us, even happens on us, in a way that an object presented for sight is not, the experience of hearing something with one's own ears is much more importunate and encroaching than seeing it with one's eyes."[5] It is important, then, to examine the conditions behind earwitness accounts of such alarming transformations. Imbedded within the listener's cochlea was a sonic memory of a miraculous event, one that I won't attempt to explain *away* but will explain *within* a context of nineteenth-century understandings of voice.

The story of Young's transfiguration has some problems—namely, that it likely didn't happen, at least not the way it is commonly told. First, even though more than 120 witnesses confirmed some version of a transfiguration in journals, diaries, or other personal recollections, none of those remembrances were contemporary. Most versions of the transfiguration story were recorded decades after Brigham Young led the company of Saints to modern-day Utah and had become their actual prophet-president.[6] Yet in the convoluted annals of Mormon history, much depends on Brigham Young's succession. Whether because of a miraculous transfiguration or not, most of the Mormons followed Young two years later when he led the first company of Mormons west across the Mississippi River and toward the Rocky Mountains. Thousands of others were not as convinced, however, and either stayed in Illinois waiting for a different leader or dissipated into various splinter groups. Because the efficacy of Young's succession is not apparent beyond this miraculous transfiguration, with dozens of other competing factions laying claim to true Mormonism, there is a tremendous pressure on the transfiguration narrative to prove the reality of *the* Mormon Church. Without the authority of the transfiguration, the Mormon Church is simply another member of the larger Mormon faith movement.

The second issue with the veracity of the transfiguration is Brigham Young's particular set of talents and interests. According to apostle Orson Hyde, Young was "a complete mimic, and [could] mimic anybody."[7] Young was also a great supporter of the theater. Under his leadership, one of the first permanent buildings erected in Salt Lake City was a theater, and Young himself took to the stage as both impresario and actor. It seems possible, therefore, that even if the accounts are true—that witnesses indeed saw and heard Joseph when Young was speaking—what they saw and heard was a convincing recital by a gifted actor. Richard Van Wagoner sees things similarly: "The force of Young's commanding presence, his well-timed arrival at the morning meeting, and perhaps a bit of theatrical mimicry swayed the crowd, rather than a metaphysical transfiguration of his physical body."[8] In a

36 · CHAPTER 1

sense, Brigham Young *performed* Joseph the best—better than Rigdon or any other vying for the title—and through that performance rose to the position of God's anointed. A similar performance continues today among Young's successors, as we will see.

But first, these accounts should be understood within a particular framework of early Enlightenment reasoning. Early Mormon converts, like others at the time, shifted somewhat uneasily between a magical and rationalist worldview. In the words of Gordon Woods, it was a time when "everything was believable" and thus "everything could be doubted."[9] Newly endowed with the possibilities of reason, nineteenth-century Americans were skeptical of intellectual or authoritative pronouncements. Yet they often failed to see the extent of their own gullibility and naive reasoning skills and "could be easily impressed by what they did not understand."[10]

It is out of this environment that acts of vocal duplicity, like mimicry or ventriloquism, begin to take on new meanings in American popular culture. In his history of ventriloquism, Steven Connor introduces the concept of the "vocalic body." Built on the premise that the voice is created *by* a body but in turn also *produces* a body, Connor's concept may help connect the practice of ventriloquism to the seemingly metaphysical transfiguration of Brigham Young. Connor claims that the power of the vocalic body can actually reshape listener's perception of the body out of which the voice emanates:

> In fact, so strong is the embodying power of the voice, that this process occurs not only in the case of voices that seem separated from their obvious or natural sources, but also in voices, or patterned vocal inflections, or postures, that have a clearly identifiable source, but seem in various ways excessive to that source. This voice then conjures for itself a different kind of body; an imaginary body which may contradict, compete with, replace, or even reshape the actual, visible body of the speaker.[11]

Connor's vocalic body is the product of what I am calling the vicarious voice. The conjured body loses precedence to the resounding voice, however, even if the bodiless voice in a sense demands our attention and undoes notions of vocal authorship. Along those lines, the very existence of a vocalic body is a gesture of theatricality—a kind of competition between multiple realities confirmed, yet also confused, through physical bodies.

Mormons were not immune to this fascination with the theatrical voice. Joseph Smith's life rather naturally fits within this narrative of theatricality. "Madly," writes journalist Avi Steinberg, "[Joseph] turned his whole life, every aspect of it, into high literature and literature into life, casting himself as the hero of a recklessly improvised live-action epic."[12] Joseph could be easily carried away by the theatrical quality of his communion with God or Jesus Christ, John the Baptist, or Moses. Some found Joseph's dramatic penchant unseemly for a prophet—"recklessly improvised"—and used Joseph's theatricality against him. Early on, people associated Joseph's vocal channeling of God with the duplicitous qualities of mimics. One anti-Mormon book written shortly after Joseph's death lists the "pretended prophet Joe Smith" among other such "remarkable characters in the annals of religious imposture" such as mimics, a horse whisperer, and the famed "Lame Beggar of London"; the book even includes a written account of a would-be initiate describing the secret and abominable rites of the Mormon temple ceremony.[13] An illustration of the impostor Joseph dressed in elaborate costume and gesturing wildly in a theatrical manner, like a hysteric barker hocking his goods in the religious marketplace, accompanies the story.

More amazing is the story of Book of Mormon scribe Oliver Cowdery's "confession"—later determined to be a hoax—that when Joseph baptized him in the Susquehanna River in 1829 and John the Baptist appeared and conferred upon Joseph and Cowdery the Aaronic Priesthood, Cowdery heard from John the Baptist the voice of Sidney Rigdon.[14] The account suggests that while Cowdery's eyes were closed and the hands of John the Baptist were laid upon his head, the voice Cowdery heard conferring the Priesthood was that of Sidney Rigdon. Cowdery at this point had not met Rigdon, nor supposedly had Joseph (although one theory suggests that Joseph and Rigdon conspired early on to concoct and write the stories in The Book of Mormon).[15] Later, when he met Rigdon for the *first* time, Cowdery distinctly remembered his voice as being identical to the voice of John the Baptist. Unwavering in his convictions, Cowdery ventured the guess that perhaps Rigdon's role was to prepare the way for Joseph in the same manner as John the Baptist's was to prepare the way for Jesus; with hints of the reincarnate made possible by a proxy, Cowdery concluded that the same voice matched the same divine responsibility.

This story was taken from the confession by Oliver *Overstreet*, the feigned Oliver Cowdery, but the confession itself was also a hoax. Known as "the Overstreet Letter," this story survives as an early example of fierce anti-Mormon propaganda and evidence of the intense turmoil and infighting that continued within Mormonism despite Brigham Young's impressive performance as Joseph Smith. As the story goes, a man named Oliver Overstreet was hired in 1848 by Mormon officials to impersonate Oliver Cowdery in order to preserve Cowdery's witness of The Book of Mormon (the real Cowdery claimed

38 · CHAPTER 1

that he saw the original brass plates of The Book of Mormon before an angel took them to heaven, but he had since apostatized from the Church several years earlier). Fake or not, Overstreet's confession reads like an endorsement of Mormon leadership's high appraisal for convincing impersonation:

> I personated Oliver Cowdery at Council Bluffs, Iowa, on the 21st day of October, 1848 in a conference at which Bro. Orson Hyde presided [. . .]
>
> The facts are these: Bro. R. Miller came to me with an offer from Bro. Brigham Young of $500.00, cash in hand paid, to pose as Oliver Cowdery, the first of the "three witnesses" to the Book of Mormon. [. . .]
>
> He insisted that I resemble Cowdery so much in form and features, notwithstanding our differences in tone of voice that I could easily personate him without danger of being caught and exposed. [. . .]
>
> To enable me to know what to say and do, Bro. Miller had me read some articles written by Cowdery and also gave me some voice drill, assuring me that he would make a verbatum [sic] record of my remarks, while personating Mr. Cowdery to be preserved for futur [sic] use under Bro. Brigham Young's direction; and that my part in the matter he was confident would never be known or suspected.[16]

While this story exists within a complex narrative of fraudulence, it survives for substantive reasons. Even though both Young's transfiguration and Cowdery's/Overstreet's confession are outside the bounds of historical veracity, these examples of impersonation and deception draw attention to a particular theological undercurrent within Mormonism that sustains vocal deception and vicariousness as emblems of godliness. In fact, despite the familiarity and prominence of Joseph's First Vision for Mormons today, I would argue that the most important sonic miracle for Mormonism was not when Joseph conversed with God and Jesus in the grove of trees near his family farm but rather the moment Joseph's voice was heard breaking forth out of the mouth of Brigham Young. It is in this instance where a theology of voice is first put to use by an aspiring leader, one heard and understood as a divine sign by the faithful, and that established vocal vicariousness as a quality of all prophets and not just a peculiar ability of Joseph Smith.

The possibility for mimed voices or impersonation was not only a part of the nineteenth-century American milieu, it was also a distinct part of Mormon theology. Given the storied prominence of Young and Cowdery's remarkable examples of vocal mimicry, perhaps nineteenth-century Mormons were willing to play along with impersonations and clever acts of deceit. People are never as good at masking their voices as they think they are, anyway. Jody Kreiman and Diana Sidtis write that "it is very difficult indeed to reproduce a voice so accurately that it is actually mistaken for the target, and true impersonation usually requires a credulous audience to succeed."[17] Since any act of vocal vicariousness is also an act of duplicity, one's ears can easily be fooled if not properly attuned to the qualities of a divine voice.

The Voice of Laban

If the possibility exists for a mimic Brigham Young, it stands as all the more convincing because of another Mormon story of feigned identity and vocal impersonation: the story of Nephi and Laban in the opening pages of The Book of Mormon. The Book of Mormon begins in Jerusalem shortly before its destruction. A prophet named Lehi (a contemporary of Jeremiah's) is warned by God to take his wife and family into the wilderness to flee persecution. This departure eventually lands the family on the American continent. Before they can make the trip overseas, however, Lehi instructs his sons Nephi, Laman, and Lemuel to go back into Jerusalem and obtain some scriptural and genealogical records held by Laban, the family's ecclesiastical leader. Laban is apparently a wicked and greedy man. When Lehi's most obedient and faithful son, Nephi, confronts Laban and offers payment of the family's fortunes in exchange for the records, Laban greedily takes the money and tries to kill Nephi. The faithful son escapes, and later tries a second time to gain the records.

On this second visit to Laban, Nephi finds him drunk and passed out in an alley outside his home. In an exchange remarkable for its ethical vibrancy, God commands Nephi to take Laban's sword and kill him. Nephi obeys—he cuts off Laban's head, puts on Laban's clothes, and enters the house of Laban looking for the sacred records. Like Brigham Young, Nephi is apparently a brilliant actor and mimic, for he speaks "in the voice of Laban" and is costumed in his "garments and also the sword girded about [his] loins."[18] Nephi-as-Laban convinces Laban's servant Zoram to retrieve the sacred records, allowing Nephi to escape with them and thus preserve the records from destruction (see figure 2.3).

Avi Steinberg asks the right question when he first reads of Laban's beheading: "The Hebrew Bible begins with the creation of heaven and earth; the New Testament begins with the mysterious birth of a boy god. What kind of bible starts off in a dark creepy alley, with a sleazy drunk guy and a gruesome murder/robbery?"[19] There *is* something grizzly about a divinely

40 · CHAPTER 1

endorsed beheading and mugging; the story is unsettling, no matter how it is sliced.

Although Nephi feels justified murdering Laban and then lying about his identity to rob his victim, his actions likely sit uneasily on the Mormon conscience. Perhaps the ends justify the means; without the sacred plates Laban is keeping for himself, Lehi and his sons feel they cannot proceed with God's directives. And, as Mormons know from the Old Testament, Jerusalem is about to be destroyed; it is unlikely that Lehi and his family would have survived the attacks had they not escaped when they did. Still, Nephi's duplicitous actions call for scrutiny. As the faithful hero of The Book of Mormon, Nephi is exemplary, obedient, loyal, and courageously willing to do what he is asked regardless of the personal costs. His theatrical guise here may have been ethically dubious, yet pretending to be Laban is what allows him access to the sacred plates.

One would think this story would make Mormons ambivalent toward theatricality, the way Andrea Most argues was the case for Jews who, with the story of Jacob and Esau, are also faced with a Genesis story built around duping others. Disdain for the theater is not the case, however, for either group today. Jews and Mormons have instead both used the theater to assimilate into American ideologies and, especially with Jewish figures such as Richard Rodgers, Oscar Hammerstein II, Stephen Sondheim, and Leonard Bernstein, even create new American ideologies from the theater. If God has a hand in shepherding either group, it appears He is content with allowing theatricality to move things along.

Moral ambivalence aside, it seems significant that Nephi is instructed to kill Laban in the way that he does. Surely a less messy way exists for obtaining garments than decapitation. Yet to strike off the head—at the very point of vocal delivery—signifies the removal of authority, of the voice that speaks for another, and is an action echoed throughout mythical and biblical stories. When it comes to mediating the interior Self and the exterior Other, the head is paramount. It contains not just the vocal mechanism but also the teeth, lips, tongue, palette, and mouth we use to engage the world with our voice. As Brandon LaBelle has written, "the mouth has already initiated a confrontation with the forces surrounding and penetrating us, leaving their deep impressions firmly upon the tongue and hence our psychological life."[20] There is even in Mormonism a modern inverse of Laban's murder: according to one legend, after Joseph was killed and his body had fallen from the jail's second story window, his attackers tried to cut off his head as a souvenir (and possibly redeemable for bounty) but were thwarted by electrical shock.

THE VOICE AND MORMON THEATRICALITY · 41

These two tales of impersonation and mimicry are foundational mythologies in Mormon lore. Both Young's transfiguration and this moral of Nephi and Laban act as Genesis stories for the Mormon faith, catalysts that shift the action of the story from one location to another: Illinois to the Great Salt Lake for one, Jerusalem to a pre-Columbian American continent for the other. Taken together, these tales of mysterious theatrics and mimicry give the capacity of voicing someone else a unique position in Mormon lore.

Attuning the Ear to God

The power dependent on voice in both stories confirms the etymological meaning of obedience, which comes from the Latin *audire* (to hear). Inherent in obedience is a kind of willful theatricality, and inherent in hearing is obedience. In the annals of heaven, kingdoms rise and fall on the merits of a listening ear. Therefore, it is through the attuned ear that God proves the faithful; the ears of the unfaithful or disobedient, by contrast, may easily be fooled by God's theatrically sophisticated elect. In exceptional instances, as with Brigham Young or Nephi, the ability to speak and hear on behalf of another person provides the means to miraculous ends. Yet even in normative circumstances, Mormons practice a kind of vocal vicariousness. This is how faithful Mormons fashion themselves as proxies for the dead in the Mormon temple ceremony and how Mormon prophets came to speak with sameness the voice of God.

Mormonism is built around The Book of Mormon, a written document with sonic origins, and therefore may best be understood as a conceptual space where *vocality* orders the heavens and the everyday practices of its members: a training ground for how to perform one's place in eternity through vocal sound—in effect, a *theology of voice*. Such a theology is practiced in two ways in Mormonism. First, Mormonism's roots are sonic, so all policies and dogma arguably emerge from the sound of the voice. Joseph's experiences with angels, God, and other divine beings are grounded in conversation: he heard God call him by name, he dictated to scribes The Book of Mormon (which likewise refers to itself as a "voice speaking out of the dust"), and he instated a temple drama where speaking on behalf of the dead transforms everyday Mormons into "saviors on Mount Zion."[21] In his study of The Book of Mormon's sonic qualities, Peter McMurray even suggests that The Book of Mormon be considered both in *medium* and *message* to be about sound.

> The Book of Mormon contains numerous events in which sounds play a crucial role in formulating, transmitting, and representing sacred knowledge

42 · CHAPTER 1

and action. It frequently becomes a site of contestation between believers and non-believers. But perhaps most importantly, it functions as a key marker of divinity and an object of aspiration, as prophets and other believers aspire to attain a sonic existence more like that of God and his angels.[22]

Fundamentally, then, Mormonism is the product of a certain kind of vocal vicariousness, a good that will be rewarded in heaven. The Book of Mormon proclaims it, Joseph's life exemplified it, and Mormons today continue to practice it.

Mormons perform a theology of voice secondly by materializing long-lasting metaphors in Mormon scriptures where speaking and hearing a spiritual message are the primary measures of conversion to the gospel. Joseph boldly proclaimed that "no unhallowed hand can stop the work from progressing" until "it has penetrated every continent, visited every clime, swept every country, and *sounded in every ear*."[23] Towers from which messages could be proclaimed are frequently erected and destroyed in The Book of Mormon amid cycles of peace and violence. In the early twentieth century, the Church adopted radio and television to spread its message—a practice some saw as an electronic extension of those ancient wooden towers. "What mighty towers has our Heavenly Father permitted us to have in this dispensation through the use of radio and television," exclaimed Fred C. Esplin. "Surely they are more powerful instruments beyond imagination, to help the gospel message 'sound in every ear' on this planet."[24]

Given these two dimensions for voice in Mormonism, it is unsurprising that Mormons have developed ways to practice their religion by drawing attention to the voice, even in the face of rather drastic policy changes over many years. Voice in imitation gives buoyancy to the faith, and performance on stage—whether ritualized in the everyday or in musicals—helps sacralize it.

Imitating God

Vocal performance involves not only the voice but also a repertoire of gestures, postures, and, most important, an intention to deceive. Deception need not always carry a negative connotation; many religious texts actually seem to promote it as a pious practice. In addition to stories in The Book of Mormon about disguise or mistaken identity, such as the Nephi and Laban account or the wandering and immortal Three Nephites, Mormon scriptures and the Bible are replete with instances of theatrics as apparent signs of divinity. As noted, Andrea Most has written about the ambivalence Jews have felt toward the theater since Jacob, namesake for the entire Hebrew nation, hoodwinked his father and stole the birthright from his brother Esau.[25] The New Testament is no less cautious about duplicitous behavior. Paul warns against "false prophets, deceitful workers, transforming themselves into the apostles of Christ"; he places a fine point on the matter by adding that "Satan himself is transformed into an angel of light."[26]

Other scriptures send mixed messages on this topic, however. "Put on the whole armor of God," Paul writes.[27] Paul's association between a new identity and godly behavior sets a standard for imitation as an emblem of discipleship. For many ages, then, Christians have had concerns about modeling holy behavior. Coincidentally, the uneasy relationship between pious Christian denominations and the theater suggests scriptural endorsements of imitation or duplicity are classified by religious practitioners as something different in kind, not degree, from what happens on a theatrical stage. In this regard, Mormons set themselves apart, as Mormon leaders have celebrated and modeled theatricality since the religion's founding (see chapter 2). Still, it seems that for the most part, religious imitation or modeling of God is understood as something patently different from the happenings of the theater.

Indeed, early Mormons found themselves caught within a web of imitative practices, including some that were not always welcome. The angry mob of local vigilantes, religious zealots, and disgruntled Mormons that charged Carthage Jail and murdered Joseph and Hyrum Smith, for example, were disguised in blackface. When confronted by the prospects of harassment by a reckless U.S. Federal Army—one scholar noted that tensions between the Church and federal government during the nineteenth century "resembled comic opera more than a political battle"—one band of Mormons dressed as Native Americans raided and killed a party of 120 men, women, and children passing through on the way to California.[28] Patrick Q. Mason details how, when Church leader Brigham H. Roberts was charged with retrieving the bodies of two missionaries murdered in Cane Creek, Tennessee, he disguised himself as a tramp before stealing away the bodies undetected.[29] These were common happenings and reduced the gap between reality and the playacting in circumstances far removed from the footlights of a theater. Mormons were on the cusp of changing sensibilities in America, as the principles of minstrelsy and speaking on behalf of God became harder and harder to separate in practice.

In line with Paul's somewhat cautionary embrace of mimicry, religious thinkers have continued to imagine God's relationship with humans in theatrical terms. Augustine, for example, believed God communicated to humans

44 · CHAPTER 1

through a form of mimicry. Because any manifestation of God to humans is contingent on God having a material body—a belief today held almost exclusively by Mormons—Augustine understood theophany instead to be a divine theatrical act. For Augustine, God's dramatic presentation raised the stakes for who God is and who humans are in relation to Him. As John Durham Peters writes of Augustine, "If God appeared to appear, he was resorting to deception, donning a disguise to meet the crudity of human sense organs. Theophany is either deception (of humans) or debasement (of God)."[30] In Augustine's words, "For as the sound which communicates the thought conceived in the silence of the mind is not the thought itself, so the form by which God, invisible in his own nature, became visible, was not God himself."[31] What the prophets and apostles have come to know, fear, love, and worship is, for Augustine, just a mock-up, a Something-Else pretending to be what we have come to know as God.

In the fifteenth century, Thomas à Kempis first published *De Imitatione Christi* (*The Imitation of Christ*), in which he argued that internal modeling of Christ's attitude, rather than a physical imitation of his life as measured by friars, is what is meant by becoming like God. "Whoever wishes to understand fully the words of Christ must try to pattern his whole life on that of Christ," the book reads.[32] In the nineteenth century, Kierkegaard refocused Augustine's notion of a God "incognito," who lives out the principle that concealing one's identity and purpose may be necessary to maintain purity. For Kierkegaard, disciples must confront Jesus as a deceiver, as part of a contradiction, justified because paradox is what can save us from the falsity of direct communication.

In the twentieth century, C. S. Lewis turned the tables on deception and encouraged believers to "pretend," to "dress up as Christ" when praying. This is far from pretense for the sake of fooling yourself or another person, he argues. Rather, theatrics is an important means for followers to come closer to God and Jesus. Lewis writes,

> Now, the moment you realize "Here I am, dressing up as Christ," it is extremely likely that you will see at once some way in which at that very moment the pretense could be made less of a pretense and more of a reality. . . . You see what is happening. The Christ Himself, the Son of God who is man (just like you) and God (just like His Father) is actually at your side and is already at that moment beginning to turn your pretense into a reality.[33]

In this passage, Lewis argues for duplicity as a religious necessity, requisite to achieving the proper state of humility before approaching the divine.

Tucked within this pretending is the notion of vicariousness. Acting and praying on behalf of Jesus makes humans the agents of godly communication. This is how humans for millennia have been able to make God in their own image, a practice that continues today. In her book *When God Talks Back*, anthropologist Tanya Luhrmann discovers a direct application of Lewis's counsel in the attitudes of modern American evangelicals. She finds that in seeking an immediate and personal experience with God, evangelicals resort to playacting in order to make an invisible and scripturally distant God seem closer and empathetic.[34] Thus evangelicals pretend to have coffee with God, go on lunch dates with God, and in general act as if the unseeable God is interested in and present for the ins and outs of their everyday lives.

Taken together, such propositions are paradoxical, suggesting that reality can be understood best when unrealistic measures are taken. These purposeful and respected guises don't belong solely within the domain of religion, however. Viktor Shlovsky in his infamous gem that art exists "to make one feel things, to make the stone stony" similarly sees value in how artifice provides a distance to reality which, in turn, allows people to reconnect to that reality in a more real way.[35]

Mormon practices of vicariousness are fundamentally different from what most Christians have practiced and in fact serve different theological ends, since playacting for Augustine or Lewis is a private, even pious affair, while pretend in Mormonism depends on the presence of an audience. Yet Christian understandings of playacting and vicariousness do serve as useful comparisons to Mormon theatricality. For example, Lewis's words echo those in an instruction manual the Mormon Church published in 1980 as guidelines for local congregations planning theatrical events: "Vicarious experiences that confirm truth while entertaining an audience can make good theatre." There is a tremendous message packed within that one sentence. Implicit in this perspective is that God, truth, or divine immediacy may be ascertained by humans only through the process of pretending. Augustine presumes the inverse is true as well, that God interfaces with humans only by donning the character of "God." A child's imaginative playacting draws her closer to a world otherwise unknown to her, and in the same way a believer may draw closer to heaven through vicarious enactments of someone or something else. In this framework, Jesus's teaching that "except ye be converted, and become as little children, ye shall not enter into the kingdom of heaven" takes on a new meaning.[36]

Even though these examples demonstrate that Mormons are not alone in the attention they give to a theatrically possible theology, stories of a

46 · CHAPTER 1

transformed person, a god in disguise, or mistaken identity greatly inform the Mormon faith. The favorite model of transformation seems to be none other than the singular Jesus himself; after all, Jesus concedes to the theatrical necessity of discipleship. Modeling human life after divine beings is central to Jesus's teachings in both the ancient world and the new world. His biblical counsel to "Be ye perfect, even as your Father which is in heaven is perfect" elevates the ability to perform, and to do it well, to the realm of utmost divinity.[37] Even more, in The Book of Mormon the resurrected Jesus asks the Nephites "what manner of men ought ye to be?" He answers his own question with "Verily I say unto you, even as I am."[38] Most crucial, however, may be Jesus's act of surrogacy in taking on the sins of every individual and dying on the cross for them all (Mormons refer to this as the "substitution" theory of atonement, in which Jesus literally "acts" on behalf of all humans). This tremendously powerful testament to vicariousness defines the relationship many Christians have with Jesus, who, in turn, teaches them how to act and speak for one another.[39]

His reliance on parables, a genre notable for the way meaning is disguised by clever rhetoric, also makes Jesus a slippery figure. In fact, Jesus has a remarkable ability to disappear and then reappear in unexpected places throughout scripture and mythology. The resurrected Jesus is mistaken for a stranger by his disciples on the road to Emmaus, thought a gardener by Mary at his own tomb, and, in the song "The Poor Wayfaring Man of Grief," which was reportedly sung to Joseph in the hours leading up to his death, a story is told of charity given to a stranger who, in the final verse, is revealed to have been Jesus in disguise. "Then in a moment to my view/ The stranger started from disguise./ The tokens in his hands I knew;/ The Savior stood before mine eyes."

Perhaps Jesus's shape-shifting is not a cheeky stunt to test human credulity but rather a training session on how to be more like the God he vicariously represents. Mormons take this attribute of Jesus's very seriously. The base of Mormon theology is that mortal life is preparatory for godliness and that men are something akin to gods-in-training. Lorenzo Snow's oft-quoted couplet "As man is, God once was; as God is, man may become" succinctly captures this belief in both the materiality of God as well as the godly potential of all mortals.[40] Mormons thus take C. S. Lewis's counsel to ends that far exceed his vision of Christian humility. If Jesus and other biblical figures were so favored and skilled in the art of disguise (or frankly, in some cases, deceit), perhaps within the Mormon impulse to perform is the instinct for the apprentice to model the master.

THE VOICE AND MORMON THEATRICALITY   ·   47

Braden Bell's 2010 novel *The Road Show* illustrates this point well. Road shows are short musical comedies that for many years were integral to the Church's youth programs; Mormon congregations plan and perform road shows together, often in friendly competition with neighboring congregations.[41] Bell's novel tells how one Mormon congregation was changed in the process of such a theatrical venture. Scott, the road show director, is a young Mormon struggling with a pornography addiction. He battles depression and intense feelings of unworthiness throughout the process of writing and directing the play. Scott performs the role of a leper and Curtis, his priesthood leader, plays Jesus. Scott and Curtis both have transformative experiences on stage when the actual Jesus speaks through Curtis—a Mormon overwhelmed with Church responsibilities—and directly to Scott—a man who is very aware of his personal failings. For Curtis, "In that instant, it all came together. As he stood on the stage dressed as the Savior, saying the Savior's words, he felt that he stood on holy ground. He felt honored and almost overwhelmed to be in that position. He was full of reverence and awe. And most of all, he felt love."[42] Scott, meanwhile, finally found relief from his shame and guilt as Curtis's portrayal of Jesus somehow became more than just a performance. "He knew the figure above him was merely Curtis in a wig, but there was more going on. Somehow, Curtis was a focal point, a mirror reflecting a far greater presence. Curtis, Scott's priesthood leader, represented the Savior. Scott knew he was clean."[43]

This story is fictional but nevertheless points to the transformative power Mormons grant to impersonation, mimicry, and performance. An otherwise common theatrical experience turns out to be the means by which faithful Mormons come closer to Jesus, in this case through impersonating him as well as learning to see (and hear) Jesus in another person. So much of Jesus's identity seems a clever affront for a hidden god within human form, but for Mormons this quality makes Jesus more immediate, relevant, and accessible. And as theatricality gives Mormons a glimpse into their biggest role as someday-gods, an opportunity to perform as Jesus on stage is just the beginning.

With One Voice

In 1897, Church president Wilford Woodruff recorded his testimony on a wax cylinder in Salt Lake City, Utah, becoming the first Mormon prophet to record his voice. Mormons have long understood the prophet to be the literal mouthpiece of God. This phonographic encapsulation of a prophet's voice, then, is the capturing of God's voice. And since Woodruff's is the first prophetic voice we have on record, this initial foray into phonographic magic is a starting point for understanding not only the language but also the vocal essence—what Robert Frost called the "oversound"—of the prophet and, presumably, God Himself.[44] It is here where the voice of the prophet becomes real to modern Mormons, and it is to this point where Mormons attune their ears and voices in the practice of vocal vicariousness.

For all that Woodruff could have used his precious few minutes of wax cylinder space speaking to, he chose to testify to events from 1844 that affirm Brigham Young's rightful place as successor to Mormon prophet and founder Joseph Smith. As they were the day Joseph's voice came sounding out of Young's mouth, the stakes here for Woodruff are quite high. No doubt, as Joseph's son Joseph Smith III was putting pressure on Latter-Day Saints in Utah to join the "true" Mormon faith—the Reorganized Church of Jesus Christ of Latter Day Saints, now Community of Christ, headquartered in Independence, Missouri—Woodruff felt it important to strike down any insurgency from that splinter group. Woodruff specifically testifies that Joseph met with the twelve apostles and "delivered unto them the ordinances of the Church and kingdom of God" and confirms that the temple endowments were received directly by the hand of Joseph, rather than a later development or invention of Brigham Young's—two contestable claims that the rightfulness of the LDS Church hinged upon.

Mormons were awestruck by the implications of a recorded voice. In an 1897 editorial in the Mormon-owned *Deseret News*, one writer wonders at the technological powers of capturing Woodruff's voice. He even goes so far as to suppose that God must use an instrument similar in design to render perfect judgment in the afterlife.

> If mortals can manufacture instruments that can register the tones of the human voice with such fidelity as they are produced by the gramophone, what may not be presumed of the capabilities of the higher powers, even on perfectly natural principles, to bring forth to the dismay of the wicked, pictures and sounds of deeds and sayings which they cannot deny, to confound them in the presence of the Eternal Judge. "Out of thine own mouth shalt thou be judged," may turn out to be something more than a mere figure of speech.[45]

As remarkable as this editorial is, Mormons weren't the only ones quick to connect phonographic powers with eternal powers. Media theorist Friedrich Kittler reports that *Scientific American* decreed in 1877 of Edison's invention, "Speech has become, as it were, immortal" under the headline "A Wonderful

THE VOICE AND MORMON THEATRICALITY · 49

Invention—Speech Capable of Infinite Repetitions from Automatic Records."[46] Ceaseless repetition, it seems, made the heavens more proximate than ever before imagined. God has been listening, the editorial almost hysterically hisses, and He can listen with exactness by tuning in again and again and again. The repetitive potential of the phonograph explained how God's listening ears might be infallible, and for the first time ever, humans could be made to hear the way God Himself has been eavesdropping on his creation all along. By the early twentieth century, some had even come to believe that technology could capture every voice that was ever uttered because, as the theory goes, the voice was still vibrating the air but at too low a frequency to be audible. Guglielmo Marconi, the Italian inventor of long-distance radio transmission, argued that the wavelengths from Jesus's Sermon on the Mount were still bouncing through the air and could be heard if a sensitive-enough microphone were ever developed.[47] Even into midcentury, science fiction spun tales of technology as mundane as the telephone that allowed the living to speak and listen to the dead, as depicted in *The Twilight Zone* episodes "Long Distance Call" (1961) and "Night Call" (1964).[48] Recording technology has thus created a paradigm shift among religious listeners, Mormons included. As Kittler suggests, "technology literally makes the unheard-of possible."[49]

It's perhaps unsurprising then that Edison's invention was commonly known as a "talking machine," a moniker that admits of the machine's immediate usefulness to those unaccustomed to preserving human speech. This is how Woodruff himself refers to the phonograph in his own recording. Because people once lived without the expectation that voices could be preserved, they developed listening techniques to retain the voice in human memory with as much fidelity as possible. In her humorous but poignant search for the voice of celebrated actress Sarah Siddons (who died decades before the phonograph was invented), Judith Pascoe acknowledges that straining to catch Siddons's voice is not so much out of an interest in recovering the voice per se but rather an effort to "understand how people listened in the romantic period and how that style of listening influenced what they heard."[50] "Even as the voice has become ever more easily recordable, transferrable, and portable," she laments, "it may have slipped farther out of memory's reach."[51]

It is increasingly unfathomable to imagine a vanishing voice that simply cannot—and will never be—recalled. People today can retrieve images and sounds with the press of a button; consequently, we may not be listening as closely as people once did to the voices around us. We may in fact be

50 · CHAPTER 1

unknowingly suffering from this condition, having in effect solved the riddle of immortality with the capability of hearing any voice on demand by bargaining away our attention to voices sounding around us in real time. Stephen Connor calls this assumption of permanency "the loss of the loss of voice."[52]

Without Marconi's ultrasensitive microphone, we have no recording of that infamous outdoor meeting in 1844, so we cannot know for certain what Brigham Young's voice sounded like, or Joseph Smith's for that matter. This seems an unfortunate absence in today's world where seemingly every word is embalmed by digital recorders upon delivery. The fragility of the human voice was certainly something early Mormons were aware of, and because of their awareness we have a fairly good idea of how those now-lost voices were once heard. Especially after Joseph's death, when it began to seem that Jesus's return to earth may not be as soon as most followers were initially led to believe, Mormons became much more vigilant about recording and preserving the words and actions of their leaders who, as proxies for the voice of God, were vessels of divinity on earth. The voluminous diary and journal entries attesting to Brigham Young's transfiguration are proof of this recording frenzy. Mormons today continue to diligently record their words and actions for posterity. Still, as much as speech may be captured on paper and the ways of listening preserved on record, the voice itself remains irretrievable without recordings.

Enter Wilford Woodruff's wax cylinder. Woodruff's recording not only preserved *a* prophet's voice, but it truly may have captured *the* prophet's voice. If Young was able to carry forward the voice of Joseph as a matter of vocal principal, then perhaps Woodruff too, as another prophetic successor, modeled in his testimony the speaking voice of his predecessors and, ultimately, the Mormon founder. In the words of Truman G. Madsen, "Notes are often misplaced and forgotten. But this recording preserves indelible firsthand experience. With transparent clarity, [Woodruff] blends Joseph's words with his own. This, Joseph's last testimony to the Twelve, became his own."[53] Even in death, then, Joseph may continue to shape the church he founded through the vicarious voicings of subsequent prophets.

We might take Pascoe's mission to "understand how people listened in the romantic period" as our own, using Woodruff's recording to determine the voice Mormons attuned their ears toward when they listened for the voice of God, but we might also view it as a litmus test to gauge how prophets *did* (and perhaps *ought to*) speak even still today. Mormon leaders and laity today continue to base their mode of speech upon a vocal model encapsulated through recordings of the prophets. Mormons gather twice a year at General Conference to listen to Church leaders (commonly referred to as General

Authorities) speak; what they hear is a unified voice providing a unified message. Listen backward into the twentieth century and you will hear that virtually all General Conference speakers sound alike. Numerous YouTube compilations of Mormon prophets bearing testimony make this comparison a simple process. The cadence, breath control, inflection, and length of pause between phrases mark the speech as sacred or prophetic (rather than mundane—or profane, to use Durkheim's dyad) as much, if not more, as the similarity among any words or phrases themselves. Clearly there is some kind of listening technique at work whereby subsequent prophets, perhaps enabled by the offices they hold or else as the result of years of hearing prophets speak this particular way, match vocal inflections to a historical standard.

Anthropologist Nicolas Harkness has noticed similar impersonation trends among Christian communities in Seoul, South Korea. Harkness observes that South Korea's remarkable transition from one of the poorest countries in the world to one of the wealthiest in but a few decades has left a sonic imprint on the Korean voice. Koreans today speak of the voice as "clean" or "unclean" in reference to a changing sound quality that emerged during the country's radical reinvention. Harkness hears how this new aesthetic has reached the evangelical Christian practice of glossolalia, as well as the operatic conventions in classical vocal training. As a singer studies with a master teacher in South Korea, for example, the student is expected to take on the vocal sound, or *qualia*, of that teacher. The vocal modeling is understood as an act of submission and respect. "The disciple is supposed to be of service to the teacher," he writes, "and likewise the disciple's voice should replicate qualia of the teacher's voice. By doing so, students index the teacher's authority through the qualia of the voice itself."[54] Similarly, he notes that moments of collective effervescence during Korean religious services are often moments marked by vocal attunement—bodies gradually match pitch and tone during tongue-speaking, even though such experiences are upheld as supremely individualistic and personal.

Within this larger Christian context, some argue that this ability to give voice to experiences with God is written into our DNA. Stephen Webb, in his book *Divine Voice: Christian Proclamation and the Theology of Sound*, claims that all human speech is a priori of and for God. The theological necessity of hearing God's word, whether given by Jesus, a prophet, or another medium, gives meaning to our ability to speak to Him.

> Theologically construed, speaking is not a trait projected upon God by analogy to human experience. We do not speak first and then think about God as speaking too. On the contrary, we can speak only because God created us

> to be hearers of God's Word. We are created in God's image, but that image
> is more like an echo than a mirror. God spoke us into being so that we too
> might have the joy of sharing in the spoken Word.[55]

For Webb, human vocality is intrinsically imitative since God's presence is tucked within every human utterance; in a prayerful cry for supplication, God effectively is speaking through the supplicant to Himself. Webb's concept of God as a divine feedback loop is different from the Mormon perspective that God delegates vocal power not for His own sake (though fundamentally this may be the case) but rather in pursuit of a standardized, broadcast message to all who may hear. It is for the sake of the hearer that the Mormon God permits vocal vicariousness. As a result, Mormons are much less interested in why God allows them to speak or hear than they are in fulfilling God's commandment to act as His surrogates to as many people as possible. It is in God's best interest, then, to establish a mechanism whereby Mormons may learn and then practice for themselves the voice of God as given to the prophets.

Given the scriptural pronouncement that "whether by mine own voice or by the voice of my servants, it is the same," it is unsurprising that everyday Mormons inevitably appropriate this common, prophetic voice in their religious speech acts. Anthropologist David Knowlton has pointed out this trend in terms of grammar choice, noting that on the local level, Mormons adhere to the form and structure in testimony or prayer that is used by the prophetic leaders. "Most Mormons can reproduce the style, and probably do when they bear testimony," he writes, "and usually they are not conscious of doing it. We are native performers, experts, and do it unawares."[56]

Indeed, the Mormon vocal model goes beyond mere syntax and is inscribed in the vocal product itself, as any comparison of prophets speaking will show. What Mormons do is not just impersonation or rhetorical matching, although those are important components of the standard prophetic voice. Rather, Mormons in essence demonstrate their righteousness by ventriloquizing the voice of their leaders. It is important to note that God's delegation of voice in Mormonism is not one-directional or contained only within the prophet-deity relationship; in effect, this ventriloquism exploits both the experience of speaking through and of being spoken through. As Stephen Connor has argued, the history of ventriloquism is a history of the tension between "the power to speak through others or as the experience of being spoken through by others."[57] Therefore, Mormons use the prophetic voice to lend authority to their own experiences with the divine, or, inversely perhaps, the prophet speaks vicariously through each member to confirm for listeners the truthfulness of such accounts.

THE VOICE AND MORMON THEATRICALITY · 53

Regardless of the phenomenological apparatus at work in Mormon mimicry, relying on "sacred codes" in their prayers and testimonies allows Mormons to get a feel for what it is like to speak with divinity even as that "divinity" gets channeled through the voices and bodies of those devout members. Even more, by picking up and modeling the standardized vocal patterns of the prophets, Mormons can and have learned essentially to speak on behalf of God. Samuel Brown argues that verbal standardization in fact makes prophets out of spiritual paupers, writing that "uttering God's actual words allows the worshippers to become mouthpieces for the divine Word."[58] Speaking a certain way is thus a marker of belonging, an emblem Mormons employ to broadcast that they have staked a claim in the institution and agreed to willingly make the voice of the prophets the voice of their own, and thereby sound inflections of God.

Even though the process of speaking a standardized voice may seem instinctive or natural for many Mormons, a lot depends on this vocal modeling. Inaccurately voicing the pattern and sound of Mormon leaders is an aural admission of dilettante status. Knowlton understands the stakes in a Mormon testimony meeting when he writes, "Performance, like it or not, becomes the critical means of determining whether a given individual is righteous or spiritual."[59] Failure to perform an accurate portrayal of the standard makes the novice easily classifiable—a forgivable grievance if in fact a novice you are, though highly suspect if you are a familiar, long-term member. The disciplining of the Mormon voice, even if done without much attention to itself, is what Mormons attune their ears to whenever anyone steps up to the microphone at a testimony meeting and begins with the familiar phrase, "Brothers and sisters, I'd like to bear you my testimony."[60]

*   *   *

From Woodruff's wax cylinders of 1897 to today, a standardized voice emerges as a sonic emblem of divinity that Mormons model to show piety. Members construct this chain of vocal vicariousness—speaking with the voice of the prophet, who is likewise speaking the voice of God—in an effort to pattern more closely their lives in godliness. As with the example of Brigham Young, the closer a Mormon can sound to the model, the greater his likelihood of ascending the Mormon hierarchy—it is but a small exaggeration to say that an everyday Mormon becomes a prophet by successfully voicing Mormonism. Spending enough time in a Mormon congregation and listening to how the men speak, one learns that those who sound more like the model will be the next in line for local leadership positions.

54 · CHAPTER 1

The Mormon hierarchy comprises exquisite performers, all devoted to honing the craft of theatrical virtuosity in their role as proxies for God. Moreover, each faithful Mormon is invested in listening and voicing techniques to move them closer to the divine through carefully calculated performances. As Mormonism has evolved, members have made the small leap from their vocal performative theology to embrace many of the conventions of American musical theater. The unfolding story is that Mormons have therefore gravitated toward musical theater not merely as a source of entertainment but also as a mode of communication, a venue of religious practice, and an opportunity for social acceptance. Voice is of utmost concern in musical theater where, as with Mormonism, the voice on a musical stage serves a utilitarian purpose in channeling a person's ideology, personality, allegiances, and capabilities. In a genre where to sing is to belong, musicals inhabit a world where Mormons too want to belong: a world where the voice can show who can be trusted, who someone really is, and what that person longs to be. The Mormon devotion to and practical consideration of musical theater starts with the simple, everyday practice of listening for God in the voice of the prophet—his vicarious voice at once acting as a buttress of the Mormon status quo and as a clear reminder that becoming like God is an act, and that the show must go on.[61]

2

Promised Valley, Integration, and the Singing Voice

And he said, It is not the voice of them that shout for mastery, neither is it the voice of them that cry for being overcome: but the noise of them that sing do I hear.

—Exodus 32:18

Thy watchmen shall lift up the voice; with the voice together shall they sing: for they shall see eye to eye, when the Lord shall bring again Zion.

—Isaiah 52:8

Singing carries a certain magical power in the service of death. Choirs of angels may be expected in those final moments, a sonic hand grasping ahold of the faithful and pulling them toward their final reward. On the other hand, the sirens ushered unwilling mortals to their death through beautiful singing. In some versions of the story, the mournful song of Orfeo stops even Sisyphus in his eternal peddling of the boulder up and down the mountain. But voice, like music more generally, has also occasioned mistrust. Mladen Dolar felt that singing signaled a kind of semantic death: the death of meaning. "Singing represents a different stage," he writes. "It brings the voice energetically to the forefront, on purpose, at the expense of meaning. Indeed, singing is bad communication."[1] If bad communication is the result of the intoned voice, then it seems the musical stage would be the last place a group could find meaning.

Yet this is the story of how Mormons found great meaning and renewed purpose through exactly such a place. Chapter 1 explored how Mormon vocality emerged as an emblem of divine vicariousness. This chapter looks at how the Mormon voice became magnified when Mormons moved to the

56 · CHAPTER 2

musical stage—the platform from which voice is perhaps the most consequential. From the mid-nineteenth century to the mid-twentieth century,
Mormons regularly found themselves lampooned on the stages of New York,
Boston, London, and elsewhere. As the Mormon Church attempted to create a more acceptable image for itself and its members in the early twentieth
century, however, it turned to musical theater as the venue for achieving
broader acceptance in American life. I trace the legacy of musicals in and
about Mormon life from the nineteenth century through the commission of
the musical *Promised Valley* in the 1940s. The show helped Mormons cash
in on a particular kind of American identity, but it also illustrates how vocal
discipline became the means by which Mormons vied for broader acceptance
from the country they once fled.

Brigham Young and the Salt Lake Theatre

When Brigham Young spoke with the voice of Joseph Smith outside Nauvoo, Illinois, in 1844, he not only initiated a practice of vocal modeling still
in use today, but he also revealed glimpses of his theatrical side. The hardy
image Brigham Young enjoys today—sire to fifty-six children, unflinching
zealot with a sizable beard, and an emblem of benevolent American frontier
stock—hardly seems commensurable with that of a thespian. Yet Brigham
Young may be thanked for the tremendous outflow of theatrical and musical culture that permeated the otherwise barren Salt Lake Valley. When
Mormons made the thirteen-hundred-mile trek across the plains and over
the Rocky Mountains into present-day Utah, Young made sure they were
accompanied by a brass band, and theatricals sprang up at almost every
juncture. In Nauvoo, when Joseph was still alive and Mormons enjoyed less
desperate times, plays, dances, and musical evenings were common. En route,
theatrics were meant as diversions, perhaps as much protection during their
challenging journey as their threadbare coats and sole-less shoes. Theatricals
put on by Mormon pioneers made the harsh winter stay in Winters Quarters,
Nebraska, somewhat more bearable. Young looked at the situation matter-
of-factly. "The people must have amusement," he once said. "Human nature
demands it. If healthy and harmless diversions are not attainable they will
seek those which are vicious and degrading."[2]

Once in the Salt Lake valley, Mormons began planning their new city
around a new temple. Plans for the Salt Lake Temple were announced almost
immediately when the Mormons arrived in 1847, but construction on the Salt
Lake City Temple did not begin until six years later. Not until 1893—almost

two decades after Young's death—was the temple completed. In the meantime, Young set to work on building the Salt Lake Theatre, which opened in March 1862. Dubbed Young's "Thespian temple" by the *New York Times*, the Salt Lake Theatre was heralded as "the greatest material wonder of Utah."[3] The building was not overly large or grandiose, seating around fifteen hundred people, but it served an almost divine purpose. In the Theatre's dedicatory prayer, Brigham Young's counselor Daniel H. Wells prayed,

> As the unstrung bow longer retains its elasticity, strength and powers, so may Thy people who congregate here for recreation, unbend for a while from the sterner and more wearying duties of life, receive that food which in our organization becomes necessary to supply and invigorate our energies and vitality, and stimulate to more enduring exertions in the drama of life, its various scenes and changes which still in Thy providence still await us.[4]

Clearly, the Salt Lake Theatre was more than just an entertainment venue for early Mormons. The Theatre represented the culmination of a promise given to the faithful by those weary performers who on the frozen plains nightly spun out intimate tales, skits, songs, and dances that contrasted sharply with the enormity of the trek westward. These performances "without a doubt were the first causes, the germs from whence sprang the widespread interest in the drama among the Utah pioneers," one writer recalled.[5] It was in that building where feelings of isolation were diminished by the antics of traveling performing troupes and where the musical and theatrical qualities of Mormons themselves began to blossom.

The Deseret Musical and Dramatic Society was formed out of the brass band and outfit of performers who entertained during the slow march of the pioneers. Soon, a great artistic culture blossomed in the desert valley. When a *New York Daily Tribune* article ran a review of Utah poet Sarah E. Carmichael in 1865, the reviewer could hardly contain his surprise.

> Can any good thing come out of Nazareth? The utter isolation, the iron social and mental limitation of this community would seem to render it the last place in the civilized world favorable to mental development, but talents, like gunpowder, must have vent, and the poet once born, no Medusa can strike him dumb.[6]

Many other Mormons began to excel in the arts, and those ever-streaming converts from the East Coast and Western Europe brought with them musical skills and an eagerness to share their cultural artistry. But as impresario and actor, Young seemed to enjoy the stage perhaps more than most others.

58 · CHAPTER 2

Young played the role of "High Priest" in Richard Sheridan's 1799 play *Pizarro* in Nauvoo shortly before Joseph was killed. If Young was a convincing actor in Nauvoo, it seems the part of religious zealot rather grew on him in the following decades. Director Thomas Lyne humorously "regretted having cast Brigham Young for that part of the high priest" because, as the new prophet and controversial militant leader, "he's been playing the character with great success ever since."[7] *Pizarro* was also the first play produced in the Salt Lake Theatre, and, as Jeremy Ravi Mumford claims, the show "went on to become something like the Mormons' national play, a reliable favorite over the decades."[8] Nineteenth-century Americans likely saw in Sheridan's tale of Spanish conquest in Peru a familiar trope of America's colonizing Native American lands. Once again, Jacksonian ideologies of self-fashioning, white supremacy, and fierce independence come through in the Mormon instinct to perform.

Young's love for the theater further distances him and his followers from other nineteenth-century religious groups who, at the time, held a much less favorable opinion of drama. Renowned minister Henry Ward Beecher held a particularly poor view of actors, whom he uncharitably dismissed (possibly with homophobic prejudice) as "tickling men."

> They eat, they drink, they giggle, they grimace, they strut in garish clothes—and what else? They have not afforded even useful amusement; they are professional laugh-makers; their trade is comical, or tragical, buffoonery—the trade of tickling men. We do not feel any need of them before they come; and when they leave, the only effects resulting from their visits are unruly boys, aping apprentices and unsteady workmen.[9]

The Mormon prophet, on the other hand, unapologetically supported the theater and took great interest in all its wonders. Theatrical guise won him his religious office, after all. Young may have won the bet on Mormon leadership by a well-thrown voice, but he also ensured that the cultural trappings of the Mormons' abandoned home weren't lost for good. One prominent actor in the Salt Lake Theatre once described Young as a "champion of the drama and friend of the actor," confidently adding that he "did more to elevate the drama and encourage the histrionic art, in his day, than perhaps any man in America."[10]

As we know, Young demonstrated his support of theatricality in more ways than just what appeared on the rough-hewn stages of the Salt Lake valley. Vocal theatricality and disguise were continually practiced by Mormon leaders throughout the nineteenth century, typically in defense against perceived threats to Mormon religious liberty. Mormon leadership and laity alike continued to find reason or excuse to mask their identity in the face of intrusions by outsiders. Perhaps the most repulsive example of Mormon deception is the infamous massacre near Mountain Meadows in southern Utah. In 1857 a group of Mormon militiamen disguised themselves as Paiute Native Americans and attacked an emigrant party en route from Arkansas to California. In what some describe as a horrific example of war hysteria from the Utah War, or perhaps in retaliation for previous transgressions against Mormons—including the ambushed murder of seventeen Mormon men in the 1838 Hahn's Mill massacre in northwestern Missouri—the Mormon militia commenced to slaughter around 120 men, women, and children, their bodies hastily buried and surviving children given to Mormon settlers to raise. It remains unclear what degree of responsibility Brigham Young had in the massacre's planning, execution, and aftermath.

The Mountain Meadows massacre is a sad reminder of the violence by which early Mormons defined their relationship with outsiders. Isolated examples of Mormon violence or stories of other Mormon peculiarities only fanned the flames of anti-Mormon sentiment. By 1865, with the rest of the country looking to heal deep wounds left by the Civil War, Mormon practice of plural marriage, or polygamy, had become a rallying cry of many Americans; as Patrick Mason has argued, eliminating polygamy became one of the first topics of mutual interest for otherwise bitter communities in the North and South.[11] The feverish fight of American moralists to eradicate polygamy and slavery had erupted nine years earlier at the 1856 GOP Convention when those practices were labeled "twin relics of barbarism."

In the face of continuous pressure from the United States government to desist the practice of polygamy, and with "gentiles" visiting Salt Lake City more frequently, Mormon leaders insisted that misleading or lying to those intent on destroying their way of life was morally defensible. Well into the twentieth century, Mormons and their leaders repeatedly said one thing to appease their listening enemies while really intending to do quite the opposite. As one Mormon apostle succinctly put it, "Some things that are true are not very useful."[12] Thus "lying for the Lord," as the practice became known, perpetuated Mormon dishonesty in order to protect religious leaders and others who practiced polygamy. Even so, Charles W. Penrose was not alone when he voiced concern that the "Mormon logic" (as these deceits were sometimes named) of "endless subterfuges and prevarications . . . threaten to make our rising generation a race of deceivers."[13] This practice arguably is an outgrowth of the kinds of deceptions Brigham Young performed in

60 · CHAPTER 2

mimicking Joseph Smith or the scriptural precedent of Nephi's taking on the identity of Laban, whom he has just murdered in his sleep. The vocal discipline enacted throughout nineteenth-century Mormonism further required the faithful to be carefully attuned to their leaders' voices, perhaps perpetually reminded of God's warning that "whoso receiveth not my voice is not acquainted with my voice, and is not of me."[14]

Much of the kerfuffle surrounding Mormons and polygamy dimmed with the 1890 Manifesto by Church president Wilford Woodruff, though the Manifesto was received with a wink and a nod since many Mormons considered Woodruff's concession simply a part of the act that had been perpetuated for decades. Woodruff apparently did not really mean what he said either, as he secretly continued the practice of sealing plural families in the Mormon temples and privately sanctioned many such marriages to the Mormon elite. The final nail in polygamy's coffin was secured in 1904 by Woodruff's successor, Joseph F. Smith, with his "Second Manifesto," which essentially gave teeth to the original revelation. Smith's this-time-we-mean-it manifesto made clear that any Mormons practicing plural marriage were to be excommunicated from the Church, a policy still in effect today. Once deceit is introduced into an institution, however, all communication becomes a listening test that casts doubt on every utterance. Even more, as B. Carmon Hardy worries, when the Church first decided to play into deceit regarding polygamy, it "assured today's following of fundamentalist actors who believe the play neither is nor should be at an end."[15]

Nonetheless, the Mormon culture of wit, deception, and disguise had been defined and continues to remain in effect, even after Smith's "Second Manifesto." Theatricality did not diminish in importance as the twentieth century dawned but instead shifted into a new terrain in the form of musical drama. As the site for numerous plays, concerts, burlesques, and minstrel shows, the Salt Lake Theatre also became a focal point for the newly established frontier city. As Howard R. Lamar argues, theater was a sign of civilization and therefore a demonstration against disparaging portrayals of Mormons as violent polygamist barbarians. As much as it served to signify normalcy and civility, the theater also gave Mormons a venue to practice performing a new identity—an increasingly pressing skill since the arrival in 1869 of the First Transcontinental Railroad in Utah made the isolation Mormons first enjoyed a dwindling possibility and wider acceptance an eventual necessity. When the Salt Lake Theatre was torn down in 1928 to make room for a parking lot, Lamar writes, it was without regret a hopeful symbol "that the old had made way for dozens of new theatrical enterprises in Utah."[16]

Mormons and Operetta

In 1917 the *New York Times* published a review of the new musical comedy *His Little Widows*. The show attracted a good deal of attention in part because the librettist, Rida Johnson Young, had written herself into musical theater history seven years earlier by penning the libretto to Victor Herbert's sensational operetta, *Naughty Marietta*. The wordsmith of Herbert's now-iconic song "Ah! Sweet Mystery of Life" tackled a very different topic with this musical. *His Little Widows* tells the story of a young man who is shocked to discover that, upon his uncle's untimely death in Utah, he is to be betrothed to his uncle's eleven wives. The story of a reluctant polygamist makes for a predictably farcical plot that sidesteps any moral opposition to polygamy in favor of lampooning its logistic absurdity, as the song "A Wife for Every Day in the Week" makes plain.

> One wife for Monday, who's crazy for wealth,
> One wife for Tuesday, who's not,
> One wife for Wednesday to care for your health,
> You can see where you'll need her a lot!
> One wife for Thursday to make pretty clothes
> For Friday and Saturday fair
> And Sunday? On Sunday, you'll rest I suppose
> Yes you'll rest, maybe so, but where?

Although little is remembered of it today, *His Little Widows* found a receptive audience in its time. "The new musical comedy which arrived with a bang at the Astor Theatre last evening is several times as amusing as the average of its kind," raved the reviewer. Actually, the review continues, part of what makes *His Little Widows* such a pleaser is how well displayed are "all the humors of Mormonism." Despite the show's charm in making "merry with the subject of Mormonism and plural marriage," however, the reviewer is still alarmed that audiences could so easily laugh at such serious subject matter. In the minds of many Americans, even by 1917 Mormons were still not off the hook for their past sexual deviance. Decades of vilification in media and popular culture, including musical comedy, had made Mormonism just too appealing to let go. "Then, too," the reviewer shrugs, "Mormonism is just about the only religion that can be exploited in musical comedy."[17]

His Little Widows was continuing in a tradition of operetta that "exploited" Mormonism in comedic ways. In fact, throughout the nineteenth and early twentieth centuries, Mormons and Mormonism were frequently put on display through some form of musical comedy, whether operetta, vaudeville, or the occasional burlesque. These depictions were uniformly negative. In 1871, Lydia Thompson's burlesque troupe adapted Jacques Offenbach's 1866 operetta *Barbe-bleue* to liken the infamous serial lady-killer with Mormon polygamists. In a Scottish style, Blue Beard the polygamist vaunts amorously,

> Blue Beard is my name!
> Polygamy's my fame
> For the girls I seal 'em quick,
> Mormonise them very slick.
> Blue Beard is my name

Figure 1: Broadside for a performance of *Blue Beard* at the Bush Street Theatre in San Francisco, California, 1880. Library of Congress, Washington, D.C.

Polygamy's my game
And my castle's down at Salt Lake City.

Nine years later, Dudley Buck penned *Deseret; or, A Saint's Afflictions.* Buck had given piano lessons to one of Brigham Young's sons who was visiting Boston in 1877, so this operetta may have arisen out of that fortuitous encounter. The show treats polygamy as a humorous diversion that sets the story into action, but in the end polygamous marriage is given a serious treatment. The twenty-five wives of Elder Scram join in chorus at the close of the show, singing lyrics that make it clear that polygamy was seen not only as a twin to slavery but also akin to it:

God of Love! Oh! Wilt thou never
Rescue us and make us free?
From these bitter woes deliver!
Though extreme the complication,
Let us now, before we part,
From the depths of tribulation
Hail thee sovereign of the heart!

Other operettas followed, including *The Mormons* in 1895 that featured songs with titles as telling as "The Marriage Monomaniac." However, between this production in 1895 and *My Little Widows* in 1917 came the Mormon-themed operetta with perhaps the most significance to musical theater historiography.

Girl from Utah was an enormous hit in London in 1913 and caught the attention of American theatrical producer Charles Frohman. He enlisted young composer Jerome Kern to add interpolated songs to Paul Rubens's original score and produced *Girl from Utah* in the United States in 1914. By this point in his career, Kern had been working as rehearsal pianist and occasionally would write interpolations for Frohman. This would be the first time Kern would receive billing and advance publicity for his interpolations. One song Kern added, "They Didn't Believe Me," became his first big hit and a largely unremembered force that shaped American musical theater. The tune reportedly caught the attention of such titans of American musical theater as Victor Herbert and George Gershwin, and it helped validate newer American styles and conventions that would later come to define American musical theater. Kern's biographer Gerald Bordman went so far to say that "this great song established the popular musical comedy number as it was to remain for the next half-century."[18]

"Aspirations toward Whiteness"

American and British operetta lampooning Mormons fanned the flames of growing anti-Mormon sentiment in America, but eventually this cynicism actually may have helped relieve such ethnic tension. As musical theater developed in densely populated urban areas where close-quartered ethnic groups increasingly led to violent brawls, musicals helped deflect actual violence by lampooning various ethnic groups on stage. As Raymond Knapp and Mitchell Morris argue, in pre–World War II New York City, Tin Pan Alley's ethnic songs (such as the popular "coon songs") served as a safety valve on ethnic hatred, "substituting travesty for assault and battery."[19] Similarly, hardened views of Mormonism, once displayed on stage, eventually dissipated into laughter. It may be that anti-Mormon operettas during the nineteenth century in fact helped normalize Mormon behaviors in the early decades of the twentieth century, even in the process of derision.

Acceptance and normalization, however, were still a long way off. Many nineteenth-century Americans held unfavorable views of Mormons, in part because of peculiar practices like polygamy or communal economies, but also because the great physical distance that separated them from the rest of the country made the allure of the strange faith that much greater and prospects of meeting actual Mormons that much harder. For these reasons,

Figure 2: *The Mormon Harem*, by Joseph Keppler. Published in 1884 in the magazine *Puck*. Library of Congress, Washington, D.C.

Mormons were routinely viewed with suspicion by the press, and otherwise normative dimensions of their life and faith diminished by exaggerated accounts of polygamist families. Mormon men were almost universally depicted as violent, sex-crazed tyrants, and women their brainwashed prey. These rough depictions matched well with views of other feared tyrants of the world, including Muslim men. One political cartoon from 1884 captures this connection, depicting a Mormon polygamist family as living in a harem, the tagline "I imagine it must be a perfect Paradise" hardly masking the titillation of being simultaneously abhorred and envious of a man who seemed so sexually uninhibited (see figure 2).

As the nineteenth century wore on, Mormons became more and more associable with other social pariahs, like blacks or the Chinese. Eventually, associating Mormons with other undesirable ethnicities led outsiders to suggest Mormons were in fact not white at all, but rather a different ethnicity altogether. This racial association stuck despite the fact that Mormons were overwhelmingly white and largely immigrants from Anglo-Saxon countries. Mormons tried their best to overcome these accusations, in historian Paul Reeve's words, by "respond[ing] with aspirations toward whiteness."[20] In his book *Religion of a Different Color*, Reeve argues that the crisis of whiteness forced Mormons to search out ways of assimilating into mainstream American thought. The problem, however, was that racial identity in the nineteenth century was understood to be more than just appearances. Mormons were easily categorized as an ethnic minority not because they didn't look white enough but because, for whatever reason, they did not *act* white enough. Reeve explains,

> Mormon behavior—fanaticism, adherence to theocratic rule, ignorance, sexual promiscuity, plural marriage, fawning subservience, and violence—produced race. Polygamy, when combined with Mormon isolation spawned a "new race." As outsiders viewed it, Mormon race was a performance; that is, Mormons *acted* racially degenerate, therefore they *were* racially degenerate.[21]

For Mormons to again proximate whiteness, they would need to change their behavior. Of course, for a people whose theology was built on a sense of theatricality, pretending to be somebody they weren't was more than just a matter of survival—it was a matter of religious duty.

Perhaps as a sign of solidarity with other whites, or perhaps because by this point it was in such fashion, and probably because shifting identities through the stage was by now a critical skill to be honed, some Mormons began to perform in blackface. As we know, Mormonism and blackface minstrelsy bloomed from the same flowering shoot of Jacksonian ideology. Near the end of the nineteenth century, Mormons—in parallel to other ethnic groups such as the Irish and Jews—were using blackface to capitalize on those Jacksonian beliefs regarding whiteness and self-fashioning. Michael Hicks has written about the history of Mormonism and minstrelsy, claiming that Mormons may have been drawn to blackface because it conveniently satirized sectarian beliefs—a practice for which Mormons were also quite fond. Mormons also would have been drawn to minstrelsy's frivolity and appreciated the "attention of outsiders to help reinforce their sense of self-importance and maintain their identity as a distinctive people."[22]

Most pressing, however, is that performing in blackface gave Mormons the opportunity to put on a black mask in order to whiten up. Mormons likely detected the echoing strains of self-actualization imbued within minstrelsy, recognized it as derivative of their birthright, and exploited it in order to turn the tables on the popular Mormon image. Acquiring the performance codes of demoralization—codes Toni Morrison argues are an inheritance of whiteness that press black people "to the lowest level of the racial hierarchy"—rather than merely being lampooned by them as they did as inflicted victims in operetta, must have been tinged with at least some measure of ambivalence.[23] Such ambivalence may have come from a moralist perspective, but the portrayal of blacks on stage may also have been a measured and deliberate attempt by Mormon leaders to balance perception of the religion as mainstream while also retaining a separate identity. Sociologist Armand Mauss has argued that in order to survive and prosper, Mormonism had to maintain "indefinitely an optimum tension" between greater acceptance, on the one hand, and "greater separateness, peculiarity, and militance" on the other.[24] Noting that "a religious movement must strategically reverse course from time to time as a condition of meaningful survival and success," Mauss helps contextualize why religions like Mormonism sometimes appear to behave in strange, contradictory ways.[25] Religious communities practicing minstrelsy to gain white respectability may be one of those strategic course reversals.

As noted, minstrelsy was proving useful for other marginalized groups and would later prove invaluable for Jews as they, too, used the theatrical stage to assimilate—the burnt cork creating a mask to mock blacks from behind in order to cover their own ethnic or religious stain. At the time, however, the stakes for not belonging in America were quite high. The relative passivity of mockery and satire on the stage may have seemed the lesser of evils in comparison to other forms of mistreatment coming around the corner.

For Jews and Mormons in particular, the twentieth-century musical stage took on the shape of a shield and protection, albeit from different perspectives. The Jewish-American association with the musical theater has its beginnings with nineteenth-century Yiddish theater in the boroughs of New York City, but most notably in musicals of the twentieth century, Jews "discovered a theatrical form particularly well suited to representing the complexity of assimilation in America," as Andrea Most argues.[26] Jewish identity was heralded (or, more typically, subverted) by musical composers and lyricists like Richard Rodgers, Lorenz Hart, Oscar Hammerstein II, George and Ira Gershwin, Leonard Bernstein, and Stephen Sondheim, while many beloved musicals of the mid-twentieth century, such as *Oklahoma!* (1943), *South Pacific* (1949), or *West Side Story* (1957), are often "about" Jews or the Jewish story through a thinly veiled metaphor for Jewish assimilation. This connection runs so deep, according to Most, that "the social reality of being a Jew in America is fundamentally inscribed in the form of the American musical theater."[27] Most argues that the musical stage offered Jewish performers the opportunity to display behaviors more accepted as mainstream, white behaviors, and therefore carved a niche for broader acceptance. "As long as the characters could learn to speak, dress, and sing and dance in the American style," she writes, "they were fully accepted into the stage community."[28]

Mormons gradually moved away from blackface as the century came to a close, though Hicks remarks that the practice continued in part "at least through the 1950s."[29] This parallels the drop-off in depictions of Mormons in musical theater, with negative characterizations all but stopping by the mid-twentieth century, with Lerner and Loewe's 1951 musical *Paint Your Wagon* sounding the death knell for Mormon musical buffoonery, for a time at least. Lerner and Loewe injected into their story of an almost all-male camp of California miners the polygamist Jacob Woodling and his two wives, Sarah and Elizabeth. The other men demand Jacob sell one of his wives to them, which he eventually does for $800. In their only musical moment, the Mormon trio kneels in prayer, and the two women offer up for the audience their true feelings about living with a sister wife: Sarah prayerfully declares she will make sure that Elizabeth does all the household chores, while Elizabeth fantasizes about Sarah falling through an icy lake, leaving Jacob to herself.

The scene is meant to be humorous, but its aim was faulty. *Paint Your Wagon* preys on what had by then come to be seen as archaic and insensitive stereotypes—and provides an uneasy portrayal of female slavery that must have been discomfiting even to audiences then. For all its other problems, *Paint Your Wagon*'s sly jabs at polygamous Mormonism seemed out of place

68 · CHAPTER 2

by the 1950s, and some productions today downplay or eliminate the Mormon polygamist from the show altogether.

In January 1961, NBC Opera Theatre produced Leonard Kastle and Anne Howard Bailey's television opera *Deseret*, which once again put Mormon polygamy center stage. Instead of ridiculing the practice, however, *Deseret* romanticizes polygamy, even portraying Brigham Young as a benevolent prophet and kind husband instead of a sex-crazed tyrant. Rather than force the young Ann Louisa to be his twenty-fifth wife, the sixty-year-old Brigham Young enjoys a more dignified portrayal; by the end of the opera he instructs Ann Louisa to follow her heart and marry Captain James Dee, the man she truly loves. *Deseret* enjoyed measurable success, with the *Los Angeles Times* calling it "the most expert and convincing opera yet produced by American authors."[30]

If how polygamy was treated on stage between *Paint Your Wagon* and *Deseret* is any indication of America's changing opinion of Mormonism, then by the mid-twentieth century Mormons had successfully pulled off the remarkable transition from polygamist outliers to belonging to what Harold Bloom called "the American religion."[31] Even the much-maligned Brigham Young emerges midcentury unscathed as an iconic American hero. This transition hinged on Mormons' reframing beliefs and practices that seemed unorthodox or otherwise raised suspicions of outsiders. Mormons changed behavior, altered their practices, and demonstrated that they, too, could refashion themselves on stage at the expense of those even more despised than they were.

But as the Mormon practice of blackface gradually subsided, the Mormon Church took steps to capitalize on the possibilities the musical stage afforded them. As the centennial celebration of the 1847 arrival of Mormon pioneers to Utah loomed, the state of Utah—along with the Mormon Church—needed something to shift the conversation about Mormonism away from its checkered past. The story of Mormonism, as state and religious leaders envisioned it, was inherently American, heroic, romantic, and even inspirational. With the nation's attention soon to be on Utah, leaders knew they had an opportunity to restart the conversation about Mormonism on their own terms. The challenge was to find a medium that could capture the qualities of Mormon resilience and hold them up as quintessentially American, while simultaneously drawing attention away from the religion's unpopular dogma. Musical theater offered them exactly that venue and, with Broadway's unapologetic connection with wealthy white urbanites in the East, also proved providential in affirming the Mormon identity as decidedly white. The state of Utah and the Mormon Church found all they were looking for and more in the musical *Promised Valley*.

Figure 3: Cover image from the official Utah Centennial souvenir program, 1947. Crawford Gates Papers, L. Tom Perry Special Collections, Brigham Young University.

Integration

The tremendous success in 1943 of Rodgers and Hammerstein's first collaboration, *Oklahoma!*, caught the attention of the Utah Centennial Commission, who realized the fanciful story of men and women living on the frontier was also their story to tell. It also caught the attention of most theatergoers, who recognized that *Oklahoma!* was doing something other musicals had not done before. Most plots of operettas and musical comedy up to this point were shot through with contradictions and loose dramatic scenarios that by today's standards would seem a jumble of confusion. The often-absurd plot lines were mostly vehicles for hit songs and flashy dances. Rodgers and

70 · CHAPTER 2

Hammerstein sought to build more cohesion into their new musical and so reportedly worked to integrate the songs and dance into the story rather than just have such elements run alongside the drama. The result was a kind of show whose individual parts all moved in sync to support a singular idea or moral (as Richard Rodgers famously said, "In a great musical, the orchestrations sound the way the costumes look").[32] *Oklahoma!* thus became known as the first fully *integrated musical*—although arguably Kern and Hammerstein had already achieved this in 1927 with *Show Boat*—and established a theatrical standard among musicals that continues to be influential today.

With the popularity of *Oklahoma!* in mind, the Utah Centennial Commission envisioned a new musical as the keystone to the centennial celebrations and immediately set out to create a production on a professional scale never before mounted in Utah.[33] The Commission initially approached Kurt Weill to write the music; Weill was at the time working with Langston Hughes on *Street Scene*, so he declined the offer but suggested the librettist for his 1945 folk opera, *Down in the Valley* (which wouldn't premiere until 1948), Arnold Sundgaard, as a lyricist. Sundgaard agreed, and, in a risky venture, the Church tapped twenty-five-year-old Brigham Young University graduate student Crawford Gates to write the music in lieu of a big-name Broadway composer.

By the time *Promised Valley* premiered on July 21, 1947, it was clear the Utah Centennial Commission, which was chaired by Mormon apostle and future prophet David O. McKay, expected a great deal from the musical. The show ran for seventeen performances for an audience of more than 104,000 people, at the hefty cost of $150,000 to the State of Utah—$20,000 of that spent on the stage alone. The commission looked for every opportunity to gain national attention and capitalize on their investment by drawing a connection between their state and icons of other big cities. This was no different with the outdoor stage. A bowl, similar to that built in 1929 in Hollywood, was placed at the end of the football stadium at the University of Utah to accommodate the state-of-the-art equipment ("a new stereophonic sound system, unsurpassed even by that at the Radio City Music Hall, New York")[34] needed for such an enormous outdoor production. The amphitheater design worked well, with only one performance canceled because of rain, and the University of Utah was allowed to keep the bowl to use in future productions.

The critical response to *Promised Valley* was immensely positive. "The most elaborate music-drama ever presented in this intermountain region," boasted the *Salt Lake Tribune*.[35] Another review recognized in *Promised Valley* the story of bravery and heroism the Centennial Commission hoped would be the new legacy of Mormonism: "When fatigue undermined courage, when fear bordered on paralysis, and when even the stoutest hearts had doubts, one thing—music—seemed always to beat back a final hopelessness that threatened a pioneering people."[36] A week later, journalist Lowell M. Durham wondered excitedly what was coming next for the region: "Pasadena has its 'Parade of Roses' and New Orleans' annual 'Mardi Gras' festivities attract worldwide attention each year. Salt Lake City might well become famous as the site of the world's greatest outdoor musicals."[37] While the city did not become known worldwide for its outdoor musicals, Salt Lake City did continue the legacy of *Promised Valley* when, in 1972, the Mormon Church converted an old movie theater in downtown Salt Lake City to use for church plays, renaming it the Promised Valley Playhouse. It closed in 1996, though the Church replaced it in 2000 by including a 911-seat theater in the plans for the new Church Conference Center. A shortened version of *Promised Valley* also played for tourists in downtown Salt Lake City's Temple Square every summer for eighteen years.[38]

Because of the publicity surrounding Rodgers and Hammerstein's enormous success, everyone involved in *Promised Valley* stood to benefit from connecting their show to the new, integrated style of *Oklahoma!* For the lead role of Jed Cutler, the Commission hired Alfred Drake—a deliberate if not heavy-handed attempt to siphon some of Drake's notoriety as the first Curly McLain—and Hollywood starlet Jet McDonald to play opposite him as Celia Cutler. Jay Blackton, who was the original musical director of the Broadway production of *Oklahoma!* and conductor of Irving Berlin's 1946 musical *Annie Get Your Gun*, was hired to direct music for *Promised Valley*, and celebrated dancer and choreographer Helen Tamaris, also coming off her success the year before with the premiere of *Annie Get Your Gun*, was brought on as choreographer. The manner in which professional talent was brought in to work with local actors and dancers mirrors closely the way in which professional pageant masters in the first decade of the twentieth century—men like William Chauncy Langdon—were hired by small midwestern or frontier communities to help put on pageants celebrating their region's unique history in order to better define future goals.[39] The publicity for *Promised Valley* also pushed its relationship to *Oklahoma!*, mentioning Drake's connection to the Broadway show in large print in almost every poster (figure 4).

Some members of the Centennial Commission also urged Gates and Sundgaard to include a new state song in the show—another nod to the place of honor the musical *Oklahoma!* would occupy in the state of Oklahoma. Evidently, the plan was to create a Utah state song from an existing melody Gates had already written for *Promised Valley* and incorporate that into the

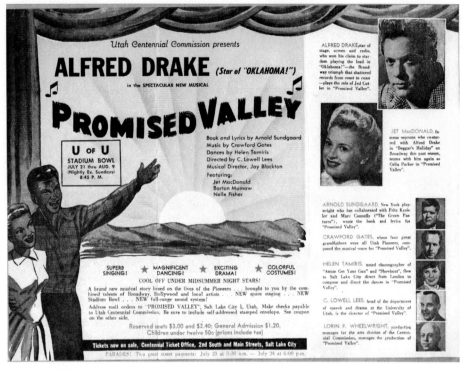

Figure 4: Publicity for *Promised Valley*. Crawford Gates Papers, L. Tom Perry Special Collections, Brigham Young University.

musical. Sundgaard and Gates tossed the idea back and forth, with Sundgaard not wanting to risk distorting the story "just to get a state song."[40] Nevertheless, in a letter to Gates dated April 20, Sundgaard refers to a group of lyrics he called "Home in Utah" that was to appear at some point after the "Choir Practice Song" and then be featured in a full reprise in the epilogue. There is no record of Gates's response to Sundgaard's last letter, and the slight changes Sundgaard had suggested to make room for "Home in Utah" were ignored in the final production, indicating that the plans for the state song evidently were dropped.[41] Ironically, the title song that in 1953 was adopted as Oklahoma's official state song and apparently was the impetus for Utah's state leaders seeking something similar in their own musical almost didn't make the cut. It was not part of *Oklahoma!* during pre–New York tryouts but was added later to emphasize the reconciliation among the story's warring factions: the farmers and the cowhands.

In hindsight, the Commission's wagon-hitching to *Oklahoma!* seems vexed. Even though the integrated technique of *Oklahoma!* has since colored the musical as a watershed in American musical theater, the historiographic prominence *Oklahoma!* enjoys has recently come into question, with its claim to fame as the first integrated musical arguably the result of a carefully crafted publicity stunt. Musicologists James O'Leary and Tim Carter both position *Oklahoma!*'s reception within the economic constraints of its producers, the Theatre Guild, who needed some assurance of the show's success in the face of mixed reviews during tryouts. Novelty would sell tickets, it was determined, so the creative staff and the show's producers began weaving a careful story of how *Oklahoma!* would be the first musical to integrate song, dance, and drama, despite evidence that what was being called integration was really nothing new. O'Leary writes,

> The term was deployed as part of a finely honed, performative act of cultural positioning; more a term of highly charged persuasive rhetoric than an objective, analyzable, or ineluctably "real" part of the work. The term became a rhetorical emblem of sophistication, deployed as part of a public-relations strategy that sought to attract or dissuade certain segments of the general theatergoing crowd.[42]

It seems, then, that the plan for *Oklahoma!* to act as the vehicle through which integration would come for Mormons was built on two well-played publicity strategies. The Centennial Commission hoped the Broadway show would bolster the success of *Promised Valley* as the latest incantation of the famed "integration technique"; likewise, the Theatre Guild had manipulated *Oklahoma!*'s legacy by selling integration as a novelty. No harm, no foul, perhaps, since both parties got what they wanted: getting in the good graces of the rest of Americans for one and financial solidarity for the other.

In spite of the integration ruse, Sundgaard attempted to cash in on the trend, telling reporters that he "found it was necessary to use every form of drama" to tell this particular story "as it should be told. . . . The spoken word and dramatic situations were not enough—integrated drama, music, and dancing were also needed."[43] Local journalists in turn gleefully reported that *Promised Valley* would feature the latest fashions of Broadway: "The drama of Utah pioneers, written by New York playwrite [*sic*] Arnold Sundgaard, will follow the 'integration' technique of 'Porgie [*sic*] and Bess' and 'Oklahoma' in that dance and song will be integrated in plot action."[44] Others were less convinced the connections between the two musicals were that manifest. "There will be a natural tendency to compare 'Promised Valley' with 'Oklahoma!' since both salute this western land, and both feature the same principal vocalist," wrote the *Salt Lake Tribune* on July 26. "Each has the same good humor, the same honest 'folk-art' quality, plus a strong similarity in choreographic

74 · CHAPTER 2

style. But the Broadway presentation was more certainly a musical comedy, while 'Promised Valley,' dealing in its first act with a serious subject, for a time took on the aura of a folk-opera."[45]

So entrenched was the association between the two musicals that, even by 1994, Mormon historian Davis Bitton still maintained that *Promised Valley* "combined words and music in the manner of Rodgers and Hammerstein."[46] Yet the reviewer's likening to folk opera was adept, for despite all the publicity and alertness to *Oklahoma!* as the model, Crawford Gates's music for *Promised Valley* bore little resemblance to that of Richard Rodgers. Instead, Gates's score is more comparable to the folk-opera lyricism of Kurt Weill, the composer Gates replaced. This can most readily be heard in Jed Cutler's opening number, "Valley Home." The tune bears some resemblance to Kurt Weill's song "My Ship" from his 1941 musical *Lady in the Dark*, both in melodic structure and lyrical message (see examples 1 and 2). Musicologist Naomi Graber has argued that Weill frequently demonstrated in his musicals and film scores of the late 1930s that anyone could be an American regardless of the path that brought them to such acceptance; this pro-immigrant theme is strongly represented in *Knickerbocker Holiday* (1938), for example.[47] Perhaps drawing a parallel between such an inclusive position and Mormonism was one reason the Commission originally sought Weill to write the score for *Promised Valley* and may help explain why Gates modeled some of his tunes after Weill's. Whatever the reason, the contour of the melodies is similar, as is the climax of both songs (see examples 1 and 2). Even the cadential gimmick in the coda for "Valley Home" is colored by a plagal extension from F major to D-flat and finally back to F major, just as it does in the final bars of "My Ship." This same cadence appears in Celia's song "The Wind is a Lion" and in several of Jed and Celia's duets and in fact seems to be a harmonic thread connecting the show's otherwise disparate musical styles.

Musical resonances aside, voice serves as a strong thematic connection between both shows. *Lady in the Dark* tells the story of Liza, a fashion editor for a magazine who is undergoing psychoanalysis to cure her depression. She continuously hears snatches of a song she learned as a child, but she can't recall it in its entirety, nor can she remember what the song is. The song comes to her in full at the end of the show after she discovers her psychological block stems from her being compared unfavorably to her mother's natural beauty. When she finally can give voice to the tune in the show's final song, "My Ship," Liza relates dreaming and singing together, almost as if song itself could create a good life bound by true love.

In *Lady in the Dark*, singing therefore is equated with emotional health and a true, perhaps hidden, self within. This isn't all that different from the

Example 1: Jed's vocal line in "Valley Home," from *Promised Valley* (1947). Music by Crawford Gates and lyrics by Arnold Sundgaard.

Example 2: Liza's vocal line in "My Ship," from *Lady in the Dark* (1941). Music by Kurt Weill and lyrics by Ira Gershwin.

community's value system in *Promised Valley*. Similarly, in "Valley Home" Jed dreams of a place where he and his wife Celia can settle down. The dream includes green land where he can "work in its fields all the day." Most significant, the first verse ends with his pronouncement "I *sing* that we're going that way," which gives an immediate connection between voice and prophesy—Jed prophesies a future home for his family through his ability to "sing" that it will happen. "Valley Home" establishes that Jed, the hero of the story, is one who sings—and who is therefore recognizably a part of the community. Liza and Jed, along with the rest of *Promised Valley*'s Mormon community, both believe in the magical power of singing to connect them with their dreams—which more generally speaks to the influence of psychoanalysis at the time, in that the subconscious can use the voice to communicate what the visible self cannot. The similarity of the melodies and message helps amplify and deepen Jed's character, placing his identity firmly within a dramatic conversation happening on Broadway (and indeed in psychiatric offices around the world) at the time. Even more, Gates's music amplifies the political message of *Promised Valley*: to sing is to belong.

"The Mormon Folk Are Singing"

The story of *Promised Valley* upholds vocality as what unites the tight-knit Mormon community. Jed and his wife Celia are temporarily stopped in Winters Quarters, Nebraska, along with their wagon train of fellow Mormon pioneers, as they wait for the icy ground to thaw. The show opens with Jed

76 · CHAPTER 2

singing on stage alone, perhaps another nod toward Curly's famous off-stage entrance singing "Oh, What a Beautiful Mornin'" at the top of *Oklahoma!* (which is in turn how *Green Grow the Lilacs*, Lynn Riggs's 1930 play Rodgers and Hammerstein modeled their show after, also begins). Listening and singing are key attributes of their relationship and are established as important practices for creating their future. Celia longs for a place to call home, tuning in to the song of the robin as a signal of spring's arrival and the journey west to continue, while Jed sings for a green valley for him and Celia to raise a family.

The plans are disrupted, however, when on the day the wagon train was to move out, a captain in the U.S. Army arrives to recruit most men from the outfit for the Mexican-American War. The men are to march down to Santa Fe and onward to California, where they will then join the rest of their Mormon company. As Duncan Emrich wrote in 1952, however, the term "California" was simply a placeholder for a Mormon pioneer's final destination because "to the early Mormons moving westward anything beyond the Rocky Mountains was termed 'California.'"[48] Swayed by the modest army salary, Jed reluctantly joins what became known as the Mormon Battalion. Celia continues with the rest of the party west, hiding her pregnancy from her husband as he leaves.

The Mormons eventually stop in the Salt Lake valley, its barren soil and harsh conditions sitting uneasy with many in the company. Nonetheless, the Mormons fall in rank and begin developing the land and building their homes. Soon after, Jed and the rest of the Mormon Battalion arrive in Utah to join their families. After having seen the fertile and green valleys of California, though, Jed wants to continue there to raise his family in the "valley home" he had once sung about. Celia convinces him to stay and honor their commitments to God and develop the land given them. The show ends with a triumphant choral reprise of Jed's opening number "Valley Home": "We pushed out across the prairie, / We walked across the plain, / And here we've found our promised home, / And forever we will remain, remain. / Our thanks be to God again!"

Singing is emphatically conveyed in *Promised Valley* as a symbol of community. In "The Upper California" a choir sings "the Mormon folk are singing, their songs will reach the sky." The Mormon community anticipates a great triumph in "the upper California" region, perhaps a total dominance over the land. Later, the ensemble sings "We'll make the air with music ring, / Sing praises to our God and King" in an arrangement of the popular Mormon hymn "Come, Come Ye Saints," another song celebrating the arrival of Mormons in the Salt Lake valley. Ironically, as Michael Hicks points out, both of these Mormon hymns included in *Promised Valley* were adapted from existing Christian hymn tunes shortly after Joseph's death, marking early examples of a now-common Mormon propensity (and indeed the primary function of *Promised Valley*) to speak through familiar popular culture models in order to demonstrate cultural fluency and to make that identity their own.[49] Showcasing Christian tunes in the mouths of Mormons on stage likewise gave Mormons the opportunity to broadcast to audiences that they were part of American Protestant culture, at least sonically. Audiences in 1947 knew that the Mormons eventually do arrive in the mountain west (this was a celebration of Utah's centennial, after all), so singing becomes tied to prophetic prescience and comes to represent the community's ability to work together to fulfill that prophecy.

It is significant that the ensemble features so prominently in this show; in fact, eleven of the musical numbers in *Promised Valley* are for chorus, including one explicitly called "The Choir Practice Song." Given the framing conceit of the show, that "to sing is to be Mormon," this song demonstrates how the people become a community through singing together, and it almost serves as a primer for building community solidarity. Choir members, here understood as a simulacrum for the larger community, pronounce all the rules of belonging: "never be late" because "the chorister's eager to lead in our singing" so their "hymns will be reaching to the skies." The song hints that romantic relationships are made in choir practice, and new members are encouraged to "please take it slowly and you'll get it perfect." Choral singing had been a staple of Mormon culture from its inception. Joseph Smith's wife Emma was directed through her husband's revelation in 1830 to compile a book of "sacred hymns. . . . For my soul delighteth in the song of the heart; yea, the song of the righteous is a prayer unto me, and it shall be answered with a blessing upon their heads."[50] Choral singing soon became a regular and prominent part of Mormon worship. This fact alone made Mormonism stand out, as Michael Hicks has pointed out in his history of the Mormon Tabernacle Choir, since for most American churches in Joseph's time, angelic choirs were the only choirs expected to be heard on earth, and only occasionally—"earthly choirs were a transgression," he writes.[51] *Promised Valley* cashes in on the rich legacy of Mormon choral singing by showing collective vocality is a representation of American grit.

The Mormon Tabernacle Choir (now known simply as The Tabernacle Choir at Temple Square) stands at the pinnacle of choral spectacle and popularity in America today, and at the time it was quickly gaining prominence as the centerpiece of the radio program *Music and the Spoken Word*, which has been broadcast continuously on radio since 1929. Dubbed "America's Choir" by Ronald Reagan (in a sense delegating American's collective voice to Mormonism), the Mormon Tabernacle Choir has become something of a de facto cultural ambassador for the Church. Because of its wide reach, the choir's repertoire has been a source of ongoing conflict, according to Hicks's research, with one side trying to maintain the choir's legacy with strictly sacred hymns and another side vying for the kind of commercial popularity that would bring wider attention to the Church and, presumably, better fill the Church's coffers. Unsurprisingly, in the 1960s, there began to be some stirrings for the choir to make an album of Broadway songs. Although the Mormon prophet Joseph Fielding Smith had once declared in an interview, "I don't think the Salt Lake Tabernacle Choir belongs on Broadway," during his presidency in 1971, the choir released an album of Broadway show tunes called *Climb Every Mountain*.[52]

In the 1940s, however, collective singing represented a kind of discipline and patriotism as the country struggled to define itself against global powers. A disciplined voice, to the ears of many, signaled a disciplined and united country. Scott A. Carter explores how America's "voice culture" became of central concern during the late nineteenth and early twentieth centuries. From roughly 1880 to 1920, America's "voice culture practitioners" attempted to "establish an ideal singing aesthetic capable of representing the nation-state."[53] This concern over controlling the sound of America was an implicit reach into the governing of the human body. Because the voice has a physical and material connection to the body, any disciplining of the vocal sound is likewise a disciplining of the body in which the vocal apparatus is housed. Unrefined voices of African Americans or immigrants from Asian and European countries were heard as "particularly vexing" to the ears of vocal aesthetes. Carter writes, "These Other voices posed for the cultured elite an aural and physical threat to what was perceived as a fragile national culture by transforming urban soundscapes into polyvocal communities beset with racial and cultural tensions."[54]

Promised Valley's attention to disciplined, choral singing therefore comes not long after a period of great concern for how the collective body of the nation sounded. If becoming American depended to some degree on sounding American, then *Promised Valley* helpfully pointed to Mormons as exemplary citizens. To further distance themselves from a perceived ill-refined sound of racial or ethnic minorities, Mormons could demonstrate a concern with vocal discipline and establish a legacy of harmonious singing in their communities. Furthermore, the communal goals of choral singing match the communal spirit of early Mormonism, where a form of wealth distribution was practiced until railroads crisscrossed Utah and more stringent capitalist practices quickly rendered the struggling communal economies outmoded. The original name for the state of Utah was Deseret—a Book of Mormon word that means "honeybee." The symbol of the beehive remains on Utah's state flag and, like the practice of choral singing, continues to inform Mormon understandings of thrift, industry, and prosperity. *Promised Valley* adamantly promotes the Mormon work ethic. As one character in the show notes, "Everyone has a job to do here. I have a job. You have a job. We all have a job. Jobs create order in the human family. Without order we lose our meaning."

Chorus thus comes to represent Mormon industry and cooperation, a simulacrum of Mormon community. The main characters come to be identified through their willingness and ability to "sing" in harmony with the rest of the community. Jed's identity as a model Mormon is confirmed by his willingness and ability to sing, as is Celia's. The oddball and comic character Fenelly Parsons, on the other hand, has a different relationship to music, which signals his outsider status. Fenelly is a widower burdened with eight sons he struggles to feed. His buoyant music, however, betrays his true ethnic identity. While Fenelly does indeed sing in the show, his action on stage is always musically exoticized by Scottish snaps, which, as Michael Pisani has argued, is the same musical language used to characterize an exotic Other throughout stage and film music.[55] The frequent frills and grace notes that accompany his songs and stage action are examples of such exoticism.

In "Golly, I'm Glad to be Alive," Fenelly reveals that he once was a piano tuner and could "make the music sweet." Yet he now finds the back-breaking work of farming too onerous a responsibility, sarcastically singing, "Golly out in Utah I'm glad to be alive. Oh, the life that we live here is great." Unlike the other characters, who embrace difficult conditions as confirmation of their faith and place in the community, Fenelly sees music as a luxury and can't find a way to reconcile a life filled with both music and hard work. Although still a Mormon, Fenelly is conveyed musically as an outsider—while he does "sing" as a character in the show, his inability to harmonize as part of the community renders him socially mute. All he can do is begrudge his particular life struggles, committing a fundamental frontier (and Mormon) sin of considering the individual's comforts over the community's well-being. His outsider status is confirmed by his "ethnic" musical accompaniment in both "The Cushioned Seat" and "Golly, I'm Glad to be Alive."

80 · CHAPTER 2

It may also be that Fenelly cannot "sing" because he lacks a wife. In Mormon culture, to be single marks someone as an outsider; to stray from the nuclear, heteronormative family dynamic is to walk the delicate bounds of Mormon acceptability. As a rule, a family must have husband and wife, and since Fenelly has no wife, he therefore cannot be completely integrated into the community. This reflects a Mormon policy that would not have been in effect during Fenelly's life but certainly was a mindset of mid-twentieth-century Mormon audiences. When polygamy was finally revoked in 1907, the Church shifted focus away from marriages as *plural* to marriages that were *celestial*—a clever turn of words that allowed Mormons to give up plural marriage as a temporal principle while still maintaining its practice and belief as the order of heaven. Since the Mormons had been in Nauvoo, the temple ceremony had taught that families could be bound together as units in the hereafter, and that those units were bound within "celestial marriage."[56] By retaining the same wording, Mormons left a back door open for polygamy to be reinstated at a future date. Nonetheless, the Church's emphasis on a nuclear family was much more palatable than rhetoric about polygamy and consequently was widely accepted and respected by the Protestant America Mormons hoped to win over. Today, monogamous Mormon families are sealed together in temples as celestial families, still abiding by the principles that once governed plural marriages.[57]

In contrast to Fenelly's outsider status, the romance between Jed and Celia is portrayed as a successful attuning, one to the other's voice. They sing that "love is their song" and "the music of our love so true will always be strong." In everything they do, whether in rising from bed or working in the fields, they sing love. Their relationship is built from the same principle Isaiah wrote of when he considered the voices of God's special witnesses: "With the voice together shall they sing: for they shall see eye to eye, when the Lord shall bring again Zion."[58] This supports what we already knew about Jed and Celia—that by singing they affirm their commitment to the community and show their willingness for hard work. The four duets between Jed and Celia confirm that we ought to understand their relationship through song, since we hear them sing together far more often than alone. Their tuneful companionship is best illustrated in "Love Is Our Song," when Celia admits, "Ev'ry song I sang, I sang for you," and asks Jed if he could hear her singing while he was hundreds of miles away from her.

It is a common conceit that musicals are endowed with an overblown optimism. This may be cause for much ridicule, but musicals need optimism to enable individuals and communities to define, rediscover, and then reimagine their respective identities when any form of conflict arises. Raymond Knapp calls such easy reconciliation the "marriage trope"; in musicals there are "couples whose individual issues mirror or embody larger ones that turn out to be what the musical in question is 'really' about."[59] Sometimes this technique involves a literal marriage, as is the case with Curly and Laurey in *Oklahoma!*, whose union serves as a metaphor for reconciliation between farmers and cowhands. Other times the marriage is implied or denied. The disrupted union of Tony and Maria in *West Side Story* nonetheless suggests both respective communities will work for peaceable reconciliation. *Promised Valley* features none of these. Though they are forced to spend time apart while Jed serves in the Mormon Battalion, Jed and Celia's union was never really threatened, nor does their relationship represent a "marriage" between two opposing forces, since they were married before the action of the musical begins and appear to be of a singular mindset. They are both Mormons and both coming to terms with the destiny of their people and their places within that new world. The tension in the musical is therefore the effect of their union and not the cause of it.

If we look beyond the confines of the actual musical, however, there is a real-life marriage trope that *Promised Valley* helps bring about: reconciliation between Mormonism and America. After decades of living on the fringe of American life, postwar Mormons actively sought out ways of assimilation. *Promised Valley*, Mormonism's true entrée into musical theater, seems well timed and purposefully designed to show Mormonism's good faith in core American enterprises—hard work, community spirit, devotion to the land and family, and, of course, the thoroughly American institution of musical theater. Previous displays of Mormons in popular culture, including musical comedy, were antagonistic, mocking, and exploitative. *Promised Valley* disrupted those conventional images of Mormon faith and life by emphasizing beloved American work ethics inscribed within Mormon vocality. Furthermore, the show played up the conventions of singing in musicals. If in musical theater to sing means to belong, then *Promised Valley* was an opportunity to prove that Mormons belonged, by establishing their mastery over the style and conventions of America's home-grown theatrical genre.

*   *   *

By the mid-twentieth century, Mormonism had finished on top in a long journey of self-reinvention. Mormons across the country filled academic posts, held prominent and successful positions in business, and were employed at the highest levels of state and national government. There was

82 · CHAPTER 2

even a Mormon appointed Secretary of Agriculture under the Eisenhower administration. By sidling up to musical theater, the Mormon Church helped change the image of Mormons from untrustworthy bandits to exemplary Americans.

They also successfully reattached themselves to the narrative of whiteness, emboldened by musical theater. The Mormon "aspiration toward whiteness" came at a price, however, as the path the rest of the country was on shifted beneath Mormonism's feet. Understandings of race were veering radically away from those held in the nineteenth century, yet Mormons continued to emphasize behavior determined by increasingly out-of-date notions of whiteness. In essence, Mormons overshot their mark, becoming in turn too white and their devotion to musical theater too strong. The subsequent Mormon affinity for carrying optimistic, unrealistic, and privileged conventions or assumptions of so-called "Golden Age" American musical theater outside the stage and into the real world could easily be mocked. Oscar Hammerstein's defense of his work's optimism might well describe Mormonism of the twentieth century: "I don't deny the ugly and tragic—but somebody has to keep saying that life's pretty wonderful, too. Because it's true. I guess I can't write anything without hope in it."[60] When Trey Parker and Matt Stone set out to portray Mormons in their 2011 Broadway hit *Book of Mormon*, they readily drew the connection between Mormons, the musicals of Rodgers and Hammerstein, and Disney, since in their minds all three groups promoted a 1950s fantasy of middle-class, white optimism, easy fodder for ridicule in the postmodern climate of the twenty-first century.[61]

As much as musical theater helped convince Americans that Mormons were now acceptably white enough, it may also have helped convince Mormons of their inseparable connection to the country that had not always treated them kindly. The legacy of Mormonism began to cement in the mid-twentieth century, while musical theater also become a set fixture in the practice of Mormonism. Just as the message of *Promised Valley* insisted that vocal discipline reflected perceived American principles of obedience and order, so too did Mormons adapt their theology of voice to fit within conventions of American musical theater. The Mormon Church took unprecedented steps toward expansions in the decades immediately following *Promised Valley*, and they carried musical theater with them as a positive emblem of Mormon behavior. Mormon understandings of musicals as innately white came along with them and helped the Church chart a course of white, religious colonialism during the last half of the twentieth century.

3

Exoticized Voices, Racialized Bodies

Lineage and Whiteness on Stage

Hearken ye people from afar; and ye that are upon the
islands of the sea, listen together. For verily the voice of
the Lord is unto all men.

   —Doctrine and Covenants 1:1

Musical theater helped solve the assimilation problem Mormons faced in
the first half of the twentieth century. Mormons showed they could adapt
themselves to the styles and conventions of white America through the styles
and conventions of musical theater—white middle-class America's cultural
surrogate. Even fundamentalist factions of the Church found musical theater a helpful vehicle for navigating their complex American identity; one
polygamous community retooled *The Sound of Music* as a piece of polygamous propaganda. Yet the mainstream Church's newfound acceptance would
need to be guarded in the ensuing years. Following the enormous success
of *Promised Valley*, the Mormon Church looked continually to musicals to
help define Mormonism as its membership grew substantially in the second
half of the century. The political and theological benefits of musical theater
had become apparent to Mormon leaders, and by the 1960s, musicals figured
into almost every aspect of Mormon life.

Mormons midcentury furthermore used musical theater to define the
boundaries between and among various races of people both within and
outside of Mormonism. This is not without some irony, since Mormons
had long been brutally degraded as ethnic minorities through the musical
stage and now were resorting to using musical theater as a means toward
similar racial categorization. With a complex doctrinal understanding of
lineage and race, Mormons took to musical theater to frame a world where
musical theater performances signaled a people's identity as "white" within

84 · CHAPTER 3

the Mormon racial hierarchy. By allowing certain groups the opportunity to voice whiteness through the conventions of musical theater, Mormons reimagined the genre as a tool to transform some minority members into exemplars of whiteness.

Mormonism's long and tenuous relationship with race in the United States undoubtedly contributed to the impulse to cleanse racially through musical theater. By the time the group immigrated to Utah in 1847, Church leaders had put in place a racial policy that prevented black men from being granted the priesthood. Church officials stringently maintained the racial policy for over one hundred years. Yet, when Mormon missionaries first sailed to the Sandwich Islands in the nineteenth century and found success converting the natives, the dark skin of the Polynesians betrayed their actual lineage (at least to the missionaries) as remnant of the House of Israel. Like Native Americans, but unlike blacks, Polynesians were eagerly welcomed as candidates for joining the Mormon ranks.

Mormon policy depended on an easy racial categorization of members and prospective members, which goes a long way in explaining the ensuing decades of racial ambiguity, racist policies and practices, and blatant exoticism of the racial Other within Mormonism. Inasmuch as the faithful Mormon has always been a performing Mormon, the theater became a helpful venue for performing Mormon racial policies. Using the evening shows at the Church-owned Polynesian Cultural Center and the Mormon musical *Life . . . More Sweet than Bitter* as case studies, this chapter offers a view into the machinations of Mormon exoticism.

Polynesia and The Book of Mormon

Somewhere in the middle of the narrative, a man named Hagoth appears in The Book of Mormon. Described as an "exceedingly curious man," Hagoth lived among the ancient American tribes of Nephites and Lamanites whose comings and goings make up the bulk of The Book of Mormon. Hagoth becomes a shipbuilder, constructing an "exceedingly large ship" that "many of the Nephites . . . did enter therein and did sail forth with much provisions, and also many women and children; and they took their course northward." Hagoth later returns and builds more ships, and even more people and provisions set out on the waters with him.[1]

The Book of Mormon picks up where it left off with no mention of Hagoth or his ships again, yet for young Mormon missionary George Q. Cannon, the story of Hagoth offered a convenient explanation for an unexpected turn of events that occurred in the mission field. It was 1850 when twenty-three-year-old Cannon and nine other missionaries were sent by Brigham Young to dedicate the Sandwich Islands for the preaching of the Gospel. The missionaries assumed they were sent to proselytize among the white inhabitants of the islands and, as such, virtually ignored the dark-skinned Native Hawaiians. Their assumption stems from racial categorization emerging within Mormonism at the time. Under the leadership of Brigham Young, Mormon policy had evolved to exclude people of African descent from proselytizing efforts. One basis for this belief lies within a verse of The Book of Mormon, where those who disobeyed God's commandments were punished with dark skin; these "Lamanites," as they were called, eventually overtook the fairer-skinned ancient Americans; today's dark-skinned Native Americans are believed to be Lamanite descendants. This means that Native Americans, who descend from a Jewish prophet named Lehi, are considered to be of the House of Israel and therefore are Jews—"chosen" and eligible for the preaching of the gospel despite their dark skin. People with African descent, on the other hand, were believed to have gained their dark skin punitively (either through bad bloodlines, choices made in the pre-mortal existence, or both) and therefore were not considered part of the House of Israel. Until the racial ban was lifted in 1978, men with any amount of African lineage were barred from obtaining the Mormon priesthood, effectively estranging them and their families from almost every meaningful social or cultural practice in the Church.[2]

The missionaries had no luck proselytizing among the whites, however, and the mission president suggested they pack up and continue their work elsewhere. But Cannon received a vision while working on the island of Maui that gave him and a few other missionaries reason to stay. Cannon saw in his vision that Hagoth, the Book of Mormon shipbuilder, had led his small group of ancient Americans to the Pacific islands, effectively populating the region with dark-skinned descendants of ancient Jews. Mormon historian R. Lanier Britsch explains that, "while at Lahaina, Maui, [Cannon] had a revelation in which the Lord spoke to him telling him that the Hawaiians were of the House of Israel. From this time on, Cannon and his associates began to preach that the Hawaiian people were an offshoot branch of Israel through the posterity of Lehi, a *Book of Mormon* prophet."[3] As the missionaries began finding immediate and substantial success converting Native Hawaiians to Mormonism, Cannon's vision seemed validated—his experience in turn rendered Polynesians not cursed but in fact chosen, not deplorable but of royal lineage.

86 · CHAPTER 3

Polynesians were no longer ignored by Mormon missionaries; rather they were acknowledged as "chosen" and thus elevated to the status all fair-skinned Mormons shared as Israelites. In her book *A Chosen People, a Promised Land*, political scientist (and former Mormon) Hokulani Aikau writes that "the revelation transformed Hawaiians from a people ineligible to hear the gospel to a people who needed the gospel 'returned' to them."[4] Polynesians were engulfed within a distinct colonialist agenda born out of a racial hierarchy where "whiteness persists as a privileged state of being and sign of salvation."[5] With Cannon's vision, Polynesians immediately joined the ranks of Native Americans and Jews, whose "chosenness" remains a characteristically Mormon euphemism for "whiteness."

As Hawaiians continued to join the Mormon faith in large numbers, the Mormon belief in a central gathering place—known as Zion and geographically positioned in Jackson County, Missouri—became a logistical complication; the Hawaiian Islands began to be thought of as a separate gathering place, thus disrupting the early Mormon conception of a literal gathering in one designated location.[6] Church leaders bought land in Hawaii during the nineteenth century to form a Mormon colony in the Pacific, providing much of the sugar bought and sold through the Mormon Church. The large Mormon presence on the Hawaiian Islands resulted in the building and dedication of a Mormon temple in Laie in 1919 and, in 1955, the Church College of Hawaii (later renamed Brigham Young University-Hawaii) was established. Both the temple and the college were built on land the Church had acquired shortly after the success of Cannon's first proselytizing mission. A separate Mormon institution closely tied to the efforts of both the temple and the college was built soon thereafter, and in 1963 the Polynesian Cultural Center opened its doors.

The Polynesian Cultural Center and Mormon Theatricality

The Polynesian Cultural Center was established to create jobs for Polynesian students at the college, to preserve some aspects of Native culture, and to help proselyte among non-Mormons.[7] Students at the Church College of Hawaii were employed as "labor missionaries" to help build and then work for the cultural center. Aikau points to problems with these goals of the center, noting that some Native Hawaiian Mormons felt that their work was less to spread the charitable gospel and more to promote the prosperity of the Mormon Church. As one student complained, his work as a labor missionary served a different purpose than what was originally perceived.

LINEAGE AND WHITENESS ON STAGE · 87

Entertainment six days a week with about the only sane thinking going on was church on Sunday and then six more days of entertaining. Whether it's a siva or pese or serving supper, lunch, and dinner, frying hamburgers, it's still a catering kind of thing for kupe (for money) from other strangers. And it didn't seem to us that the individuals there, who were performing in the various aspects of the Polynesian Center, would have any time to preach the gospel to anybody. It was just a matter of cash and carry business.[8]

This era of Mormon acculturation of American economic ideals gave the Church a distinctly capitalist rhetoric with which to perform its proselytizing efforts. The Polynesian Cultural Center likewise became the site of cultural encounter via musical theater, where identity politics were on full display.

According to the website for the cultural center, in 1959 "Polynesian students at Church College of Hawai'i had started up *Polynesian Panorama*—a production of authentic South Pacific island songs and dances."[9] That musical drama has evolved over the decades but today it is known as *Ha: Breath of Life*. Six evenings a week, visitors to the center are entertained with a dramatic production of dance, music, and storytelling—a musical drama detailing the history of the Polynesian islands. The center and its evening show frequently rank among the top tourist attractions in Hawaii, with one advertisement boasting, "Think Broadway, then add flaming knives."[10] Allusions to Broadway musicals aside, performances at the Polynesian Cultural Center have been praised for their authenticity, however feigned the shows may be. It seems odd to use perhaps the most brazenly *inauthentic* genre to pass off these performances as authentic, but similar marketing logic works on those seeking an authentic New York experience by taking in a Broadway show, and many take the bait. One reviewer states, "It is by far the best Polynesian entertainment in Hawaii," and the *Honolulu Advertiser* sees in *Ha* "authentic pageantry teeming and throbbing with the syncopations and synergy of the south seas culture."[11]

In promoting the center as authentic, student-performers must walk a delicate line between tradition and Mormon prudence. Since the early part of the twentieth century, both men and women must adhere to standards of modesty outlined by the Church. Mormons therefore have kept strict rules governing the body and its appearance. Performers at the cultural center necessarily break these standards when the men entertain shirtless and the women dance in hula skirts and bikini tops. Traditional tattoos among Samoan or Fijian performers are also very common—fake tattoos are even given to tourists as emblems of authenticity—but in Mormonism they are considered a defamation of the body. Chiung Hwang Chen points out that while both Brigham Young University-Hawaii and the Polynesian Cultural

88 · CHAPTER 3

Center are owned by the Mormon Church, "they have two different sets of rules."[12] Principles of white, American propriety in the service of authenticity thus place performers somewhat uncomfortably between Mormonism's desire for acceptance and the need to retain a distinguishable identity.

Central to the center's authenticity, therefore, are the performing Native bodies themselves, once ignored and then championed precisely for their racial qualities. This carries strong colonialist pretensions deeply embedded within Hawaiian history, though not entirely unique to its relationship with Mormonism. As political scientist Haunanu-Kay Trask writes, "Because the selling of Hawai'i depends on the prostitution of Hawaiian culture, Hawaiian and other locals must supply the industry with compliant workers. Thus our Hawaiian people—and not only our Hawaiian culture—become commodities."[13] Aikau likewise takes issue with Hawaiian tourism altogether, arguing that "the tourism machine sells race, workers perform race, and tourists buy race. Within this framework, Hawaiian people sell more than their labor for wages; tourism relies on their gendered racial bodies to sell race to tourists."[14] What emerges from the center's production, then, is a dazzling and celebrated musical spectacle undergirded by race and the mythology of the "happy Native" that plays directly into the hands of those who sell, perform, and buy race through the musical stage.

It is difficult to ignore a link between the Mormon interest in a theatrical story about Polynesians and other musicals with similar themes. Rodgers and Hammerstein had already explored American values in *South Pacific*, *Flower Drum Song*, and *The King and I* in the years preceding the cultural center's opening. In all three Broadway shows, race was treated forthrightly, if not haphazardly. For example, despite Lieutenant Joe Cable's conviction that "you've got to be carefully taught" to have racial prejudice, Rodgers and Hammerstein fail to depict the Polynesians in *South Pacific* with much dignity or respect. Similarly, *The King and I* moralizes a world where Western imperialism is celebrated, even as it inoculates Siam from its traditional moorings. Anna Leonowens's European values (conveniently standing in for American values in the musical) prove too much for King Mongkut, who struggles to keep up with modernity and creeping Western influences in his country. When it becomes apparent to the king that he will never be able to assimilate into Western ways, he dies of a broken heart.

Musicals have never been much on authenticity. For all the lip service they give for progressive values, musicals rarely model any overtly liberalized ideology. Privileged assumptions about Pacific island cultures were hurtful, but equally insensitive were depictions of frontier life in *Oklahoma!*

or domestic violence in *Carousel*. Oscar Hammerstein's dramatic scenarios were just that—fictionalized plots devised for New York audiences. In fact, backhanded liberalizing gestures well define Hammerstein's dramatic output. His progressive attitude toward dynamic issues like race resonated with elite audiences then and now, but by today's standards such thinking barely shines through the stereotypes he simultaneously perpetuates.

Critics picked up on Rodgers and Hammerstein's messy portrayals of "exotic peoples in general." "It seems to have worried neither Mr. Rodgers nor Mr. Hammerstein very much that the behavior of war torn Pacific Islanders and nineteenth-century Siamese might be slightly different from that of Chinese residents of present-day California, where *Flower Drum Song* is fictionally sung," wrote one reviewer in 1958. "The assumption, which may be justified, is that the audience will not notice the difference."[15] "Hammerstein's compromise," as Raymond Knapp calls the paradox, may have made liberal ideology less than unequivocal, but these three exotic musicals nonetheless drew attention to other cultures that was not altogether negative.[16] For Bruce McConachie, inasmuch as all three musicals allowed American audiences to "cloak their racism as benevolence and their lust for power as entitlement," Rodgers and Hammerstein also used musical theater to humanize Pacific Islanders and attack prejudice of all kinds.[17] McConachie even argues that these musicals helped soften feelings toward Asians and Asian Americans as the United States military prepared to contain Communism in Vietnam and Korea.

South Pacific, *The King and I*, and *Flower Drum Song* all premiered between *Promised Valley* in 1947 and the opening of the Polynesian Cultural Center in 1963, and, given the attention Mormons gave to *Oklahoma!*, it is unlikely the musicals' messages did not in some way influence the Church's decision to theatricalize Polynesian culture. In fact, King Mongkut's demise at the end of *The King and I* may have struck a particular nerve with some Mormons since his portrayal as mercurial and polygamist tyrant bears a strong resemblance to the menacing Mormon of nineteenth-century operetta. Nonetheless, Mormons were hoping to continue *Promised Valley*'s success and continue earning cultural capital with a musical at the Polynesian Cultural Center.

The Mormon Church continued the practice they began with *Promised Valley* in looking to Broadway for help spearheading the production. In 1963 they hired Hollywood star Jack Regas to choreograph the new evening show, which at the time was known as the "South Sea Revue." Regas, a non-Mormon, got his start as a dancer in the original cast of *Oklahoma!* and danced "in every major MGM musical between 1943 and 1948" before becoming known in

90 · CHAPTER 3

Hollywood as choreographer for the *Jack Benny Program*, the *Dinah Shore Show*, and, later, *Laugh-In*.[18] Like the professional credentials Alfred Drake and others brought to *Promised Valley*, Regas brought Broadway gravitas and white, middle-class respectability to his training of the Polynesian performers. "They didn't know a time-step from a happily hippy bump," he told reporters, "but we got along beautifully." [19]

For Mormons, performing musicals becomes a complex theological display. Teaching Polynesians how to sing and dance in the musical theater style seems in this instance like a deliberate attempt to illustrate that Polynesians, like white-skinned Mormons before them, could perform away any racial stigma by adopting conventions of American musical theater. After all, white Mormons had successfully used musicals to prove *their* whiteness in the opening decades of the century. The Polynesians' Jewish lineage could now be implicitly demonstrated through the performance of musicals, no matter how unalike Polynesians and Jews may seem (or in fact may actually be). Furthermore, as musical theater augmented Mormon ideals of vocality, granting the same privilege to other groups further extended the rights of vocal vicariousness as a token of conversion. Through musicals, Polynesians could speak with the voice of whiteness—their bodies fulfilling the promise in The Book of Mormon that Lamanites, once converted, would undergo a racial transformation from having a "skin of darkness" to being "a white and delightsome people."[20] The voice therefore sounds what the bodies cannot show: a conversion to Mormonism, to whiteness, and to a new identity as theatrical apprentice.

I'm speaking of a "white voice" here only figuratively, since any effort to distinguish a white voice from a black voice is problematic in that it suggests the white body is physiologically different from a nonwhite one. The voice is often assumed by listeners to be a stable object—unchanging and distinct from the body from which it emerges. The voice is also thought to signify subjectivity and interiority. These assumptions lead some to hear racial characteristics in a voice, concluding, for example, that black singers are only being authentic or honest when listeners hear a racialized timbre. The voice is not a stable identifier, however, if you consider that the body (which includes the larynx) is always changing, reacting and adapting to changes in the environment, and aging. To sound "white," therefore, has little to do with the quality of the voice singing. Instead, the listener has some predetermined criteria in his or her mind for what white sounds like and "authors" the voice as such. The way we hear and categorize voices by race therefore is a reflection of age-old racist ideologies about dark-skinned bodies. As Nina

LINEAGE AND WHITENESS ON STAGE · 91

Eidsheim writes, "no ear is innocent. Each cochlea curls around its past, and this past resonates with the present."[21]

In this instance, dark-skinned bodies dancing and singing in a white musical style, following white musical conventions, might stand in for this perception of a white vocality, but it is important that the voice itself cannot become white since it cannot become what does not exist. Rather, the dark-skinned Polynesians indicate a conversion to Mormonism by displaying whiteness through musical theater. If some audiences hear whiteness in the sounds of the Polynesian performers, then we must assume that they, too, find easy association between Mormonism, musical theater, and seeing on display what are presumed to be white values.

The Church didn't stop with the Polynesians; musical theater was used to perform chosenness in others as well. In 1971, Brigham Young University professor Jane ("Janie") Thompson founded a performing ensemble called "The Lamanite Generation." The group of Native American, Polynesian, and Latin American students, which continues to perform today under the name "Living Legends," toured the United States and other parts of the world throughout the 1970s and 1980s, performing songs and dances that reflected their heritage in a theatrical manner. The song and dance routines of "The Lamanite Generation" helped reinforce the narrative of colonialism, using the bodies and voices of nonwhite performers as emblems of Mormonism's newly established role as purveyor of white domination.[22] Thus, performing musical theater became a convenient way for certain dark-skinned Mormons to erase racial heritage by acting white. If a person's heritage revealed a person to be "chosen," then he or she could perform away any actual racial identity and affirm a sense of surrogate whiteness by performing on the musical stage.

Brigham Young once said, "If I were placed on a cannibal island and given the task of civilizing its people, I should straightway build a theatre."[23] It took more than one hundred years, but the Mormon Church eventually made good on Young's intention. While the Hawaiian tourist industry encompasses much more than Mormonism, the prominence the Polynesian Cultural Center holds within Hawaiian tourism highlights and exacerbates contentious Mormon understandings of race. And finally, as Brigham Young's statement attests, the transformative power of the stage is very real, very tangible for Mormons. By presenting Polynesian culture as a Broadway-style musical drama, the Mormon Church uses the musical stage to forge a connection between the dark-skinned Polynesian people and white-skinned Mormons living in the United States—making evident through performance the hidden qualities of whiteness within the Polynesians. Inasmuch as *Promised Valley*

92 · CHAPTER 3

stages the remarkable story of Mormon pioneers, the shows at the Polynesian Cultural Center likewise offer a similar musical and dramatic connection between Mormons and the history of the Polynesian people. Hidden slyly behind the Mormon conception of chosenness rests the racial purposes and intentions that uphold that conception. Far from just being an innocuous venue for frills and campy humor, musical theater thus helps Mormons categorize their complex world of racial identity, and, as the remainder of the chapter illustrates, allows some to feel a connection to broader American values—the soft lullaby of old Broadway becomes in the mouths of the dark-skinned performers a sure way of becoming white, even if in sound only.

Mormons and Jews

You can scarcely hear from all the screaming. It is 1974, and five men wearing pastel colored polyester suits shimmy and snap fingers to a groove provided by an on-stage band. All smiles and energy, the men singingly yearn for riches and women—and women there were. The Dionysian frenzy of screaming teeny-boppers erupting in front of and below the stage could scarcely have thwarted the performance, however. The band backs up the tight, chromatic shifting of their front men as they happily soak in all their devotion—testimonies to a truth this audience believes in mightily. These particular songs are not about vindications of religious truthfulness. Not like this. And these performers are in truth mere placeholders for any available version of the male celebrity body capable of enraging the hormones of a room crammed with young women. The truth of this moment rests not with the singularity of the music or the performers but rather with the relative ease with which both are synthesized as cultural products.

These five men are pop icons, but they also happen to be Mormon, and the songs they sing are pop songs, but they also happen to be about a Jewish community on the verge of extinction. If this cultural mishmash seems unlikely or perhaps a little too tidy, maybe it is. To be fair, the brotherly act The Osmonds and the hit musical *Fiddler on the Roof* probably should not be seen as entirely representative of the faith traditions out of which they emerge. Still, this moment of cultural collision—Mormon brothers singing a medley from *Fiddler on the Roof*—does point to a curiously remarkable site of common ground both faith traditions share: the musical theater stage.

In significant ways, Jewish identity is deeply woven into the fabric of musical theater and its history. Yiddish theater, as some scholars have argued, may have provided the fertile ground and cultural fervency that allowed

LINEAGE AND WHITENESS ON STAGE · 93

musical theater to take root among the increasingly diverse urban American communities; in this interpretation, Yiddish theater serves as the genesis of a distinctly American musical genre. If the Americanness of musical theater rests on its Jewish beginnings, the disempowered social place of Jews in nineteenth-century America hardly bespeaks that significance. As Andrea Most has argued, however, perhaps it was precisely that position as outsider that empowered musical theater with a distinct American flavor of resiliency.

> Indeed, the experience of being an outsider—even one not explicitly Jewish—comes to be defined by a narrative trajectory from exclusion to acceptance, a trajectory codified by Jewish writers of musicals. For all sorts of outsiders, the way to become American is, in other words, a Jewish way, and those who follow that path perform—wittingly or unwittingly—a Jewish story, which is to say, an American story, indeed *the* American story.[24]

Not only do musicals signal the Jewish experience in overt or more subtle ways, but Jews themselves are largely responsible for shaping the genre into what it is today. Virtually all of the most canonical and well-loved musicals of the last century were created by Jewish writers, including *Show Boat* (1927), *Oklahoma!* (1943), *Street Scene* (1947), *South Pacific* (1949), *West Side Story* (1957), and *A Little Night Music* (1973); many others carry specific Jewish themes or characters, such as *Parade* (1998), *Spamalot* (2005), and of course *Fiddler on the Roof* (1964).

Mormons, too, have used the musical stage to assimilate and propagate their own theological implications of vocality. Yet as deeply imbedded as musical theater is within the Mormon culture, even more a part of Mormonism is a strong sense of kinship they feel toward Jews. Significantly, this kinship pertains to the salvation of all mankind. Mormons believe in "the literal gathering of Israel and in the restoration of the Ten Tribes; that Zion (the New Jerusalem) will be built upon the American continent; that Christ will reign personally upon the earth; and, that the earth will be renewed and receive its paradisiacal glory."[25] Either through direct lineage—revealed through a patriarchal blessing, usually administered during adolescence—or through adoption by baptism, all Mormons consider themselves "Jews" from the lines of either Joseph or his son Ephraim. Consequently, Mormons consider Jews as descended from the tribe of Judah. This conception is uniquely Mormon, one derived from the moment God commands the Old Testament prophet Ezekiel to join two "sticks" into one.

> Moreover, thou son of man, take thee one stick, and write upon it, For Judah, and for the children of Israel his companions: then take another stick, and

write upon it, For Joseph, the stick of Ephraim, and for all the house of Israel his companions:

And join them one to another into one stick; and they shall become one in thine hand.

And when the children of thy people shall speak unto thee, saying, Wilt thou not shew us what thou meanest by these?

Say unto them, Thus saith the Lord GOD; Behold, I will take the stick of Joseph, which is in the hand of Ephraim, and the tribes of Israel his fellows, and will put them with him, even with the stick of Judah, and make them one stick, and they shall be one in mine hand.[26]

To Mormons, the "stick" of Judah is the Bible, and the "stick" of Ephraim The Book of Mormon. The Book of Mormon, which is an ancient text Joseph Smith purportedly translated by the power of the Holy Spirit, begins with the story of a prophet named Lehi, a contemporary of Jeremiah's, who, upon seeing a vision of impending destruction, fled Jerusalem with his family, eventually sailing over the sea to the American continent. Righteous descendants of Lehi were commanded to write down revelations and experiences on brass plates that they carried with them; these brass plates, which traveled with these ancient Americans over the course of several thousand years, are what Joseph Smith found buried within a hill near his home in Palmyra, New York. The text makes it clear that Lehi descended from the tribe of Manasseh—the brother of Ephraim—yet, historically, Mormon leaders have taught that the coming forth of The Book of Mormon as the "stick of Ephraim" signals that the time has come for Ezekiel's prophecy to be fulfilled.

Mormons, therefore, see Jews as distinctly different from the rest of the world. Perhaps even more confusing, the Mormon concept of the "Gentile" as anyone not Mormon also strips Jewishness from actual Jews. Sociologist Armand Mauss has argued that the evolution of Mormon understandings of race parallel efforts of the Church during the twentieth century to assimilate into mainstream America. Mormons needed a recognizable and friendly heritage different from the racially suspect identity given them by others. As a result, Mormons developed and promoted an understanding of lineage that connected them to ancient Israel. The relationship Jews already enjoyed with musical theater made the work of Mormon assimilation doubly coded. This enabled Mormons "simultaneously to carve out for themselves a special niche and a special connection to the whole redemptive history and destiny of God's chosen people and to claim a favored identity that would belie the identity imposed on them by their enemies," as Mauss suggests.[27] Under this "identity work," as Michael Schwalbe has called it, Mormons became Jews, Jews became Gentiles, and by the teachings of a young frontier prophet, chosenness was recast as an explicitly Mormon title.[28]

"Who God Wants You to Become"

Although *Fiddler on the Roof* premiered on Broadway in 1964, it seems to have really taken hold of the Mormon imagination shortly after Norman Jewison's 1971 film adaptation. This becomes readily apparent when looking at official Church publications and talks given or written by Church leaders, or General Authorities. Beginning in 1971 and continuing to as recently as 2012, *Fiddler on the Roof* was referred to by General Authorities eighteen times. Aside from Mormon scriptures, no other text receives anywhere near that amount of attention from Mormon leaders. Mormon appreciation for the musical is hardly unique, of course. Many faith and cultural traditions have found resonance within the musical's more general themes of resilience, tradition, and the challenges of modernity among the faithful. Sister Mary Immaculate of the National Catholic Theater Conference once remarked, for example, that *Fiddler on the Roof* was "the most catholic—small 'c'—show I ever saw."[29]

This notwithstanding, what makes the Mormon preoccupation with *Fiddler* distinct is how Mormons moralize or adapt the story to fit changing Mormon concerns. Of those eighteen references to *Fiddler*, Mormon leaders used the film (typically) as a point of departure, employing Tevye's musings with God almost always in the service of a unique Mormon theological or political conception. In 1971, apostle Thomas S. Monson noted that *Fiddler on the Roof* was one of his favorite musicals. Monson frequently used Tevye's comments loosely to point to particular issues of concern; this occasion—the first recorded Mormon reference to *Fiddler on the Roof*—was no exception. In an article titled "The Women's Movement: Liberation or Deception?" Monson counsels Mormon women not to adhere to the "idiotic and blatantly false philosophy" of women's liberation. "Error, sin, lust, envy, and evil thrive in the midst of today's prosperity," Monson writes.

> More than $5 million a year is spent on pornographic literature by which vile men try to "dig gold out of dirt." Magazines, movies, television programs, and other mass media are utilized to lower moral standards and behavior. Crime and delinquency are rampant, and spiritual values are questioned. Our interests are centered in ourselves. We are preoccupied with material things. Many

of us are more concerned about conquering space than about conquering ourselves. We are more dedicated to material security than to inner purity. We give much more thought to what we wear, what we eat, what we drink, and what we can do to relax than we give to what we are.[30]

Monson coolly shifts this litany of moral deprivations into a discussion of prescribed gender roles, roles that Mormons consider eternal and divine. After citing an exchange between columnist Ann Landers and a disgruntled mother who would rather give her son up for adoption than quit smoking the cigarettes that are causing her son's breathing difficulties, Monson responds, "Have such mothers become liberated? Have they achieved freedom? Equality? No. They have not been liberated. They have been deceived."

The rhetoric takes a curious turn here, as Monson introduces *Fiddler on the Roof*'s Tevye the milkman as an addendum to his council.

> One of the fine musical comedies of recent years is Joseph Stein's *Fiddler on the Roof*. This tells the story of an old-fashioned Jewish father in Russia who is trying to cope with changing times brought forcibly home to him by his beautiful teenage daughters. The gaiety of the dance, the rhythm of the music, the excellence of the acting all fade in their significance when the father speaks what to me becomes the message of the musical. He gathers his lovely daughters to his side and, in the simplicity of his peasant surroundings, counsels them as they ponder their future. "Remember," he cautions, "in Anatevka each one of you knows who she is and what God expects you to become." You, beloved sisters of the Church, know who you are and what God expects you to become. Your challenge is to bring all for whom you are responsible to a knowledge of this truth.

Monson concludes by challenging women to "first, sustain your husband; second, strengthen your home; third, serve your God," then promising "as a servant of the Lord, that as you do, the blessings of heaven will attend you."[31]

It seems strange to hear the words of Tevye the milkman amid this rebuttal of women's liberation. Admittedly, the single line Monson pulls from the musical—"in Anatevka, each one knows who she is and what God expects you to become"—is vague enough to blanket an associative moral onto perhaps any issue. It is rather remarkable that Church leaders fixate on this line at all since Tevye's statement on traditional roles and expectations is pointedly called into question by much of what actually happens in the musical. Still, this cherry-picked phrase has been used by Church leaders to rhapsodize on topics as varied as female modesty; the unique Mormon principle of abstaining from alcohol, coffee, and tea; cautions against a "secular lifestyle," which includes "secular knowledge"; and scriptural mastery.[32] Brigham Young University president Jeffrey R. Holland, speaking in Provo, Utah, at a 1987 BYU devotional titled "Who We Are and What God Expects Us to Do," makes an even more explicit Mormon connection to the trials of Tevye. Just before reading Tevye's line of dialogue cited by Monson above, Holland says, "I wish to invoke Tevye's help in recounting and reminding very briefly truths taught to most of us since kindergarten and before. Here's Tevye on 'tradition.' When he says 'Anatevka,' think 'Provo.'"[33]

This collapsing of cultures—of seeing the trials of Anatevka taking place within the Wasatch Range in the western United States—illustrates a Mormon propensity to seek out and canonize moralizing stories from other cultures for the benefit of its members. The thirteenth Article of Faith, penned by Joseph Smith in 1842, states explicitly that "if there is anything virtuous, lovely, or of good report or praiseworthy, we seek after these things."[34] A foundational tenet of Mormonism is that all truth may be "circumscribed into one great whole,"[35] that since Mormons conceive of their faith as the original religion taught to Adam, all faith traditions alive today carry remnants of that whole. Through the process of discernment, Mormons believe they have the tools to ascertain truth when encountering a foreign concept, culture, or principle, thereby preserving for themselves a greater degree of truth and knowledge requisite for celestial exaltation.

Life . . . More Sweet than Bitter

It is unsurprising, then, that Mormons have latched on to the moral principles they discovered within *Fiddler on the Roof*. Since the film release in 1971, Mormon leaders have consistently used the story of Tevye the milkman to illustrate one doctrinal principle after another. This association comes in part from a strong affinity Mormons have for the Jewish people, although Mormon cosmology actually displaces Jews from their normative self-realization. Mormons consider themselves Jews and, consequently, everyone else—even actual Jews—Gentiles. The Mormon conception of lineage, which makes the distinction between blacks, Native Americans, and Polynesians a matter of scriptural exegesis, locates race as a physical manifestation of a spiritual gift or curse. Racial categories, particularly for Mormons prior to 1978, matter a great deal. For this reason the creation in 1977 of a new Mormon musical modeled after *Fiddler on the Roof* signals a distinctive understanding of Mormon cosmology and helps frame a discussion of Mormon conceptions of the racialized Other through the guise of musical drama.

98 · CHAPTER 3

Referred to by composer Michael Perry as "the Mormon Fiddler," *Life . . . More Sweet than Bitter* (written by K. Newell Dayley and Pat Davis) reconstructs the familiar story of the villagers in Anatevka but with a decidedly Mormon spin.[36] Although the Mormon musical is based on the true story of Maurice Warshaw, the similarities between the Broadway hit and this local flavor make for an interesting comparison. *Life . . . More Sweet than Bitter* follows the story of Maurice and his family who, faced with persecution against Jews, flee Eastern Europe in the late nineteenth century and eventually arrive in Salt Lake City. Maurice marries a Mormon woman, converts to Mormonism himself, and opens a successful chain of grocery stores, the latter a clever modernizing of Tevye's simple dairy business in *Fiddler*. This elevation of the Tevye character out of his Jewishness and into a Mormon body (and a capitalist, no less) allows Mormons a cultural victory over the Jews, converting the Jewish emblem not only to the Mormon faith but also to a distinctively twentieth-century Mormon socioeconomic ideology.

Textually and dramatically this makes sense. The stories collide in obvious and interesting ways, and the appearance of the Mormon musical in the same decade as the film release of *Fiddler*, along with the numerous injunctions from the Mormon pulpit about the Broadway show, act as a convenient corollary to this unique Mormon conception of Judaism. Even more interesting, and perhaps subtler, though, are the ways the Jewish subject is treated musically. Musical exoticization depends on a number of signifiers and cultural tropes; like ventriloquism or vocal impersonation, successful exoticism requires a willing and knowing audience to "play along." Sometimes these signifiers can be obvious, like the choice of key or mode to gesture toward Jewishness—a common practice in *Life . . . More Sweet than Bitter*.

Musical figures, too, can signify the exotic, particularly when the music is understood to offer a glimpse into the subconscience of its creator. Gustav Mahler's music, as an example, has captivated listeners who hear in his scores a "Jewish accent." Mahler's conversion from Judaism to Christianity—as was the case with Felix Mendelssohn's conversion to Catholicism the generation before Mahler—was perceived to be politically motivated rather than earnest, and some scholars have claimed to hear in his music a resistance to Jewish assimilation.[37] Closer to home in American musical theater, Richard Rodgers's Jewish heritage was thought by some to be written into his scores, despite the distance Rodgers tried to keep between himself and Judaism. "I can always tell a Rodgers tune," wrote Cole Porter. "There's a certain holiness about it."[38]

LINEAGE AND WHITENESS ON STAGE · 99

More prominently and conceptually intriguing than stylized musical figurations that can be heard as "exotic," however, is the use of what musicologist Ralph Locke calls the "All the Music in Full Context" paradigm of exoticism. This paradigm, according to Locke, encompasses the more obvious "Exotic Style Only" paradigm but also takes into account the many other ways exoticism is conveyed to an audience, particularly in staged productions. Locke's broader conception of exoticism allows "many other musical passages—ones that do not differ from the prevailing musical language of the day—to be considered as contributing to portrayal of an exotic Other. They do so because they are presented in a plainly exoticizing context, such as—in the case of an opera—plot, sung words, sets, and costumes."[39]

The way one element of the dramatic context can give sway to another element hints at the organizational model of the integrated musical. Locke's "All the Music in Full Context" paradigm offers a productive lens through which to view much of *Life . . . More Sweet than Bitter*. Still, there are distinct moments of what Locke would call the "Exotic Style Only" paradigm, such as the opening number "God's Word Is Great and Holy." As the curtain rises, the rabbi stands and sings didactically to six young boys. This is the only time this tune is used in the musical, and the accompanying chimes and loose arpeggiation allow the melody, in the natural minor, to place the story aurally in another land. The rabbi becomes an emblem of orthodoxy and tradition—two contested themes in this story—so he is archetypically depicted in order to demonstrate his place within that ideological framework.

At least that is how it begins. The second number, "Life Is What You Make It," is introduced by the rabbi but becomes an anthem throughout the rest of the musical. The rabbi's counsel for obedience and making the most out of the life and circumstances given you extends full circle; by the end of the musical it is the grown Maurice who is singing a reprise of the song, moralizing with it the lessons from his life. The rabbi (and, by extension, orthodox Judaism) physically occupies the stage only in the opening scenes, and so becomes translated into a musical modality vicariously. By returning in the final scene, the rabbi's tune signals that Maurice's cultural heritage was not lost upon his conversion to Mormonism but rather will work in tandem with his new religion (see example 3).[40]

This is further illustrated in the musical journey Maurice takes in the show. As time lapses and the story moves across the ocean and further into the center of the American continent, so too do the Jewish qualities in the

Example 3: Excerpt of "Life is What You Make It," from *Life . . . More Sweet than Bitter* (1977). Music by K. Newell Dayley and lyrics by Pat Davis.

music become diluted and Americanized. The most prominent site of cultural negotiation occurs when Maurice and his future wife, Inez, go to a dance. The script dictates that "the music starts up louder on new dance, rhythm similar to 'Yes, We Have No Bananas.'" That song, notably covered in blackface by Al Jolson for the 1930 film *Mammy*, brings a rich set of cultural codes to the musical. It is nearly impossible to dissociate that song from Jolson and likewise to separate Jolson from his best-known film, *The Jazz Singer* (1927), which thematized manifest tension emerging between orthodox Judaism and a modern world. The background music at this important dance deepens the moment in the story by likening the underlying conflict of Maurice the Jew and Inez the Mormon with that shared between Jolson's character and his father in *The Jazz Singer*. Moreover, Maurice and Inez's culturally strained relationship models (but inverts) Jack's taboo relationship with his shiksa girlfriend, Mary Dale.

Immediately following the dance scene, Maurice and Inez sing a duet that serves as a musical watershed for the show. Maurice has up to this point continued to sing music modeled on Jewish idioms—including the humorous, Mel Brooks–style patter song, "A Gentile Is a Gentile Is a Gentile," to be discussed later. Following his union with Inez, Maurice adopts a much more American (or less Jewish) sound, while Inez shows she has learned to sing in a parodied musical theater style, surely meant to signify the largely Jewish stylizations of Tin Pan Alley. This is perhaps best illustrated in the ensemble number "1425 Kensington Avenue" (see example 4). The crisp chromatic shadings and punchy dotted eight-sixteenth figures in the melody suggest a

Example 4: Excerpt of "1425 Kensington Avenue," from *Life . . . More Sweet than Bitter* (1977). Music by K. Newell Dayley and lyrics by Pat Davis.

popular song style normalized in the 1920s through Tin Pan Alley. While this compositional style quickly became co-opted by the American entertainment industry, those composing and "pushing" these pieces in New York City were often Jewish men—famously including George Gershwin and Irving Berlin. It seems significant, then, that Inez—the Mormon who, it should be pointed out, like her husband, frustrates her religion's view on marrying outside of the faith—should begin the number.

With Inez demonstrating her ability to perform like a modern Jew, she is also demonstrating that appropriating the musical theater style is a two-way street, and her identity as a Mormon grants her the ability to "pass" as Jewish—or, more to the point, that she in fact was "Jewish" all along. Inez and Maurice previously had been discussing a compromise between their differing religious viewpoints. Inez counters Maurice's doubts with the line,

"It's the people who divide themselves. Don't blame God again! This life is ours . . . it's what we make it." Maurice hears in her words the same counsel the rabbi once gave him, and realizes that "life itself has taught me that you and I must come to some agreement." For Inez then to begin singing this song, only to be joined by Maurice and, later, others, demonstrates musically the same conflation occurring between the Mormon bride and Jewish husband. Just as the song's musical language is a cultural mashup of Jewish and American identities, so too does Inez and Maurice's romantic intertwining represent a cultural and religious negotiation between Mormon and Jewish identities.

There is one musical theater convention noticeably lacking in this production, and it has everything to do with how the audience is prepared to frame the relationship between Maurice and Inez. Between the dance and "1425 Kensington Avenue," the Jew and the Mormon get married, but the wedding—so common a trope in musical theater happy endings as to make it a dramatic convention—does not occur on stage. Audiences instead are shown the makings of the romance and the couple's life in marriage, while the wedding itself is withheld. One explanation for the absence of a wedding scene is that Mormon weddings are typically private affairs, kept hidden away inside the walls of a Mormon temple. Maurice and Inez's wedding may be kept offstage because actual Mormon weddings generally occur offstage, out of sight for all but a few. Also, as much as Mormons foreground marriage as an institution, the Mormon wedding ceremony itself is not nearly as dramatic or familiar as that typically practiced in America. Without an easily distinguishable wedding gown, fresh-cut flowers, the bridal march, or toasts to the bride and groom, for example, the Mormon wedding seems a little too common to play well on the musical stage—not that Mormon temple ceremonies of any type are ever portrayed or even discussed outside of the temple walls, another probable reason why *Life . . . More Sweet than Bitter* skips over the nuptials.

The missing wedding matters a great deal to how this story functions within the Mormon-Jewish paradigm I have used to frame this discussion. As Raymond Knapp has pointed out in his discussion of the "marriage trope," weddings in musicals serve as a reconciliatory fantasy, an illusory gesture that suggests the union of a bride and groom as representatives of particular communities, races, backgrounds, and so on, promises reconciliation between those two communities. Musicals, like comedic plots in literature, still operate under an assumption of magical circumstances that allow *Guys and Dolls*'s high-rolling gambler Sky Masterson and Save-a-Soul naïf Sarah

Brown, for example, to, rather improbably, live happily ever after. As it was in *Promised Valley*, that kind of extreme fiction is lacking in *Life . . . More Sweet than Bitter*. Instead, Maurice and Inez's offstage wedding might be taken not as a *union* of Mormon and Jewish cultures but rather a continuation of Mormonism and Judaism as parallel entities, essentially the same in function, and endowed with the same purpose. Inez and Maurice can fit their different worldviews into a single marriage because, from a Mormon perspective at least, the worldviews are already one and the same. Thus the lack of a wedding in the musical seems less an oversight or a rock against convention and more a gesture toward the kind of union Mormonism would like to enter into with Judaism—which in truth is the kind of union Mormons believe exists a priori.

One other notable instance in Locke's taxonomy of the "Exotic Music Only" paradigm occurs earlier in the musical, as the ship carrying the Warshaw family nears the American shore and the passengers take in the sight of the Statue of Liberty. Only moments before, Maurice and his family nervously wonder about what life in a new country will be like. Those fears are quelled with the sight of the American coastline, however, and, as the stage directions dictate, everyone starts "humming and chanting as men on deck form circles and begin to dance in the old Jewish way." Similar to the music during the infamous bottle dance in *Fiddler on the Roof*, the accompanying music oscillates between a slow tempo and a tempo exactly twice the speed of the first. An illustration included in Maurice Warshaw's autobiography depicts this scene of merriment and dancing; the visual likeness between the central figure in the illustration and that of Tevye in the film version of *Fiddler on the Roof* makes plain the intended connection of the two stories. Without more specific stage directions or information from the story itself (a caption underneath the illustration simply states "They begin to dance in the Jewish way"), however, it is unclear what dance styles this music is intended to accompany. Still, the music's minor mode gestures toward a Jewish musical idea, and the written accelerando between alternating slower and faster sections likewise positions this dance within a broader exoticized Jewish sound world (see figure 5).

The musical gesture toward *Fiddler*'s bottle dance during the wedding scene serves as another generic reference to Jewish gaiety, but the celebrations on Maurice's boat are a false equivalence to those during Tzeitel and Motel's wedding reception. In *Fiddler* there is no real possibility of assimilation. Even the marriage being celebrated is a "false" one—an arranged union that tries to join butcher and dairy families, symbolically against

They began to dance in the Jewish way

Figure 5: Illustration from Maurice Warshaw's 1975 autobiography, *Life—More Sweet than Bitter*.

dietary laws that will be replaced by a "true" one disrupted by the Russian bottle dancers. Still, it's really important that the possibility of assimilation in *Fiddler* is so powerfully and joyously presented by the bottle dancers, so much so that most people conveniently forget that it has no foundation in Sholom Aleichem's original stories of Tevye the milkman that the musical is loosely based upon.[41]

Locke contends that musical exoticism can take place in the particular, as I have demonstrated in these examples so far. However, he also argues that exoticism can be manifest in otherwise Western-sounding music if that music is couched within other forms of exoticism—stage directions, set design, or costumes, for example. This is exactly what happens in Maurice's patter song "A Gentile Is a Gentile Is a Gentile" (example 5). Maurice explains in a letter to his father, who is then living in Cleveland, Ohio, that his new Mormon neighbors in Utah are kind to him but strangely enough consider him—a Jew—a Gentile. Aside from the rabbi's songs from the beginning of the show, this number is one of the few comedic songs in the musical. The absence of many funny moments is a big departure from *Fiddler on the Roof*, a story whose levity requires much grander comedic gestures than needed in *Life . . . More Sweet than Bitter*. Though the music harbors no particular Jewish allusions, the patter style is an example of familiar fast-talking numbers throughout the history of musical theater, perhaps most notably the often parodied "I Am the Very Model of a Modern Major General" from Gilbert and Sullivan's *The Pirates of Penzance*. Given the topic of the song's text and the identity of both the character reading and writing the "letter" as ethnically suspect, one could conclude that the musical material is exoticized even though it does not "sound" exotic at all. Dramatically, the scene captures something exotic about Jewish presence in Mormon country while not relying on music to explicitly do that work on its own. Ironically, in this kind of situation it is the music itself that becomes exoticized, made in context to appear estranged in its Westernness even as it is designed to do just that.

Example 5: Excerpt of "A Gentile Is a Gentile Is a Gentile," from *Life . . . More Sweet than Bitter* (1977). Music by K. Newell Dayley and lyrics by Pat Davis.

106 · CHAPTER 3

Locke's conceptualization of musical exoticism helps illuminate ruptures in racial constructs inherent to Mormonism. Even as Mormon creators of musicals sought to align their beliefs with this Jewish Other, their appropriation of exotic musical topics and tropes—both explicitly and implicitly—helps tease out a complex system of racial constructions so deeply embedded within Mormonism as to obfuscate that gap between official Mormon thought and the everyday lived experience of Mormonism.

To add one further note of comparison, the latent issue at hand in Locke's "All the Music in Full Context" paradigm is that something can function as exotic while appearing quite normal. This same situation haunted nineteenth-century Americans convinced that Mormons were an inferior race. Outwardly Mormons appeared white, though inwardly their degenerative lifestyle and depraved morality corrupted that pure white status. In other words, the exotic machinations of the inward Mormon soul betrayed the normalcy of everyday appearances. As much as the Mormon body was contested on racial grounds during the nineteenth century, Mormons continue today to come to terms with that contestable and racialized body through the prism of the theatrical stage. In these musicals, the Mormon performer literally embodies the racially Other, sings his exotic music, and dances steps familiar to his feet. In ways uniquely peculiar to Mormons, this process of theatrical imposture serves as a direct link between the adoptive Jewishness of Mormons and the literal lineage of the House of Israel. In a way, then, musicals like *Life . . . More Sweet than Bitter* allow Mormons to act themselves on stage, to see the exotic bodies made common, and thus transform the musically estranged into something normative, familiar, and altogether their own.

As the Mormon Church used the momentum of a postwar economy to transform its reputation from nineteenth-century polygamous outliers to a twentieth-century emblem of traditional family values, the Church likewise adopted a trenchant capitalist ethic to replace the cooperative socioeconomic system of its founders. The story of *Life . . . More Sweet than Bitter* thus illustrates two significant roles the Cold War–era Mormon Church performed: that of cultural colonizer and sensible capitalist. Inasmuch as Mormons have used Tevye for their own purposes, through Maurice's story the new-and-improved Tevye could do that and be Mormon too; Holland's challenge to substitute Provo for Anatevka effectively became a reality with *Life . . . More Sweet than Bitter*. The convenient narrative of Jews as Gentiles and Mormons as Jews found its complete fulfillment in the musical conversion of their beloved Jewish father into an exemplary Mormon capitalist.

"A Bird May Love a Fish, but Where Would They Build a Home Together?"

The Mormon conception of chosenness effectively ties together Polynesians, Native Americans, Jews, and Mormons, united in purpose to bring about "the gathering of Israel from the four parts of the earth, and the leading of the ten tribes from the land of the north."[42] This gathering began with the publication of The Book of Mormon and will be accomplished only when the various tribes of Israel are assembled in their appropriate geographical location: Judah to Jerusalem and those "among the Gentiles" to the city of Zion, which is somewhere near Independence, Missouri, according to Mormon lore. To this end, Joseph Smith received the following revelation in 1831:

> Call you solemn assemblies, and speak often one to another. And let every man call upon the name of the Lord.
>
> Yea, verily I say unto you again, the time has come when the voice of the Lord is unto you: Go ye out of Babylon; gather ye out from among the nations, from the four winds, from one end of heaven to the other.
>
> Send forth the elders of my church unto the nations which are afar off; unto the islands of the sea; send forth unto foreign lands; call upon all nations, first upon the Gentiles, and then upon the Jews.
>
> Let them, therefore, who are among the Gentiles flee unto Zion.
>
> And let them who be of Judah flee unto Jerusalem, unto the mountains of the Lord's house.[43]

Significantly, Smith's revelation addressed the entirety of the human population—including even "the islands of the sea"—and laid out the plan for gathering the whole of Israel preparatory to Christ's return and millennial reign on earth. The literality of this gathering principle and the geographic importance of the American continent was made manifest in 1921 by David O. McKay, who at that time was a high-ranking Church official and would later become Church president, when he visited Laie, Hawaii: "America and the Church of Christ will truly make of all nations one blood. May God hasten the day when this is accomplished."[44]

Perhaps it is no surprise that this gathering principle has been met with some resistance. I turn again to Mormon-Jewish relations and examine more recent antagonisms and cultural intersections. As much as Mormons would like to see themselves in harmony with—or even the same as—Jews, the Mormon gathering principle has imposed upon Jews in significant ways. The tensions I will address are issues of the body and space. As the theater is a

108 · CHAPTER 3

manifestation of the body in a particularly hallowed space, and as much as the Mormon body is a particularly racialized body, I argue that these tensions should be seen within the larger discourse among those who sell, perform, and buy race. This conceptual theater of Mormon-Jew entanglement provides a unique position from which to observe these cultural interactions play out. Nonetheless, as much as Mormons crave a sense of shared identity with Judaism, these two worlds seem irreconcilable. In Tevye's words, "A bird may love a fish, but where would they build a home together?"

In 1841, a mere eleven years after the Church was organized, apostle Orson Hyde traveled to Jerusalem, knelt at the Mount of Olives, and offered a prayer of dedication. Hyde's prayer came to him in a revelation and focused on the gathering of Judah, the building up of Jerusalem, and the erecting of a Mormon temple in the land. It was this speech act that solidified Hyde's role in the gathering of Judah but also came as a fulfillment to a vision he experienced in 1840.

> The vision of the Lord, like clouds of light, burst into my view. . . . The cities of London, Amsterdam, Constantinople and Jerusalem, all appeared in succession before me, and the Spirit said unto me, "Here are many of the children of Abraham whom I will gather to the land that I gave to their fathers; and here also is the field of your labors."[45]

Mormons look to Hyde's vision and subsequent mission to Jerusalem as explanation for Mormonism's investment in and adoration of Judaism. "It is no coincidence that historical annals point to the 1840s as a period of awakening among Jews dispersed throughout the world," writes Mormon political scientist David B. Galbraith. "Out of this new dawn arose men of influence like Moses Hess, Joseph Salvador, Moses Montefiore, Leo Pinsker, and Theodor Herzl. Having been touched by the spirit of gathering, they began to instill in Jews everywhere the desire to return to their ancient homeland."[46] The "spirit of gathering" Galbraith refers to is Zionism, a fundamental concept not only for Jews but for Mormons as well. Mormons support Zionists and in fact see such a gathering as their principal work as members of the House of Israel. Joseph taught that in the last days there will be two gathering places, one in Jerusalem and another in a city called Zion (the "New Jerusalem"), a community they have traditionally held will return to earth from heaven and will be located in Jackson County, Missouri.[47] Therefore, the Mormon support of Zionism might be understood as an oblique support of American nationalism, their presence in Jerusalem a rehearsal for their work in an American city yet to be built. Hyde's dedicatory prayer thus serves as a dramatic entrance into Judaism, but a presence that masks a subtler Mormon investment in American nationalism. After all, The Book of Mormon was about *leaving* Jerusalem, not arriving—a fact that doesn't exactly offer a simple explanation for Mormon interest in an ancient city that has otherwise been a holy destination for hundreds of years.

Hyde's voyage to Jerusalem signaled an important relationship between Mormons and Jews, but the Church largely maintained a nonpresence in Jerusalem until 1988, when the Brigham Young University Jerusalem Center for Near Eastern Studies was opened. Sitting upon Mount Scopus, the BYU Jerusalem Center was established as a satellite campus for students and faculty at the main BYU branch in Provo, Utah, to study the "Old and New Testament, ancient and modern Near Eastern studies, and language (Hebrew and Arabic)."[48] As might be expected, the center houses a domed theater—by now a requisite space loaded with assimilative potential among both Jewish and Mormon people. Though the center was not intended to be a used to evangelize the Mormon faith, Church leadership hoped its presence would foster among Jews a greater understanding of the Mormon faith and its theological tenets. Ronald Staheli cited Howard W. Hunter, Church president at the time of construction, as saying, "Our mission [for the center] was not to harvest, probably not even to plant, but to clear away a few more stones."[49]

Still, controversy erupted. Many Israeli individuals and religious groups—including American Jews and Jewish organizations as well—warned against the Mormon presence in Jerusalem; central to their concerns was the evangelizing zeal Mormons maintain at the core of their beliefs. "The Mormon organization is one of the most dangerous, and in America they have already struck down many Jews," one publication counseled. "At the present the Mormons are cautious because of the tremendous opposition their missionary activities would engender, but the moment their new Center is completed, we won't be able to stop them."[50] Another group of Israeli intellectuals joined in: "We are convinced that this group wishes to Mormonize the people of Israel."[51] As the Mormon faith was seen as distinctly American, others saw the Mormon presence as yet another intrusion of American principalities into the area.

Part of this controversy may have to do with the timing of the construction. Daniel H. Olsen and Jeanne Kay Guelke have pointed out that the Mormon Church was not considered a threat or an intrusion "until it attempted to establish a more prominent and permanent landmark in the Jerusalem landscape."[52] They add that the "*timing* of a particular intrusion and the *history* of a particular place have a lot to do with whether a minority group is seen as 'in place' or 'out of place.'"[53] Olsen and Guelke argue that dominant groups tend to associate ideologies with a constructed meaning of place as a way of controlling others. New or outsider groups threaten to disturb the balance

110 · CHAPTER 3

of those ideologies, and such groups are therefore labeled "transgressive." "Transgression," they write, "occurs when people in authority criticize something they judge to be deviant (e.g., an action, group, or behavior) in order to strengthen their own ideological position."[54] The BYU Jerusalem Center thus engendered a "spatial transgression"—forcing the dominant groups to reevaluate the proximity of ideology with actual space.

Although the Church made its intentions explicit, the construction of the BYU Jerusalem Center has been shrouded with distrust. The Mormon desire to foster a greater awareness of itself among Jews was met with reticence and, in some cases, vitriol. That the contestation was over space seems particularly apt; I consider the musical stage as a space of cultural intermeshing, in this case involving a very eager Mormon culture intruding upon a more or less indifferent Jewish one. As the space of cultural interaction continues to be debated, the role of the Jewish body in Mormon theology puts a fine point on the issue at hand: the staging of Mormon imperialism.

As early as 1995, Jewish and Mormon leaders began meeting to discuss what was for Jews a disturbing fact. At some point in time, and reportedly unknown to Mormon leaders until after the fact, genealogical records taken from lists of Holocaust victims were uploaded to the Church's genealogy database, and temple ordinances were performed on the behalf of these deceased Jews. Mormons have been practicing baptisms for the dead since the 1840s, when temple rites were introduced as ordinances for salvation both for the living and the deceased. All who have ever lived, Mormons believe, must either perform these ordinances in life or have them performed for them vicariously in order to achieve exaltation—the opportunity to live in the highest level of heaven, the Celestial Kingdom, which is inhabited by God and Jesus Christ. Official Church policy states that Church members may enter names of only their own ancestors for temple ordinances. The case for these Holocaust victims, however, was systematic and seems to be the result of an eager and well-intentioned Mormon or group of Mormons bent on extending salvific opportunities to individuals so ruthlessly treated in life. The Mormon Church hurriedly apologized for the oversight and removed those names and ordinances from their records.

Abraham Foxman, director of the Anti-Defamation League, initially met the Jewish outrage with a calm hand, yet clearly conveyed the severity of what was at stake with these ordinances:

> We believe the Mormon Church is trying to act in good faith to live up to its agreement to prevent the names of any Jewish Holocaust victims from being submitted for posthumous baptism. They understand that this issue is extremely important to the Jewish people, as Holocaust victims died pre-

LINEAGE AND WHITENESS ON STAGE · 111

cisely because they were Jewish. Listing Jews as "Christian" on one of the most researched genealogical sites in the world inadvertently aids and abets denial of the Holocaust.[55]

Foxman's tone turned more severe a few days later: "Holocaust victims' only crime was that they were Jews. Now [the Church] is basically killing them again by eliminating their Jewishness."[56] Mormon temple ordinances, such as vicarious baptisms, were perceived as actually removing Jewish identity from the dead bodies of Holocaust victims. This anxiety over the Jewish body again thrusts into the forefront the centrality of the racialized body in Mormon discourse. Baptisms for the dead don't involve the actual bodies of the dead, naturally; rather, the rites are administered vicariously upon a living Mormon body. A Mormon pretends as if he is the deceased person, following literally Jesus's teaching that "except a man be born of water and of the Spirit, he cannot enter into the kingdom of God."[57] Therefore, cultural cleansing of this kind happens through theatricality. By acting as proxies, Mormon temple goers in these cases could embody a Holocaust victim and undergo the ordinance, effectively allowing the living Mormon to act out the role of a deceased Jew and, at least in some important ways, "eliminating their Jewishness."

Although Mormons believe the deceased person ultimately has the choice in the afterlife to accept the ordinances or not, the perception of Mormon embodiment of Jewish identity is fraught with issues of cultural preservation and identity politics. Furthermore, the ritualized space of the Mormon temple—which many members feel is more holy than even the Holy Land itself—serves as the mediated space upon which these theatrical conversions take place, further displacing Jewish identity from the nexus of monotheism, Jerusalem. The theater of the Mormon temple in effect stages a complete Mormon conquest of the Other through ritualized ordinances. Unlike the figurative conversion of a Jewish Tevye into a Mormon capitalist in *Life . . . More Sweet than Bitter*, these conversions symbolize a much more ambitious task yet are no less theatrical or significant. In the case of the Holocaust victims, if outrage emerged out of cultural insensitivity or perceived corruption of agreements between Jewish and Mormon leaders, perhaps the premise behind such fury involves the telling of a story in which the actors (Mormons) misrepresent the plot (religious identity) that the beloved characters (Jews) were never meant to perform in a space (Mormon temple) ill-conceived for "clearing away a few stones" in the first place.

* * *

112 · CHAPTER 3

From the adoptive qualities of the Abrahamic covenant whereby Tevye the milkman could be rendered Mormon through the work of musical theater, to the performance of whiteness at the Polynesian Cultural Center, Mormon conceptions of conversion are rooted in embodiment. Furthermore, the very theatrical qualities of Mormon temple rituals enshroud the faith in an aura of the dramatic and the spectacular and, as such, can easily offend. The Osmonds's iconic performance of selections from *Fiddler on the Roof* may seem an innocent cultural nod of approval from one faith group to another—and it very well may be just that. But there is something deeply troubling to me about that medley and the kind of work it appears to be doing, and it has taken me a while to put my finger on it. Maybe it has something to do with how easily these Mormon boppers slip into Jewish characters, or even that Tevye's humble musings on wealth sound in the mouths of The Osmonds like a credit card marketing ploy, or perhaps it is because the musical styles get twisted around and seem to represent something else entirely. It is that "something else" that seems bothersome. In any act of appropriation is a dual performance—one a performing into existence a new possibility, and the other a performing away of what once was. In The Osmonds's performance, as with *Life . . . More Sweet than Bitter*, the Polynesian Cultural Center, and even the temple ceremony itself, it isn't so much the slip into Jewishness that seems so problematic; rather, it's how easily we forget that actual identities have effectively been erased and replaced with a "something else."

Ta-Nehisi Coates's moniker for Donald Trump as "the First White President" is not unrelated here. By this, Coates means that the white supremacist and white nationalist values that opened up the presidency to Donald Trump are built upon the careful dismantling of all efforts by Barack Obama, America's first black president—ironically diminishing the efficacy of whiteness just as it demonstrates its power.[58] Similarly, Mormonism may be considered America's first white religion. Since Mormon ideals so clearly prefer whiteness as a demarcation of purity and achievement, yet whiteness as an ideology gains its power only as a deflection against the racial Other, Mormons embody an impoverished ideological tradition that continually reinforces its identity with each new cultural encounter with dark-skinned peoples. Perhaps in no clearer way does Mormonism reveal its ideological roots in Jacksonian-era value systems, values that connect America's religion with America's musical theater tradition as dual emblems of whiteness.

4

"I've Heard That Voice Before"

Reprising the Voice in Sacred Time

To remember is to risk despair; the past tense of the verb
to be must infer the reality of death.
   —George Steiner, *After Babel*

In some ways, being able to forget is almost as valuable
as being able to remember.
   —Franklin D. Richards, "Be a Peacemaker"

Chapter 2 opened with Wilford Woodruff's recorded voice as a point of departure in a discussion of how voices are routinely mediated by other people and things. The phonograph and wax cylinders serve as material reminders that a voice can travel, be muted, or continue to sound over and over again, all without a person's consent or control. The voice might well serve as an emblem of immortality. Woodruff's voice continues to speak and be heard through the powers of recording technology, even though Woodruff the man has long since been dead. The recorded voice is no respecter of persons; it continues to speak through a technological proxy for all who have ears to hear. As Jonathan Sterne has argued, sound recording in the nineteenth century "preserve[d] the bodies of the dead so that they could continue to perform a social function after life."[1] This necrophiliac arrangement leads to Jason Stanyek and Benjamin Piekut's observation that "being recorded means being enrolled in futures (and pasts) that one cannot wholly predict nor control. Crucially, having a future means having an effect."[2]

Likewise, the voice in Mormonism speaks beyond the grave. The iconic Mormon rock musical *Saturday's Warrior* (1973; film 1989/2016) suggests the voice is a stable identifier transcendent of time. In important ways, *Saturday's Warrior* extends the Mormon fascination with vocality into the pre-mortal world. *Promised Valley* may have been built upon the concept of voice as the

114 · CHAPTER 4

glue binding communities, but *Saturday's Warrior* goes further by implying voice can also bind together families across metaphysical spaces. The musical puts pressure on historiographical idealism that has been emphasized in Mormon theology since 1960, when the Church began streamlining the faith's central theology in a process known as Correlation. Correlation reinforced the centrality of male priesthood authority and extended that authority to all segments of Church activities. Remarkably, *Saturday's Warrior* sidestepped Correlation—which represents the authority of modern Mormon leaders— and injected into Mormon culture a form of folk doctrine that continues to inform Mormon views of cosmology, even though those beliefs remain unsanctioned by Church leaders. Finally, I return to the act of vocal modeling discussed in the first chapters and argue that Correlation created an environment of unity and sameness that consequently reshaped how Mormons speak. Under Correlation, the Mormon voice becomes an emblem of exactness and a material demonstration of Mormon mastery and faithfulness.

Performing Sacred Time

In 2002, Mormon president and prophet Gordon B. Hinckley told members, "I knew a so-called intellectual who said the Church was trapped by its history. My response was that without that history we have nothing."[3] As this statement makes clear, a pronounced interest in historical events in Mormon history, as well as key moments where Mormons or proto-Mormon ideals intersect with other historical narratives, is a defining quality of faithful Mormons. There may be several explanations for this interest in history which, as Hinckley's statement attests, is the crux upon which all of Mormonism succeeds or fails. The Book of Mormon was originally peddled as a history of the Native Americans; it wasn't until the late nineteenth century that it became principally a key document in Mormon theology and secondarily a history of the American continents.[4] Consequently, being able to testify to the literality of Joseph's version of the miraculous events leading to the unearthing of the ancient plates and their translation process have become a proving ground for Mormon acceptance. The consensus seems to be that the stories either happened the way Joseph said they did or they didn't happen at all. Mormons are taught from a young age that Mormonism represents the pinnacle of truth and that God's guiding hand throughout history to establish the Mormon Church through Joseph Smith can be easily recognized. The Book of Mormon itself suggests that Christopher Columbus was an instrument in the hand of God for this exact purpose.[5] Mormons also conduct extensive research on their ancestors in order to perform saving ordinances for them in one of the Mormon temples. This act ultimately situates everyday Mormons at the pinnacle of history and the purpose of life: by uncovering forgotten names and vicariously ensuring saving ordinances on those people's behalf, Mormons become "Saviors on Mount Zion" and are effectively cast alongside Jesus in the role of Savior in God's grand theater.

Mormons are well attuned to the parallels between their history and biblical events. The exodus west to Utah, led by a leader who would later famously be known as the "American Moses" and faced with many travails and hardships, came to be recognized as the kind of refiner's fire familiar to ancient Israelites in the Old Testament, deepening the camaraderie Mormons felt *toward* and *as* Jews. The mythical quality of their exodus and persecution shaped Mormon identity in ways that are still present. As Mormon scholar Jan Shipps describes it, when Brigham Young led the Saints out of Illinois, "he led them not only out of the hands of their midwestern persecutors but backward into a primordial sacred time."[6]

Mormons enjoyed a relatively isolated existence for several decades, where they could erect through plural marriage a boundary system similar to the purpose circumcision served for ancient Jews. Polygamy became a performance of Mormon identity—one that not everyone partook of but that still was so recognizably Mormon as to be defended at all costs. Therefore, Wilford Woodruff's 1890 proclamation ending plural marriages became "the effective point of division between the past and the present" in Mormonism.[7] "Thus, whatever else it did," Shipps continues, "the Manifesto announced that the old order would have to pass away."[8]

Following the 1890 Manifesto, Mormons were jettisoned from sacred time and found themselves living in what amounts to profane time. Considering Durkheim's argument that moments of collective effervescence help religious communities navigate the boundaries between the sacred and the profane, it is unsurprising to see post-Manifesto Mormons paying increased attention to dramatic enactments of the past. Shipps points to newer revelations around this time that reinforced or added information about temple ordinances for the dead as "occasions of returning periodically to sacred time through the medium of the ritual performance of sacred ordinances."[9]

Other religious communities have navigated the duality of sacred time and profane time; modernity demands some reconciliation between the two. Anthropologist Lara Deeb has written about the problems Muslims face "when Muslim communities are not granted the same historicity or the same possibilities for complexity of change and temporality that other communities

116 · CHAPTER 4

are."[10] She suggests that Muslims are not talking literally about time travel when they make reference to a "return to the past." Rather, she argues that what is being voiced "has more to do with notions of what is modern, valued, contemporary, and/or progressive than about the structure or experience of time itself."[11] Living within "multiple temporal frameworks" is how Deeb refers to this kind of artful placement of religious identity within modern or otherwise contemporary value systems.

Like Islam, Mormonism too is concerned with these "temporal frameworks" and is continually looking over its shoulder to be reassured that current practices can be seen in line with those demanded by its histories. Mormons throughout the twentieth century responded to modernity by placing themselves within acceptable historical narratives and, as with *Promised Valley*, claiming them as their own. The Mormon prerogative that "without our history we have nothing" needs to be considered a performative statement rather than simply partisan boasting. A more accurate wording might be, "Without the continual *performance* and constant *revisiting* of the one particular historical narrative we claim as our own, we have nothing."

By performing temple ordinances, and through other performative events such as pageants or musicals, Mormons can sustain memory of what life was like during a mythical sacred time. As Pierre Nora explains in his article "Between Memory and History: *Les Lieux de Memorie*," spaces or ritual events become significant "places of memory" if remembrance is threatened or otherwise no longer present among members of a community.[12] It is the performative aspect of history making that seems to be what primarily guides Mormon narratives of history. Mormons enter history as interlocutors and see the historical landscape as malleable in their hands. Thus Mormons conceptually move in and through time to recreate it in the manner most fitting to their needs, all while being sanctioned, implicitly and sometimes explicitly, by leaders who likewise suggest that the chaos of the past can be made sensible through the prism of Mormonism.

As memories of pre-Manifesto Mormonism lost vibrancy, Mormons responded by constructing events and ritualizing sites through performances of early Mormon life. Performance, not memory, allowed sacred time to be recalled long after it had ceased. The temple ceremony, pageants, parades, and historical monuments and markers that celebrate the pioneer heritage or early stages of Mormonism came to define the Mormon experience of the first decades of the twentieth century, similar to how cultural practices have contributed for centuries to a sense of nationalism in numerous European contexts. Davis Bitton claims that when nineteenth-century Mormons realized they were cut off from an identity outside of themselves, "they needed ritualistic supports for their legitimacy."[13] "By mid-century," he continues, "the visual representations of Mormon history numbered in the thousands—all contributing to the process of ritualization by establishing a sense of the past that was primarily emotional, appropriable, and not primarily concerned with accuracy."[14] The "almost feverish activity" of erecting monuments and creating historical enactments during the 1930s and 1940s reached a pinnacle with the centennial celebration in 1947. *Promised Valley* was thus a major "sonic" monument to Mormon ideals of the past—as romanticized and calculated as the history the institution claims as its own.

During these opening decades of the twentieth century, enormous outdoor pageants sprang up. Many, like the Hill Cumorah Pageant in upstate New York or the Mormon Miracle Pageant in Manti, Utah, continue today as grand demonstrations of the effects of musical drama and spectacle on Mormon religious identity. These musical pageants not only allow a performer's body to become an "implicit contract of authenticity and authority," to use Scott Magelssen's description for bodily performance at living history sites, but they also focus Mormon attention on how performance evokes collective values like heroism and resilience, particularly in response to religious persecution and the harsh and rugged landscape of the western United States, where most Mormons chose to settle.[15] Pageants are such an established part of contemporary Mormonism, in fact, that one episode of the HBO television series *Big Love* (2006–2011) even featured the polygamist family on a pilgrimage through Church historical sites that culminated with attending the Hill Cumorah Pageant.[16]

Orson Scott Card's short story "Pageant Wagon" illuminates the ethic of performing sacred time that for decades pageants have upheld for Mormons. Card is known outside the Mormon world as the author of science fiction classics *Ender's Game* (1985) and its sequels, including *Speaker for the Dead* (1986)—the latter a story empathically concerned with quasi-religious figures who, as the title suggests, speak vicariously for the dead. Card earned a separate reputation within Mormonism in 1988 for writing a new script to accompany Crawford Gates's music for the Hill Cumorah Pageant. In "Pageant Wagon," Card melds his science-fiction ethos with a hard-won Mormon perspective on American ideology, even in a dystopian setting. A cowboy named Deaver comes across a family of actors who travel from town to town to entertain through their "pageant wagon." Deaver is taken with the family's

118 · CHAPTER 4

kindness (they are Mormon, of course), but, given they are professional actors, he is deeply suspicious of their intentions.

> And then he thought how when he was little, somebody told him that if you cross your eyes too often they'll stick that way. What if acting all humble and sweet worked that way? What if it got to be such a habit you forgot you were acting, the way Marshall's and Scarlett's fancy acting voices came out of their mouths even when they were picking up a range rider in the middle of the night. Do you become whatever you act like?[17]

Deaver's reasoning speaks to the power of performance and vocal vicariousness that Mormons uphold. One paradox of performance is that the more often a performer pretends to be something or someone else, the blurrier the distinction between truth and fiction—"Do you become whatever you act like?" This seems to be something the Mormon Church realizes, since they printed in their *Theatre Manual* that "vicarious experiences that confirm truth while entertaining an audience are likely to be good theatre."[18] As Mormons began in the twentieth century to enact their history as a part of, rather than at odds with, American history, they came to see the American story as their own—so much so, it has become difficult for one narrative to be separated from the other. Even Deaver found it "a little strange that a show called *Glory of America* should have an equal mix of Mormon and American history." But, he reasons, "to these people . . . it was all the same story. George Washington, Betsy Ross, Joseph Smith, Abraham Lincoln, Brigham Young, all part of the same unfolding tale. Their own past."[19]

The sacredness of America in Mormon theology and the virtues of perseverance amid great hardships that Mormons celebrate about their heritage often make the ritualized performances of pageants, musicals, and even the temple ceremony in the service of a nationalist agenda. By focusing on supposedly historical performances, especially performances using conventions of musical theater, Mormons construct a nationalist identity that lets them be distinct and different from most Americans but also, in drawing upon American musical theater practices in their pageants, allows them to actively perform an accepted, mainstream American identity. A common language, after all, was the principal concern of early nationalist thinkers like Johann Gottfried Herder and Johann Gottlieb Fichte; the Mormon acquisition of American musical theater conventions certainly allowed them to couch their history within a language common to many Americans, if only figuratively.[20] The fluency with which Mormons can speak the language of American musical theater also suggests that the positive message of reconciliation endemic to musical dramas—especially in post-apocalyptic worlds like Deaver's—may rub off on Mormons who play the role so frequently and so well.

Reprising Sacred Time

Pageants, parades, ritual enactments, musicals, and other spectacular monuments to the pioneer spirit that imbued sacred time are essential for Mormonism to remain vibrant in contemporary times—even, paradoxically, as fewer and fewer members today can claim that pioneer heritage. Yet even more than other performance rituals, musicals offer Mormons the opportunity not only to inhabit sacred time, but also to extend its reaches through the conventions of the genre. For example, in integrated musicals, the reprise is a regular enough convention that not to repeat at least one song sung earlier in the show seems a dramaturgical misstep. These repeated moments do more than just recall a familiar tune, however. In effect, the reprise suggests that temporality can be undone, that the past can be transplanted into the present in a way that confuses the difference between the two. In his book *Cosmos and History*, Mircea Eliade claims that repeated events imitate an archetype of "the exemplary event." Furthermore, he adds, "through this repetition, time is suspended, or at least its virulence is diminished."[21] In the context of musical theater, the reprise offers such a repeated event that simultaneously points backward and forward through time. The reprise consequently does for musicals what a musical does for Mormons: it suspends time, allows disparate ends to resolve, and thus slows down the faith-choking creep of modernity.

There are two types of reprises in musical theater: one that reasserts an earlier truth and one that reconfigures it. The first type of reprise often provides thematic bookends for the musical, as is the case in *Life . . . More Sweet than Bitter*, when Maurice reprises at the end the rabbi's opening song "Life Is What You Make It" in order to affirm the musical's message of hope, resilience, and an Emersonian bootstrap ideology popular among Mormons. By repeating the rabbi's opening number, the now-Mormon Maurice also shows his resolve to retain his Jewish heritage, even though the show works to conflate Judaism with Mormonism.

The second type of reprise usually clarifies that the earlier formation was not entirely truthful, even though the audience knew it all along. Consider how this type of reprise works in the song "People Will Say We're in Love" from *Oklahoma!*. Curly and Laurey first sing this to one another as a flirtatious and fickle expression of desire kept within a protective distance. The song is heard early in the show, so even though audiences know that Curly and Laurey are the confirmed heterosexual couple that the rest of the show must spend great energy to unite, the song's premature placement ensures that an appropriate amount of tension must yet define the relationship before it can be confirmed and formalized. And in fact this happens exactly. The reprise of "People Will Say We're in Love" comes right after Curly has proved himself over Jud as the more eligible man for Laurey. The reprise—its lyric now rewritten to "let people say we're in love"—confirms for the audience that the initial tension has been resolved and that reconciliation is in sight.

Some reprises directly tie the present to the past by reasserting earlier truths, while other reprises distinguish between the past and the present. Although not all reprises perform a similar kind of time travel, in all cases whatever happened in the past gets set against the needs of the present. The function of the reprise thus fits well within Mormonism's desire to return to sacred time through dramatic rituals. Beyond simply satisfying a reconciliatory narrative in musical theater, the reprise may well chart the sonic path by which Mormons can navigate sacred time, even in shows with no perceivable context of pioneer or even Mormon themes. The reprise offers a way for voices from the past to permeate the present, giving the impression in some cases that the action between them had never happened. Performers can reach back in time and make the past resonate again (literally) by putting into the mouths of characters words that previously held different meanings but in a new context can reinforce a particular historical narrative. In a radical act of vocal vicariousness, the reprise allows characters to speak on behalf of their former selves and with those words draw into the present what had since been forgotten.

In a suspiciously reincarnate manner, the reprise also brings back to life what before may have been laid dead. For a religion concerned primarily with the kind of temple theater that transforms the dead into agents of the present—and of restoring ideals of the past to today, however curated those ideals may be—the reprise in musicals does the kind of salvific work that Mormons do in their temples. The reprise is thus far more than a convention: it is the material evidence for Mormons that sacred time can and will be accessed eventually, and that a happy return to the Mormon theater of polygamy and continued revelation will finally be realized.

Speaking the Canon Open

"Church tradition and oral history," claims Megan Sanborn Jones, "are considered period documents and valid merely through repetition."[22] Indeed,

Mormons have long been dependent on the voice to provide the moments of repetition requisite to entering sacred time. Beginning with Joseph Smith and continuing today with his spiritual heirs, Mormon prophets have spoken revelation to the gathered public; the revelation, subsequently, is understood to be scriptural. Although Mormons believe in a concrete set of scriptural books (the Bible, The Book of Mormon, Doctrine and Covenants, and the Pearl of Great Price, collectively known as the Standard Works), they also understand the role of a living prophet on Earth to make known the relevant will of God to His believers. In this way, Mormons lay claim to an "open canon" of scripture, one that is continually added upon with each subsequent leader's prophetic utterances.

Twice a year, every April and October, up to one hundred thousand Mormons assemble in Salt Lake City's Conference Center to hear the words of their prophets, typically culled from fifteen men—twelve apostles and a three-man General Presidency, with the Prophet-president at the helm. Other leaders of the Church sometimes speak at these conferences as well, including in recent decades some women who are presidents of "auxiliary organizations" for children, adolescent girls, and women. All who speak are considered General Authorities who, by virtue of their positions, are endowed with special privileges to commune with God and receive direct knowledge and wisdom from Him. These leaders speak on a variety of topics; their speeches, or talks, are then broadcast via satellite, radio, and now over the internet to some fifteen million members of the Church around the world. The talks are later transcribed and published online and in print, and serve as material for Sunday school lessons for the following six months until the next conference.

What makes this practice interesting is the complex thinking regarding orality and the written word. In 1842 Joseph Smith proclaimed that "whatsoever you record on earth shall be recorded in heaven, and whatsoever you do not record on earth shall not be recorded in heaven; for out of the books shall your dead be judged."[23] In an earlier revelation, Smith claims that vocally testifying your faith brings you blessings, "for the testimony which ye have borne is recorded in heaven for the angels to look upon; and they rejoice over you, and your sins are forgiven you."[24] Similarly, one Book of Mormon passage cites a command from God that all men "write the words which I speak unto them; for out of the books which shall be written I will judge the world, every man according to their works, according to that which is written."[25] Even today, faithful members are encouraged to keep a journal, to "let no family go into eternity without having left their memoirs for their children, their grandchildren, and their posterity."[26] It would seem from these

122 · CHAPTER 4

and other statements, then, that the literary is of ultimate concern as Mormons confront the sacred.

This certainly aligns with current thinking on the canon as a religious materiality, one born out of a conviction that the text, as T. S. Eliot suggests, makes the writer "acutely conscious of his place in time."[27] The written word grounds the writer, which all faithful Mormons are encouraged to become through journaling, in their own "contemporaneity" and, as the statements above are in agreement, the writer's "appreciation is the appreciation of his relation to the dead poets and artists."[28] The written word offers Mormons a link to their posterity, a heavenly account of their good works, and a means of attaining salvation not only for themselves but also for and on behalf of others already dead.

But the principled place of the written word is complicated by the Mormon dependence on and fascination with the spoken word. Brigham Young reportedly said of the scriptures:

> When compared with the living oracles those books are nothing to me. Those books do not convey the word of God directly to us now, as do the words of a Prophet or a man bearing the Holy Priesthood in our day and generation. *I would rather have the living oracles than all the writing in the books.*[29]

Mormons today would likely cringe at Young's quick dismissal of their religious texts, but his privileging of the prophet's instruction stands consistent with the primacy of place of the spoken word. "Just because it is written in a book does not make it more of an authority to guide us," warned President Harold B. Lee.[30]

In addition to General Conference addresses, for example, one Sunday service a month is devoted to "bearing one's testimony" aloud in front of each congregation. These typically are not recorded (on earth at least) but are valued precisely for their vocality. Every Church talk or sermon ends with some variation of a testimonial affirmation of key convictions of Mormons, which includes the truthfulness of The Book of Mormon, the validity of the current prophet and apostles, and his or her personal knowledge of Jesus Christ's living presence. This last part also amplifies a central and curious tenet of Mormonism: that of personal revelation. Faithful members can expect a direct line to God to receive guidance within that person's sphere of influence. A father, for example, would expect to receive revelation not only for his personal doings but also for those of his family, who are believed to be under his care and judgment. By this same logic, leaders of the Church then receive revelation for the entire body of the Church, as determined by the sphere of influence that position occupies.

This complex understanding of the written and spoken word is neatly paralleled by the theater, where lines that are written down exist somewhere off stage, out of sight, and are mystically created and then immediately erased by the actor uttering its words. This gives the illusion of immediacy with the portrayals on stage but also distorts the relationship between the orator and his text, helping to frame a complicated cultural practice of forgetting. To put it another way, by vicariously voicing a character, the performer pushes the limits of our believability while simultaneously allowing us to suspend disbelief (to "forget") that who we are watching and listening to is actually a character and not a ventriloquizing actor moving his lips to memorized lines. The voice in performance can be *seen* as well as *heard*, felt materially just as much as imagined sensually. As Stephen Connor writes, by the end of the eighteenth century, "the theatre, etymologically the place of seeing, would sediment the visibility of the voice."[31]

Yet in seeing the voice on stage, audiences are permitted to forget events as they are actually taking place before them. This frames forgetting as a necessary quality of audiences for the fantastical, magical, spectacular, or otherwise theatrical performance. We need only recall how those watching and listening to Brigham Young in 1844 were convinced they heard the voice of Joseph, even though, in all likelihood, those witnesses heard and saw what they wanted to hear and see—they forgot themselves and eventually came to believe this padded historical narrative, forgetting that they "forgot" in the first place. In their now-classic article "On the Semiotic Mechanism of Culture," Yuri Lotman and George Uspensky argue that forgetting is a central practice of a culture, one in which "fixing certain events which are translatable into elements of the text and forgetting others, marked as nonessential" helps forge the mechanization of culture, whose role is to aggregate texts for its own realization.[32] They later comment that, "in this sense, every text furthers not only the remembering process, but forgetting as well."[33] What Lotman and Upsensky suggest about texts we can infer about the voice—it is a malleable event that sticks and slips through memory banks willy-nilly. That is the voice's greatest strength and source of perplexity.

Perhaps the clearest example of the coalescing of memory, forgetting, the spoken word, and the written word is in the Mormon temple ceremony. This most sacred ceremony is open only to select members with a "recommend," or a card noting that they have proved their worthiness to enter into the House

124 · CHAPTER 4

of the Lord. The temple rite is conducted exclusively as an oral tradition; though the script for the rite does exist in written form within the temple, those texts are used in a special room only to teach "temple workers"—or members who have been called to positions inside the temple—and as such, the script never leaves the temple. For the general membership, the temple rite is taught orally and then performed from memory. And, as historian Kathleen Flake has observed, among the membership "it is not generally acknowledged that a script of the ritual exists."[34]

Flake argues that the use of what she calls "oral traditioning" within the temple rite facilitates a "forgetting and transmuting [of] inconsistency" allowing, in other words, for a degree of change to occur within the temple ceremony without disrupting the purportedly ancient character of the script itself.[35] As the Church has adapted certain aspects of the temple ceremony over time—mostly, as she claims, in order to soften language that exacerbates gender differences—these changes have not affected the perception that the temple ordinances "are those taught by an angel to Adam."[36] Flake feels that by keeping the rite solely within an oral tradition, the Church "shield[s] its core canon from the divisive effects of discursive thought and public debate."[37] Moreover, Flake sees foul play in the Church's "strategy":

> Approaching this phenomenon with the assumptions of a textually literate and ritually illiterate society, it is possible to conclude that LDS use of oral conventions to adapt and forget is, at best, secrecy in service to willful ignorance or, at worst, deceit in service of social control.[38]

Using nondiscursive measures to attain social control, according to Flake, keeps the Church from "jeopardizing its sense of a shared universe as whole, immune to human history," thus "enabling the entire community to 'misrecognize' change for stasis and to peacefully reorder itself."[39]

Mircea Eliade wrote that "the memory of the collectivity is anhistorical" and reminds us of "the inability of collective memory to retain historical events and individuals except insofar as it transforms them into archetypes—that is, insofar as it annuls all their historical and personal peculiarities." Oral traditioning within the temple rite thus provides a practical measure for altering cultural memory—perhaps even subverting memory as "anhistorical"—through repetition. Outside the temple ceremony, too, the spoken word offers an opportunity for cultural change to take place without drawing attention to itself, further contributing to the illusion of historical continuity that Mormons assume of their faith. We may well remember Eliot's argument that every new piece of literature forces a reordering process on all the others that came before it. As such, every General Conference address contributes to a canon not bound by pages but only by the limits of human memory.

Correlation

Amid the furor of radical theological viewpoints, differing opinions on historical and doctrinal matters among General Authorities, and the pressure to erect borders during the ongoing culture wars of the Cold War era, Mormon leaders in 1960 began the ongoing process of radically stripping down (or "correlating") the key doctrines and policies of the Church. Historian Matthew Bowman actually identities the roots of Correlation beginning during the progressive movement in the first decades of the twentieth century, as Mormons grappled with a postpolygamy identity. "Correlation, broadly defined," he writes, "came to replace plural marriage as the animating force of the Mormon quest for salvation: the structure through which they imagined what gaining heaven looked like."[40] Like minstrelsy before and musicals after, Correlation became a means of achieving harmony in the various enactments of what needed to be seen (and heard) as Mormonism. As it grappled with modernity, Joseph's religion, where "all truth can be circumscribed into one great whole," needed to temper itself into something less malleable in order to translate in a rapidly changing world.

Mormons post-Correlation experience their faith much differently than those of earlier generations. As Bowman writes, "If you've ever wondered how Mormons went from beard-wearing polygamous radicals (think Brigham Young) to your well-scrubbed, wholesome, and somewhat dorky next-door neighbors (think Mitt Romney—albeit with not quite so much money), the short answer is 'correlation.'"[41] Anthropologist Daymon Smith continues the humor when he notes the effect of Correlation as such: "The nineteenth-century Jesus was a polygamist, communist, revolutionary. The twentieth-century Jesus wears pastel colors, holds sheep, and caresses children's hair."[42]

Although Correlation is no secret among membership—the system is even touted within Sunday school manuals as a divine system of ordering—its mediating effects are often masked by its reach. Speeches or instructions from prophets pre-Correlation are only selectively chosen, which perhaps explains why the Church makes available online only conference addresses that were delivered after 1971, well after Correlation had taken effect. Today a Correlation committee filters all Church communication, ensuring that all official Church materials, publications, and even conference talks adhere to the guidelines set forth during Correlation. No single leader is above the

126 · CHAPTER 4

Correlation committee, not even the prophet. This is striking, since the basic presumptions of revelation and living prophets rest on being able to voice communications God has for a changing world, yet Correlation presumably prohibits just that from happening, since it is designed precisely to do the opposite. "Correlation creates nothing," says Paul H. Dunn, a General Authority who served from 1964 to his death in 1998.

> That's the process. It has no authority to make a statement that creates a position or direction. . . . Since the 1970s, I've seen that drift, where correlation now is telling me, if I write something to get through correlation, "You can't say that." And I write back and say, "Why?" And they say, "Well, because we think this is the interpretation." And I write back and say, "You're not the interpreter." . . . And that's where we get lost. . . . So, while I think correlation is good, I think it's gone past its original commission.[43]

Dunn's remarks characterize Correlation as machine-like in its precision but also with regard to the lingering question of agency in an increasingly posthuman world. Anthropologist Daymon Smith also alludes to Correlation as a complex machine. The reader learns that Smith's book *The Book of Mammon: A Book about a Book about the Corporation That Owns the Mormons* is actually the product of Correlation, that the convoluted syntax is simply a demonstration of how Correlation rehashes old messages and presents it as new over and over and over again.[44] Another Mormon blogger used a coding engine that continues Smith's portrayal of a Correlation machine. The blogger enters old general conference addresses given by actual Mormon leaders into the engine, which then cuts and pastes those phrases into new messages. The hosting website, GenConPreview, markets those fake conference addresses as "previews" of the upcoming General Conference and preys on unsuspecting, less scrutinizing Mormons to believe they are getting important revelatory information ahead of the game. To round out the charade, the site is hosted by "Conference Preparation Coordinator" Kevin D. Porter—a fictitious person whose image, in keeping with the data mining project, is a composite General Authority created by digitally overlapping the faces of existing prophets and apostles.[45]

According to the blog site, this mockup of conference talks convinced several it was the real thing, at least for a while. Those Mormons who initially took the bait eventually questioned not the *content* of the message, but the *medium*. They didn't question what the message contained, in other words, but asked why official Church material would be published on a personal blog rather than on official Mormon sites. Chapter 5 will address more specifically the problem of sifting the true messages of Mormonism from chaff like GenConPreview, but as Daymon Smith observes, the site is able to dupe Mormons because the mechanism for creating these fake talks and the way actual General Conference talks are prepared is essentially the same, in that:

> former talks are cut up, arranged according to topic of theme, which is then found in some scripture decontextualized from another story, and these are arranged into a talk. What is the difference? Is there so much more intelligence, spirit, and light going into the cut-and-paste and add-a-story material we hear every spring and fall than there is when a computer does the same thing? Where is the difference found? In the content, or the delivery? Or is a General Conference talk only partially known by its content, and everything else—its real power—comes from the assumption of an audience, and a venue for its delivery, and the endless circulation of that talk as it fragments into other talks, commodities, and imagination?[46]

As Smith points out, Correlation is fundamentally a policy about communication, a broad disciplining of the Mormon voice—what it can say, how it can say it, and how it is heard. Even Church leaders fall prey to its machinations, mimicking themselves and other leaders in a circuitous act of vocal vicariousness. Thus the mode of "forgetting and transmuting inconsistency" pervades even the highest levels of the Mormon hierarchy and, in turn, Mormon leaders utter revelations hewn from a perverted sense of memory and dispense wisdom designed only to be forgotten in its perfect recapitulation of all that has been said before.[47]

Mormon Rock Musicals

Zion Theatricals—a licensing company for Mormon plays and musicals— displays a lengthy, though not exhaustive, list of musicals written by and for Mormons. As of this writing, there are more than forty musicals listed on the company's website.[48] In his short article "The Theatre as a Temple," Zion Theatricals owner and theatrical composer C. Michael Perry argues for the sanctity of the theater, going so far as to claim that "the theatre is the best place for the exploration of belief."[49] Even more, Perry writes of the power of the theater and its particularly Spirit-filled place in building the Kingdom of God:

> Theatre is one of the greatest missionary tools ever invented. Minds are enriched, hearts touched and spirits enlivened through the power of the spoken word on a stage. Seeing—witnessing—the experiences of others on stage brings us closer to understanding, empathy, and compassion in a non-threat-

ening atmosphere. It is all a fiction. Nobody is in real peril. There is no real danger, immediate or otherwise, of someone really losing their testimony, or life, or principles. The stage is a supposition. The actors are players in a match of wits and wills. They are imitators of life, not life itself. This is the loving atmosphere we can create within the walls of the second type of Temple—a Theatre.[50]

After pointing back to the temple ceremony as a performance in itself and overlaying the theatricality of the Hill Cumorah Pageant with twelve-year-old Jesus's confounding religious leaders in the temple, Perry concludes by asking, "What more of a Temple experience is there than an audience seeking enlightenment, even if it is through the means of an entertainment?"[51]

Perry's high valuation of theater underscores what I have noted about Mormon reliance on and love for the theater as a unique space for spiritual edification. He even refers to Brigham Young in the matter, quoting him as saying,

> The stage can be made to aid the pulpit in impressing upon the minds of a community an enlightened sense of a virtuous life, also a proper horror of the enormity of sin and a just dread of its consequences. The path of sin with its throne and pitfalls, its gins and snares can be revealed, and how to shun it.[52]

As much as the temple is a space for instruction in matters timeless, the theater likewise complements the temple in that it creates a space where that instruction and the challenges of modern life can be easily negotiated. And, as Perry reminds us, the tremendous appeal for Mormon theater works is that this can all be done in the relative safety of fictional theatricality.

This theater-as-safety-valve position helps explain the odd cultural pairing of rock and religion on stage in the closing decades of the twentieth century. *Hair, Tommy, Godspell*, and *Jesus Christ Superstar* are the four primary rock musicals of the late 1960s and early 1970s, and all four are framed by Christian ethos. The latter is perhaps the most consequential in establishing an overt religious narrative in musical theater; indeed, in bringing together rock and religion, *Jesus Christ Superstar* forced audiences to reassess assumptions about authenticity represented both by organized religion and the popular genre. In the words of theater historian Henry Bial, *Jesus Christ Superstar*'s use of rock provoked outrage in part because rock "had established itself as a site of authenticity in self-conscious opposition to the perceived emptiness of late capitalist social institutions including, but not limited to, organized religion."[53] Mormons, too, gravitated toward the rock musical during this time to express specifically Mormon sentiments and perhaps to take advantage of the genre's liminal position between established modes of authenticity that opened up space for alternative expressions of American values, despite significant pushback from Church officials. Amid conflicting ideals about rock music espoused by Mormon leadership, these rock and pop musicals emerged nonetheless and became significant cultural touchstones in Mormonism. One rock musical in particular, *Saturday's Warrior* (1973), addresses the issue of memory and forgetting endemic of Correlated Mormonism by suggesting that the material evidence of memory lies embedded in the voice itself. In the remainder of this chapter, I analyze *Saturday's Warrior* and explore its cultural reach within the broader context of a changing and growing Mormon Church.

Saturday's Warrior and Eternal Voices

Two men, worlds apart in position and ideology, are largely responsible for shaping Mormon perceptions of rock music in the 1970s and 1980s. In December 1971, Apostle Ezra Taft Benson warned Mormon youth against the "pornophonic sound" of rock music.[54] Such music, he argues, "crushing the sensibilities in a din of primitive idolatry, is in glorification of the physical to the debasement of the spirit." Benson also has no patience for what he calls "religious rock" (what presumably includes the Broadway and Off-Broadway musicals listed above), which in his mind simply replaces one idolatrous problem with another: "A review of religious rock materials unmasks an insidiously disguised anti-Christ. By reducing revealed religion to mythology, rock assumes the mantle of righteousness while rejecting the reality of sin." "Haunted by its black shadow," he adds, "[the hedonist] trades the useful, happy life for the bleak forgetfulness of drugs, alcohol, sex, and rock."

These were not uncommon sentiments for the time. Mark Sullivan reminds us that the rise of the Religious Far Right was in large part due to exacerbated remarks made in 1966 by John Lennon that the Beatles were "more popular than Jesus now."[55] The fallout was tremendous. Sullivan examines Christian fundamentalists Reverend David A. Noebel and Bob Larson's entrenched position that rock music was part of a Communist ploy to lure away unsuspecting youth. A member of the John Birch Society, Noebel was convinced throughout the 1970s that rock music was being exploited by Communists, and in the 1980s he only slightly tweaked his assertion that rock was more generally an "assault on Christian values."[56]

Like Noebel, Benson too was an active member of the John Birch Society. The apostle, who in 1953 was appointed by President Dwight D. Eisenhower

130 · CHAPTER 4

to be Secretary of Agriculture, at that time had one of the highest profiles of any Mormon before him, and he used his position and political experience to push anti-Communist sentiment, often from the pulpit. His overt concern with Communism died down when he later became Church president, but in 1971 Benson was determined not to let the Church be led asunder by left-leaning sympathizers, whether within or without the Church. While his remarks in this talk are not explicitly anti-Communistic, within the broader discourse of 1970s anti-rock sentiments spearheaded by the John Birch Society, to be concerned with Communism was to be concerned with rock 'n' roll.

A decade later, Lynn Bryson, a music industry entrepreneur in Utah, began preaching a similar message to Mormon congregations all over the country. Bryson considered rock music potentially dangerous, claiming that "if Christians did not wield this powerful tool in their favor the devil would surely wield it in his!"[57] Bryson also held an unfavorable view of the Beatles ("When the Beatles crashed in to cash in, the world was transformed under the sheer skill of a well tooled attack"), but he stopped short of denoting its inherent Communist trappings. Rather, Bryson felt that rock music was simply being used as a tool for the devil and wasn't in itself an unmitigated evil. He writes in his book *Winning the Testimony War* that "rock music, like an ax, can penetrate to the very core of hardest resistance, so that even pure light may pass. . . . The one wielding the ax decides whether to strike a blow for good or evil. The music is merely the ax . . . not being good or evil . . . if it merely has a captivating beat."[58]

Bryson claimed to have received some measure of personal validation from unnamed General Authorities—possibly Benson himself—and throughout the 1970s and 1980s took his message about the evils of rock music to various "firesides," or irregular gatherings of Mormon youth sponsored by local congregations. He called himself a "war correspondent" reporting from the front lines of a "testimony war" in which the most valiant youth of the Church were embroiled, many unknowingly. He specifically warned against hidden messages buried within rock music that might be detected blatantly only by playing records backwards, a process known as "backmasking." Bryson felt these "hidden voices" harnessed the power of the devil to speak subliminally to unsuspecting youth.

The prophetic caution fell on deaf ears. For many young Mormons coming of age in the 1970s and 1980s, Bryson and Benson were two unlikely partners cautioning against the wiles of rock music. This was the time when Mormon performers were beginning to make a presence in mainstream pop music, with some, especially Donny and Marie Osmond and their televised road-show-inspired skits, becoming pop icons. Out of this period also came a flurry of rock and pop musicals penned by and for Mormons.

One musical in particular has maintained a significant grip on Mormon culture and brings back into the discussion Lotman and Uspensky's notions of cultural memory and forgetting. *Saturday's Warrior* follows the lives of the Flinders children from the pre-mortal life where they make certain commitments to one another through their struggles in mortality, when they no longer remember their previous existence and must rely on faith to reunite and fulfill those commitments. Based on Nephi Anderson's 1898 novel *Added Upon*, *Saturday's Warrior* depicts a pre-mortal existence where the same sociality exists that will eventually exist in mortality. Siblings, spouses, and friendships that existed before mortality get reinstated on earth. As the action in *Saturday's Warrior* oscillates between earth and the pre-mortal heavens, issues of remembrance and forgetting become a central part of the musical. Having passed "through the veil" upon being born on earth, the main characters no longer remember pre-mortal existence or the promises made to one another. The voice, however, transcends time and space and thus acts as a remedy for those suspended outside of sacred time.

Siblings Jimmy and Julie serve as the primary characters in the story, their own struggles with maintaining their commitments to relationships—Jimmy to his family and Julie to her soulmate, Tod—forming two of the primary dilemmas of the show. The third and comic leg of the plot involves two missionaries, Wally and Harold, and their hope to reunite on earth as a "fearlessly extraordinary" gospel-spreading duo. Wally and Harold bear a striking resemblance to Elders Price and Cunningham in *Book of Mormon*, as Elder Price likewise struggles to balance humility with hubris (see chapter 5). In *Saturday's Warrior* the two missionaries serve as a foil for the more serious relationships of Jimmy and Julie, but, as I will describe later, Wally and Harold's union is nonetheless structured as a romance and is crucial for the musical to resolve all other conflicts, in effect bridging the great chasm between pre-mortal and mortal worlds.

Along with their parents, the seven Flinders children (minus Emily, the youngest child who is still waiting in the pre-mortal world to join the family on earth) are part of a performing family. We meet the now-mortal Flinders family during a filmed performance profiling their newest honorific as "Riverdale's Family of the Year." In this performance of "Daddy's Nose," members of the Flinders family wear exaggerated prosthetic noses and sing about all sharing a prominent nose, apparently inherited from their father. The number serves to establish the family as wholesome and decidedly Mormon, their performance style an obvious nod to the popular Mormon performing family The Osmonds.

"Daddy's Nose" places a question mark on the family's identity, however. Unlike the rest of the rock score, "Daddy's Nose" is a vaudeville number. In a typical musical structure, the sound of vaudeville is musical coding for ethnicity, almost invariably Jewish. The song's chromatic antecedent and consequent phrases, along with the reference to vaudeville performer Jimmy Durante (whose famously big nose he referred to in Yiddish as the "Schnozzola") and the throwaway line at the end that "Mom's even got it," frames the Flinderses as ethnic character types. The physical symbol of their Otherness (even as a costume gimmick) is augmented even more by the Flinderses' musical tampering with vaudeville tropes of ethnicity (see example 6).

In the 2016 film version, "Daddy's Nose" is replaced with a reprise of an earlier number called "Pullin' Together" that the Flinders children sang in the pre-mortal world, continuing a trope in the show of using reprises to bridge pre-mortal and mortal worlds, a process that I discuss more later. While removing "Daddy's Nose" from the remake changes the ethnic connotations of the newest version, other songs are added that place *Saturday's Warrior* within other racially charged musical theater conventions. The addition of black British American singer Alex Boyé's character in the pre-mortal world, for example, who sings at the beginning of the show a gospel-inflected number called "Blink of an Eye," places *Saturday's Warrior* within a long history of musicals featuring black gospel performers singing as themselves and less as integral characters in the plot.[59]

Given the original musical's treatment of ethnicity in "Daddy's Nose," Jimmy's impulse to distance himself from the embarrassment of his family might therefore be interpreted as a typical story (with hints of *The Jazz Singer*) of religious rejection in favor of assimilation. In an eerie echo of the horrors of the Holocaust, Jimmy's friends even pointedly accuse the large

Example 6: Excerpt of "Daddy's Nose," from *Saturday's Warrior* (1973). Music and lyrics by Lex de Azevedo and Douglas Stewart.

REPRISING THE VOICE IN SACRED TIME · 133

Flinders family of being a credible danger to an overcrowded planet ("Zero Population"). Andrea Most has written extensively about the Jewish narrative of assimilation through musical theater, a process she calls "theatrical liberalism." According to Most, Jewish performers not only took advantage of theatrical spaces to self-fashion new, acceptable identities in order to become more American, but they also in the process shaped musical theater conventions still operative today that bear traces of assimilative ideology.

This same process may be at play in *Saturday's Warrior*. Through performance, Jimmy is made aware of problems with his "ethnic" identity and chooses to reject his family in favor of easy assimilation. He opts to blend in with the exaggeratedly edgy rock theatricality of his peers (the sonic evidence of Benson's jeremiad) rather than the quirky yet wholesome musical numbers his family performs. Significantly, Jimmy's rejection of his family comes on the heels of his leaving the family band and taking on a new musical persona with his friends. Jimmy leaving the family challenges the collective singing ideology that *Promised Valley* promoted; it is significant that Jimmy's coming of age, his subsequent faith crisis, and his eventual return to his family (which presumably means rejoining the family's band) all hinge on his willingness to sing with his family. Singing together means each body is vibrating together and implies that all are on the same wavelength and sending the identical message (see chapter 5). It's only a slight exaggeration to say that if he can't sing with the group, then Jimmy's eternal relationship with them is threatened.

The rest of the Flinderses likewise appear to understand the plight of their ethnic and musical identity, as they jokingly lament of the nose, "Would it be so bad if it had stayed with old Dad?" Yet through performance the mask is put on and taken off at will, blurring lines of ethnic identity. Andrea Most suggests Jewish vaudeville performers similarly "subverted the basic assumptions of eugenics" through performing the easy slip in and out of various racial categories on stage, "call[ing] into question the alleged immutability of racial bloodlines."[60] Because the Flinders children in the pre-mortal world don't sing vaudeville yet do so in "Daddy's Nose," it can be taken that ethnicity is a mortal condition and stands apart from one's true identity, that ethnicity is a kind of performance and, like the prosthetic nose, is a mask that can be put on and taken off again.

After learning of his sister Pam's death, Jimmy seeks clarity in an existential number ("Brace Me Up"). This song functions as a kind of dream sequence, another musical mainstay. There is no ballet here, as is the case typically in shows such as *Oklahoma!, Carousel*, and *The King and I*; rather, the structure

134 · CHAPTER 4

of what becomes a combination song allows multiple voices to compete in Jimmy's conscience. Jimmy's melody is augmented by musical interjections from three different groups: his edgy friends cajoling him to join them, the Flinders family begging him to not turn them away, and his yet unborn sister Emily—now joined in heaven by his deceased sister Pam—reminding him of his pre-mortal promise to his family. This musical moment reveals the edge the Flinders family is teetering on; the growing divide between them, Jimmy, and the girls in heaven is represented through musical fragmentation that seems doubly significant (here we are reminded that *flinders* means splinter or fragment). The music grows increasingly chaotic as melodic shards sung by Jimmy and the three groups overlap in combination. The musical cacophony gives way finally to silence, where Jimmy hears only an echo of his family's plea: "Please don't turn us away." As with Laurey in *Oklahoma!* and Billy Bigelow in *Carousel*, Jimmy finds his dilemma resolved through the message of the dream sequence. He returns to his family and thus maintains his pre-mortal commitment.

Meanwhile, Wally and Harold, the cocky missionaries united now as mission companions on earth, discover a man named Tod who is seeking truth and happiness, and they convert him to Mormonism. His steady, Julie Flinders, has recently dumped Wally in a Dear John letter. Over the course of that long-distance courtship, Wally writes to Julie that, after a long line of disappointing mission companions, he has been assigned with Harold—a new companion who nearly gives away the secret by surmising he may have known Wally in the pre-mortal world. In the conventions of musical theater, the broken road that leads to Wally and Harold's union is a blatantly romantic one. Just like the other couples in the story, Wally and Harold vow to find one another on earth. They also sing to one another. Their funk-laden duet "Humble Way" is meant as a comedic moment. The pair does manage to get all the other pre-mortal characters dancing, though the persistent slap bass underscoring their dialogue signifies the sexiness of funk as much as its grooviness. "Humble Way" may not make explicit claims about homosexuality, but it does embrace the more sanitized homosociality that makes the companionship's success together on earth actually work as a romantic resolution. Looking ahead to the final chapter, this also forms a counterweight to *Book of Mormon*'s depiction of missionary homosociality in the song "Turn It Off"—a tome to emotional (and sexual) repression that ties the frightened missionaries together in pious assembly. Yet while *Book of Mormon* missionaries sing and dance together as a safeguard against doubt,

REPRISING THE VOICE IN SACRED TIME · 135

Saturday's Warrior's missionaries use song and dance to bring their troubled relationship full circle into resolution.

In the 1989 film version of *Saturday's Warrior*, Wally and Harold, after their success in Tod's conversion, burst into a reprise of "Humble Way." Tod's conversion encourages a performance identical to that done in the pre-mortal world—a world they otherwise have no recollection of. Having completed their intended "mission" and fulfilled their promise to one another in the pre-mortal life, the two cannot be kept from singing a song the audience knows the characters should not be able to remember. Because the reprise allows audiences and performers to see and hear continuity across time and space, their reprise ruptures conventional ideals of history and time. Principally through voice, *Saturday's Warrior* creates a world where people can truly never die and where important relationships survive intact across lives and death. The show suggests a person's voice can serve as the catalyst that makes the forgotten past memorable again, if only provisionally. Thus singing becomes a metaphysical act that tethers one world to the other, all the while signaling that the true identity and purpose of Wally and Harold has now been realized.

Now that Julie has become disentangled from her relationship with Wally, she is introduced to Tod (oddly enough, through Wally and Harold—now serving as foil to the "real" relationship of the musical), and both immediately sense their eternal connection. Tod and Julie sing a reprise of a duet they first sang together in the pre-mortal world, "Circle of Our Love."

> TOD: I've seen that smile somewhere before.
> JULIE: I've heard your voice before.
> BOTH: It seems we've talked like this before.
> TOD: Sometime, who can be certain when?
> JULIE: But if I knew you then . . . It's strange. I can't remember.

In the opening scene of the musical, the pre-mortal couple rehearses this exact mortal meeting as they promise to find one another and get married. The Mormon instinct to perform is here portrayed as a pragmatic aspect of eternal familial bonds: Tod and Julie's actual earthly reunion is but a successful performance that has been well rehearsed and planned eternities ago. And it is through the act of performance, of singing together, that the relationship materializes.

It is significant that, for Tod and Julie, common voices give away their true identity. Their reprise of "Circle of our Love" in fact seems deliberately

136 · CHAPTER 4

reminiscent of the song "Where or When" from Richard Rodgers and Lorenz Hart's 1937 musical *Babes in Arms*, which, like *Saturday's Warrior*, is also about the feeling that some relationships may have begun much earlier, perhaps even in another dimension. Billie and Val perform the number at the top of the show, much like Julie and Tod do in *Saturday's Warrior*. As Billie sings in the refrain, "It seems we stood and talked like this before / We looked at each other in the same way then / But I can't remember where or when." While Rodgers and Hart stopped short of admitting that such feelings might have a metaphysical explanation, the creators of *Saturday's Warrior* took the idea seriously and elided the sentiment with a near-forgotten Mormon belief. By modeling "Circle of Our Love" on the song "Where or When," *Saturday's Warrior* seemingly alludes to an established trope in classic musical theater in order to set up the premise that singing transcends physical or spiritual dimensions.

As Tod and Julie get lost in one another's embrace, Harold comforts a distraught Wally and they exit the stage, their future relationship confirmed by Harold's excited comment that they "could be roommates at BYU." In the end, all three mismatched relationships are resolved—Jimmy finally returns to his family, Julie and Tod reunite on earth, and Wally and Harold enjoy the success of their "extraordinary" pairing.

While represented by all three unions, the true resolution of the show seems to come as reconciliation between pre-mortality and mortality. This seems a lopsided resolution, since no one is left in the pre-mortal world to reap the benefits of reconciliation. Unlike in most musicals, where seemingly irreconcilable worlds are united in the end through cultural and musical compromise, the pre-mortal and mortal worlds in *Saturday's Warrior* now look and sound identical—even the music is the same. Julie and Tod and Wally and Harold sing just as they had before, and presumably the Flinders family continues to perform campy songs just as they always did in the pre-mortal world. *Saturday's Warrior* sidesteps the full import of the "marriage trope" in favor of character self-realization—in this case a process that seems to resolve but really only comes back in full circle. For a religion that favors eternal progression over a static afterlife, perhaps no better musical ending could put such a fine point on the story of Mormonism.

Correlated Voices

Saturday's Warrior imagines a voice that sticks, or remains somehow intact, between phases of mortality. There is some scriptural precedent for such a claim. Mormons and Christians alike share the impression that "there shall not a hair of your head perish" between death and the resurrection of the body.[61] Mormon scripture is even more explicit about this. The prophet Alma in The Book of Mormon explains that, in the resurrection, "the soul shall be restored to the body, and the body to the soul; yea, and every limb and joint shall be restored to its body; yea, even a hair of the head shall not be lost; but all things shall be restored to their proper and perfect frame."[62]

The opening verses of the traditional Christian hymn "How Can I Keep from Singing" goes so far as to allegorize sound as an emblem of truth. Like the stickiness of voice in *Saturday's Warrior*, singing is taken in this hymn to represent a conversion to truth *heard*, not seen.

> My life goes on in endless song
> Above earth's lamentations,
> I hear the real, though far-off hymn
> That hails a new creation.
> Through all the tumult and the strife
> I hear its music ringing,
> It sounds an echo in my soul.
> How can I keep from singing?[63]

The act of singing therefore allows performers to enact truth, and choral singing (the "far-off hymn") models a disciplined vocal response to pre-mortal knowledge that "sounds an echo in [the] soul." Voice, then, as a material entity, should remain unhampered between mortality and the afterlife. This seems to be the acoustic principle from which God renders judgment, if we recall the awestruck editorial wondering about the phonographic implications of Wilford Woodruff's wax-cylinder testimony. Even Jesus made the same assertion when he said, "Heaven and earth shall pass away: but my words shall not pass away."[64] What *Saturday's Warrior* claims is that somehow, even prior to a person gaining a body of flesh on earth, a voice uttered in the pre-mortal world is traceable and identifiable on earth. The voice, as an emblem for the rest of the body, has always been.

Thus the voice in Mormonism is an ultimate "always already." For Mormons, the phenomenological assumptions about vocality raise the stakes for identity and intention, for the corrupting influences of mortality are rarely conceptualized beyond bodily sins such as lasciviousness, sexual promiscuity, violence, or gluttony. This list of physical transgressions is almost never extended to vocality. Recall that Mormons well into the twentieth century in fact had no qualm using the voice to break biblical injunctions against dishonesty by "lying for the Lord." Thus, despite the voice's apparent eternal nature, little outright attention is given to the standardized vocal behavior

138 · CHAPTER 4

in Mormonism. Rather, Mormons are known for their dietary and lifestyle restraints against coffee, tea, alcohol, cigarettes, drugs, and sexual deviance of any sort. Nonetheless, through Correlation, the voice has, over the last several decades, become just as disciplined and codified as the Mormon body and its accompanying demeanor.

The Mormon preoccupation with standardized communication predates Correlation and could be traced back to Brigham Young's pet project, the Deseret Alphabet. This thirty-eight-character phonetic alphabet was intended to make the sounds of its people reflect the utopia promised by their new-found isolation. Mormons in Utah were coming from all over the world, not just in wagon trains and handcart companies out of Illinois, many bringing languages and customs that could not always be reconciled. This cosmo-politanism consequently proved to be a communications liability. It soon became apparent that "such a far-flung utopia built upon a mixture of the world population could only be unified through literacy and a common language."[65] The Church planned a complete orthographic overhaul of the English language—similar in ambition to other language planners of the nine-teenth century, including Noah Webster—in hopes of unifying the disparate cultural factions by creating a unified voice of Mormonism. Although the Church eventually abandoned the Deseret Alphabet when the encroaching railroad made it clear that a language peculiar to Mormonism would soon be obsolete, it represents an early attempt at simplifying spelling and grammar in order to better facilitate universal communication among the Mormons. The voice was central to this utopian endeavor in the nineteenth century, no less than it became during Correlation in the middle of the twentieth century.

In fact, the Mormon practice of vocal vicariousness is both compromised and augmented through Correlation. The voice of the prophet, which has been a model for vocality from the beginning of Mormonism, has become suspect in the last few decades. When the prophet speaks, Mormons can no longer hear an unhampered voice; rather, through Correlation, prophetic ut-terance is really the mouthpiece of a committee or departmental voice—an untold number of unseen people who massage God's intended message to fit within a standardized mold established purely for the sake of continuity. Correlation democratizes the prophetic voice even as it enforces a strict top-down power dynamic among Church leaders.

Because Correlation effectively allows Mormons to look into the past and recognize it as proto-Mormon, Correlation frames a practice of his-tory making and history believing reminiscent of nationalism and that re-calls Eric Hobsbawm's well-known concept of an "invented tradition." The

REPRISING THE VOICE IN SACRED TIME · 139

invented tradition, according to Hobsbawm, occurs in moments when old traditions are weakening and newer traditions are viewed as unsuitable replacements—the crisis of modernity adding grist to the wheel of invented traditions. Instead, through repetition and a certain degree of playacting, groups of people may project an invented tradition onto the past and presume therefore its imminence as "old." In Hobsbawm's words, the invented tradition "inculcate[s] certain values and norms of behavior by repetition, which automatically implies continuity with the past. In fact, where possible, they normally attempt to establish continuity with a suitable historic past."[66]

This ends up happening with Correlation. By association with past leaders or biblical events, newer traditions or policies get passed off as "old" and their practice in times far removed from today can be recognized as in line with the continuity of Mormonism. Thus Eve may be depicted wearing modest clothing and Adam portrayed without a hint of facial hair (both demarcations of modern Mormon dress and grooming standards) if those images are projected on a screen while a prophet speaks about the importance of modesty. Correlation ensures continuity by providing the mechanism by which Mormons can project modern ideals into a past where they didn't exist and into a future where they might not belong.

The repeated voice of the prophets, perfect in their homogeneity, likewise creates a sonic reference to the reach of Correlation. As discussed in the first chapters, prophets and lay members alike may model their voices after one another in an attempt to sound authentic and inspired. Mormonism is guided by the premise that voices can and should be modeled, morphed, and made new; Correlation interrupts the vocal theatrics by insisting that Mormon voices, above all, should sound the same. *Saturday's Warrior* counters the logic of Correlation by recovering the early Mormon understanding of an eternal voice and bringing it back to contemporary times. In effect, *Saturday's Warrior* reprises the original Nephi Anderson story and brings pre-Correlated Mormon ideals into the modern world. The show itself becomes the convention it sustains and in so doing brings Mormonism a little closer to its original self that exists in an otherwise unrecoverable, forgotten past.

*   *   *

It is difficult to downplay the tremendous effect of *Saturday's Warrior* on Mormon culture. The musical has been cited from the pulpit and touted in conversion stories and testimonies, creating a generational outlook on Mormon theology that, surprisingly, is actually unsubstantiated. It seems that *Saturday's Warrior*'s success was a surprise for everyone; when I bring

140 · CHAPTER 4

up *Saturday's Warrior* in conversation with Mormons, almost without fail a sheepish grin or embarrassed laugh is the response. The show is dated, to be sure. And the 1989 film version of *Saturday's Warrior*, which is how most Mormons first encountered the show, lacks any enviable cinematography or redeemable acting. Yet those same embarrassed shrugs or sighs can quickly morph into cheery refrains of "Circle of Our Love" or "Daddy's Nose." Part of this apologetic posture may come from the disparity musicologist Mitchell Morris points to, between the music that privately animates our minds and hearts and that which makes it past our carefully constructed filter for what is seemingly respectable, or important, music.[67] Shows like *Saturday's Warrior* are terribly bad by almost any standard and probably deserving of the frequent giggles stifled on their behalf. Yet these silly shows are in effect an answer to serious but often unobserved questions—questions of memory, identity, and the constancy of voice that helps connect the two. The indefensible nature of these shows in itself does little to betray the laughter; to quote Morris, my project here is to "know more about what all this laughter defends against."[68]

Nonetheless, the deeply held belief that families existed as units before coming to Earth and that romantic relationships began before mortality were not a part of modern Mormon culture until *Saturday's Warrior* reintroduced them in the 1970s. Today, as one scholar has noted, the musical has become "folk doctrine appealing to Mormons seeking assurance that divine intentions were deeply woven into their lives and that though these beliefs set them apart from the world, they were indeed fulfilling God's plan."[69] By rehashing a story with roots well before Correlation, *Saturday's Warrior* forced adaptation in Mormon doctrine that was not possible with the tight grip of Correlated Mormonism. In order to effect change, Mormon culture stumbled upon a path through the cracks of Correlation—the path of musical theater—one of Mormonism's most reliant and resilient forms of mediation.

Other Mormon-made musicals from this era addressed similar issues of forgetting and remembering, including *My Turn on Earth* (1977) and *Don't Forget to Remember* (1981). *Saturday's Warrior* aside, the majority of these and other rock musicals are largely forgotten by those outside of Mormonism, and performances of them today remain scarce even within the Church. Yet this era of prolific rock musical creation offers a telling glimpse into the machinations of Correlated Mormonism. Many of these musicals address with urgency the dangers of forgetting pre-mortal commitments in the face of increasing secularization. In hindsight, they seem to endorse the simplified doctrine of through-the-glass-darkly religion that Correlation provides.

At the same time, growing discontent among Mormons unaccustomed or resistant to the convenient narratives of Correlation made remembering pre-Correlated Mormonism a liability.

Mormon apostle Franklin D. Richards once said, "In some ways, being able to forget is almost as valuable as being able to remember."[70] His words might just as well be applied to Correlation, which was designed to erase any problematic events or policies from cultural memory. Over the next few decades the Church did its best to silence competing historical narratives about polygamy, race and the priesthood, polyandry, Joseph's seer stones, and other dark corners of Mormon history by excommunicating vocal objectors. The issue the Church has needed to defend most in the new millennium is not truth, per se, but rather its Correlated *version* of the truth. The next and final chapter looks more closely at the effects of Correlation on Mormonism today and explores how the singular message of an unwavering, streamlined doctrine reveals a broken mechanism within Mormon communication.

5

Voice Interrupted

Book of Mormon *and the Failed Message of Correlated Mormonism*

Should a society actually succeed . . . in suffocating all
contrary opinion, then its own vital juices no longer
flow and the shadow of death begins to fall across it. No
society—ecclesiastical or political, military or literary—can
afford to be snared by its own slogans.

—Edwin Scott Gaustad, *Dissent in American Religion*

And now behold, we desire to know the cause of this
exceedingly great neglect; yea, we desire to know the
cause of your thoughtless state.

—Alma 60:6

The opening number of *Book of Mormon* features a flurry of introductions from its cast of Mormon missionaries. The song "Hello!" plays on the sonic memory of a typical first meeting with a Mormon missionary, the ringing doorbell. As each cast member enters the stage—wearing the appropriate Mormon missionary uniform of white collared shirt, simple tie, and small rectangular name badge pinned above the left breast—he sings a friendly "hello," pitched to falling minor thirds that echo the familiar ding-dong sound of a doorbell. As the song continues, the cordial yet militant hellos weave in and around one another in a canon.

The uniformity of the several men, both in body and in voice, makes the entrance of bumbling Elder Arnold Cunningham all the more noticeable. When he makes the gesture of pressing a doorbell, the sound effect audiences hear is an abrasive screech rather than the melodious doorbell tones heard when the other missionaries do the same. As with the excommunicated

Mormons discussed in chapter 4, Elder Cunningham seems out of tune with the others; in fact, all action on stage stops while he tries to deliver the scripted lines he has been taught at the Missionary Training Center. He gets his introduction wrong and is quickly chastised by an off-stage voice, who accuses Elder Cunningham of "making things up" and insists he deliver only the exact dialogue, as instructed. The song kicks back in, and the rest of the missionaries continue in perfect harmony, rhythm, and stylized choreography, delivering the approved dialogue happily, mechanically, and without error.

This opening number introduces the audience to the story's antihero, Elder Cunningham, but it also cleverly highlights the perception many people have of Mormons as homogenous, unflinching characters whose doorstep sales pitch seems just a little *too* prepared. *Book of Mormon* captures in this scene the great efforts Mormons go through to ensure their message is standardized, voices synched, and image flawlessly sharp. To fall outside of those norms, as Elder Cunningham so obviously does, is to disrupt the singular message Correlated Mormonism demands. By the end of the show, however, Elder Cunningham shows how scrambling the approved message of Mormonism frees the meaning from the message and thus offers the characters hope built upon a new and vibrant mythology.

Elder Cunningham's inability to voice Mormonism correctly in *Book of Mormon* offers a biting commentary on Correlated Mormonism and glimpses a new way of thinking about the Church's recent (and very public) excommunications. Significantly, the musical highlights the degree to which Mormons rely on and become deaf to the consequences of the homogeneity that Correlation provides.

I laid out my discussion of Correlation in the previous chapter as a streamlining process with some serious effects on the way the Mormon Church relates and receives messages from God. I want to go even further with this discussion here by thinking of the singular message of Correlated Mormonism in terms of vibrational consistency. Musicologist Nina Eidsheim recently has outlined a way of thinking about music or sound fundamentally as vibrational. By shifting the discourse on sound away from musical objects and toward the material realm of vibrations (including the bone and flesh vibrations of the human body when sensing sound), she argues that we may begin to think of musical analysis as "an investigation into relationships and community."[1] I invoke Eidsheim's claims by suggesting that one way Correlation works is by disciplining sounding bodies, and that it depends on an unchecked assumption that the way of hearing or sensing the message of

144 · CHAPTER 5

Mormonism is universally agreed upon. I suggest that vibrational theories may provide a helpful metaphor for understanding the recent excommunications of prominent Mormon dissenters—those who perceive and then vocalize a version of Mormonism that draws upon vibrations outside of the scripted phrases Correlation provides. Following Eidsheim's work, I too wonder if rethinking how people sense the vibrations of Mormonism might facilitate a renewed empathy for those whose words and bodies, like Elder Cunningham's, "vibrate" differently.

This final chapter looks at the consequences of Correlation on Mormon communication and vocality. I arc back to the beginning of this story to better understand Mormonism today. How has the practice of vocal vicariousness changed or evolved over the history of Mormonism? What are the globalizing effects Correlation has had on the way Mormons speak to one another? What about the speech of prophets and apostles? Has Correlation, as it might appear, compromised the essence of revelation and replaced the prophetic cry with an empty, failed voice? What might Correlation have to do with public dissenters and their sometimes-resultant excommunications from the Church? I analyze the 2011 Broadway musical *Book of Mormon* with these lines of questioning in mind and argue that the musical envisions how a rupture in the veneer of Mormonism's idealized vocality could point back to a humane, ethical religious experience.

Dissent and Satire

In important ways, *Book of Mormon* and Wilford Woodruff's echoing voice both speak to the communication crisis Correlation has placed on contemporary Mormonism. Both also raise doubts about the integrity of an unceasing message in a rapidly changing social landscape. The missionaries singing the opening number know only how to repeat their message in the exact way they have been taught. Even when the missionaries practice introducing themselves in languages other than English, the rigid structure of the tune (backed up by snare drum hits with military band precision) makes words like "Me llamo" or "ni hao" sound hollow and pre-programmed; their almost mechanical delivery of the text echoes Woodruff's wax-preserved testimony. Wilford Woodruff could hardly have guessed at the effect of his recorded voice or that it might someday be compared with a Broadway musical. In preservation, his voice became an object of scrutiny, a hallowed sound both inspiring and eerie yet nonetheless always available. Those waxen grooves today allow for Woodruff's voice to speak to listeners vicariously through recording technology. His voice cannot fail; it will continue sounding its identical message for perpetuity.

Yet precisely because of its perfect recapitulation, Woodruff's voice *does* fail. The record of his voice can relay a message, but that message must always stand in apology for being nondialogic. It's a peculiar quality of the dead—through recordings they can speak forever, yet forever will hear nothing. Necessarily disregarding whatever changes take place in the world, Woodruff's infinitely recycling voice will remain a faint echo of an idea, removed from its source. Yet, the *sound* of the voice can have remarkable, long-lasting reach, even though the voice itself is moored to the finite animation of its host. Woodruff's voice resounds with its own compromise—eternally present, yes; its relevance for today, questionable. Woodruff's voice thus stands synecdochally for the stifled message of Correlated Mormonism.

Book of Mormon represents a loudening critique of Correlated Mormonism from outsiders—the choice of musical theater as the platform for grievances makes a neat parallel to anti-Mormon antics on nineteenth-century musical stages. It is telling that a number of criticisms recently have come from *within* Mormonism. Even more telling is that these critics (including the musical revue *Saturday's Voyeur* in Salt Lake City and, most notably, the popular online persona Brother Jake) also have been using musical theater to draw attention to the hold Correlation has on the Mormon Church. Brother Jake, described by one YouTube commenter as "the Stephen Colbert of Mormon satire," uses musical theater to question the Church's dedication to homogeneity. He blithely carries a growing audience through fallacious explanations of controversial or historically problematic aspects of Mormonism. These explanations are presented as "Brother Jake Explains:" followed by video titles covering a number of dicey historical issues, including "polygamy," "Mormonism is not a cult," "Church discipline," and "Mormons are not racist." Similar to other satirical explanations of Church culture from within the Mormon ranks (such as the "Dictionary of Correlation" by anthropologist Daymon Smith), Brother Jake's material jocularly occupies a liminal space, protected by online anonymity, where questioning, frustrated, or transitional Mormons dialogue with one another and true-believing members of the Church, who are often labeled TBMs for short.

Brother Jake has created several satirical videos that use musical theater to tell the story of Mormonism. One, called "True Believing Mormon Dude," is a parody of Gilbert and Sullivan's "I Am the Very Model of a Modern Major General" from *Pirates of Penzance* (1879)—one of the most parodied musical comedy numbers ever. In Brother Jake's hands, the familiar musical theater

146 · CHAPTER 5

tune sends a more sobering message about blind faith he sees as prominent in Mormonism: "I feel weird when people talk about my Mormon underwear / And when I go to church I dress real nice and shave my facial hair. / And even though you might be thinking 'This guy is a giant prude,' / It's no big deal because I am a true-believing Mormon dude." Inasmuch as Gilbert and Sullivan's Modern Major General is a bumbling and laughable buffoon whose naive, self-deprecating words have charmed audiences for generations, Brother Jake's caricature of faithful Mormon men as similarly incredulous exploits Mormon's use of musical theater as a means of acceptance. If Brother Jake's video complicates an easy response, it's because Mormon cultural offense is mixed with a Mormon cultural virtue.

Another of Brother Jake's videos, titled "Meant Symbolically" and set to the tune of the song "Defying Gravity" from the 2003 Broadway musical *Wicked*, problematizes the traditionally literal interpretation of historical events in the Mormon past. Brother Jake points to this unease of figurative belief in light of a traditionally very literal Mormon worldview:

> This new approach is so exciting
> I feel a huge sense of relief
> Don't have to turn my back on reason
> In matters of belief. [...]
> I'll just say it's meant symbolically
> So I can justify it logically
> That way I'll reconcile all my beliefs
> And never be pinned down!

It also seems fitting that Brother Jake chose to base his satire on "Defying Gravity," a song empowering Elphaba, the musical's version of the infamously green-skinned Wicked Witch of the West, to break out of the confines of a judgmental society. As much as Elphaba's deluded hopes of acceptance are betrayed by her character's watery demise in *The Wizard of Oz* (a death faked in the much more sympathetic *Wicked*), so too might the Mormon conscience be pricked by the difficult position of defending theological notions rooted in a literal history no longer deemed feasible by science. As with the Wicked Witch, the same with Mormon history: a splash of pure insight threatens to melt it all away.

In another of his videos, Brother Jake satirically sings of the promises of Correlation. In a song set to the tune of the title song from *Oklahoma!*, Brother Jake opines that Correlation has been used by the Church to whitewash troublesome aspects of Church history, using its corporate muscle to choke out dissidence. With Church disciplinary actions against prominent Mormon activists Kate Kelly and John Dehlin making headlines in 2014 and 2015, Brother Jake's satire hits a particularly sore spot on the Mormon conscience. While images of Kelly and Dehlin flash across the screen, Brother Jake sings:

> Correlation, where sharing doubts just doesn't fly
> And where every hour's
> run by priesthood power
> Which is really great if you're a guy.

Brother Jake continues his unbridled critique of Church policy, concluding the song with the following lines:

> But if you don't know what to do
> Just go pick up a manual or two
> 'Cause when we say
> Only white shirts on Sunday
> We're saying we could use some homogenization:
> Correlation's the way.
> And if you say
> "Hey, there's a better way,"
> Just remember we're your only way to salvation,
> So shut up and obey.

This sort of criticism may not be uncommon, or even unexpected, in a Church of fifteen million members. It is the medium of musical theater, though, that seems to make Brother Jake's satire sting a bit more. When asked why he uses musical theater in his video satire, Brother Jake gave a response that perhaps almost any American Mormon could agree with: Mormonism and musical theater "were both intimately intertwined in my upbringing." He continues,

> Brother Jake is a character who operates in the Colbert-like nether space of imitating the heuristics of an ideological "in" group while taking no pains to soften or gloss over the harsher/more bizarre implications of the ideology itself . . . Musical theatre, with its cheesy, cheery tone and generally straightforward messaging seemed like a perfect fit. It struck me as a great vehicle for taking something that externally appears harmless and marrying it with the uncomfortable, like playing "happy birthday" in a minor key.[2]

148 · CHAPTER 5

From this account, it seems Brother Jake's intention is to discomfit. This modus operandi fits easily within general theories of satire, which P. K. Elkin argues is "a catalytic agent" whose function "is less to judge people for their follies and vices than to challenge their attitudes and opinions, to taunt and provoke them into doubt, and perhaps into disbelief."[3] "Satirists can provoke by challenging received opinion," adds Dustin Griffin. "They can also provoke by holding up to scrutiny our idealized images of ourselves—forcing us to admit that such things are forever out of reach, unavailable to us, or even the last things we would really want to attain."[4]

Of course, these are dangerous qualities for an institution to tolerate. The Mormon Church in recent years has attempted to stamp out dissidence among its membership, arguing that members have the right to voice opinions but not to lead others into disbelief. Yet it may be precisely the draconian attitude that impels the establishment of this precarious balance, that births satirical material from within the Church. Griffin has argued that "it is the limitation on free inquiry and dissent that provokes one to irony—and to satire," noting that if openly challenging orthodoxy were tolerated, then people would simply take their frustrations to the newspapers and debate openly there.[5]

As has been the case with both Kate Kelly and John Dehlin, however, it is unclear where free speech ends and inappropriate criticism begins. Following her public campaign for the ordination of women, Kate Kelly's excommunication in 2014 was explained in a letter from her bishop:

> The difficulty, Sister Kelly, is not that you say you have questions or even that you believe that women should receive the priesthood. The problem is that you have persisted in an aggressive effort to persuade other Church members to your point of view and that your course of action has threatened to erode the faith of others. You are entitled to your views, but you are not entitled to promote them and proselyte others to them while remaining in full fellowship in the Church.[6]

Similarly, the stake president[7] of prominent Mormon blogger and podcast host John Dehlin wrote in his letter of excommunication that

> this action was not taken against you because you have doubts or because you were asking questions about Church doctrine. Rather, this decision has been reached because of your categorical statements opposing the doctrine of the Church, and their wide dissemination via your Internet presence, which has led others away from the Church. . . . [Y]ou do not have the right to remain a member of the Church in good standing while openly and publicly trying to convince others that Church teachings are in error.[8]

To continue my line of reasoning from earlier in this chapter, promoting dissenting opinions of Church policy or practice makes the dissenter's crime one of being vibrationally inconsistent and not necessarily of being a heretic. Dehlin and Kelly's message was incongruent with the singular message of Mormonism, and as their outcome suggests, inconsistency is perhaps the biggest threat that today's Correlated Mormon Church cannot tolerate.

Both of these excommunications were of high-profile Mormons, and the close timing suggested to some that the Church was calculatedly silencing opposition during a time of increasing skepticism toward the validity and sincerity of many Church leaders—a conspiratorial scenario that Church officials denied. Regardless, as the official excommunicatory letters admit, the damning evidence is not doubt or disbelief but a disruption of the singular message officially delivered by the Mormon Church. Yet without dissenting voices, religious dogmas are prone to stagnation and spiritual leaders to tyranny; for society's own sake, historian Edwin Scott Gaustad has argued, it must accept that "dissent makes democracy meaningful."[9] "Society's and religion's problem," he continues, "is that amid the clanging cymbals of consensus it is frequently difficult to hear what the dissenter is trying to say. One has to make a special effort to listen. He that has ears to hear, said a dissenter of ancient days, let him hear."[10]

Dissent in the Mormon Church has increased in the internet age. Curious members can find their faith derailed by learning of inconsistencies in the historical record, which, as Gordon B. Hinckley once said, was the essence of Mormonism. Rather than do as Gaustad suggests and "make a special effort to listen," the Church has responded to criticism by silencing voices of dissent. To that end, satire like Brother Jake's musical, theater-inspired videos emerges only in environments of repression and heavy-handedness, where conceptions of free speech are curtailed and uniformity expected. Arguably, this is the environment where Mormonism exists today. Shaftesbury put it well: "'Tis the persecuting Spirit has raised the bantering one. The greater the Weight is, the bitterer will be the Satire. The higher the Slavery, the more exquisite the Buffoonery."[11]

The Excommunicated

To be excommunicated in the proper sense is to be excised from the body of believers. Christian denominations have used the blunt tool of excommunication for centuries to pry out heretics, the possessed, and targeted threats to clerical authority. Although excommunication has always been a practice within Mormonism, the last several decades have seen an increase in what

150 · CHAPTER 5

some might call persecution of members whose ideologies put them at odds with official Mormon narratives. Prominent among the excommunicated are intellectuals, homosexuals, and feminists.[12] The Mormon Church, like other traditional religious groups, maintains that it is within its right—and even responsibility—to excommunicate dissenters in order to protect both the group and dissenter from the consequences of riotous behavior. By stripping membership away from the accused, the Church feels that it is offering that individual a future opportunity to reclaim his faith, that through rebaptism and a proper order of repentance, he may eventually return to the flock as a believer.

There are more nuanced ways of looking at excommunication than merely a boundary-maintenance tool, however. Some scholars have appropriated the term "excommunication" to refer to a broader divestment of opportunities or material goods necessary for survival under certain imperialist and neoliberal ideologies. For example, sociologist Armand Mattelart argues that excommunication represents the status of most of the world's population, suggesting that excommunication "lays bare the dark zone of the pacifying and pacifist vision of communication flows."[13] For Mattelart, the excommunicated are "the cultures and cultural areas that the theologisation of the apocalyptic struggle between good and evil have inscribed in the new code of the enemies of empire since 11th September 2001."[14] Arguably, Mattelart's use of the term could and should be extended even further back in time to take into account the manner in which various peoples have been cut out of narratives of prosperity. The marginalized, oppressed, and deplored throughout the world have no effective platform for giving voice to their stories or circumstances, a position Nick Couldry suggests can only be negated by dismantling the frameworks of neoliberalism that deny the valuation of voice.[15]

Others offer a vibrational model regarding excommunication. Alexander Galloway, Eugene Thacker, and McKenzie Wark similarly theorize excommunication as a sociological phenomenon. They acknowledge that excommunication is far more than just a question of language, that it is also "a question of community, belonging, and judgment before the law."[16] In arguing that excommunication is an "anti-message," they consider ways in which the process of excommunication and the people affected by it reflect a puzzling quality of communion and communication.

> At the center of excommunication is a paradoxical anti-message, a message that cannot be enunciated, a message that is anathema, heretical, and unorthodox, but for this very reason a message that has already been enunci-

ated, asserted, and distributed. Excommunicants become this paradoxical anti-message themselves, their very material existence nothing but a residual indicator of the message.[17]

The dissenter might be said to carry the essence of excommunication as he or she resonates differently from the vibrational message of the community. At the same moment, he or she embodies an unutterable message that such messages will be sent no more.

The excommunicated in Mormonism might similarly be understood as vibrationally suspect in an increasingly singular wavelength of Correlated communication. We already have learned of the value Mormons place on the sounding body. Brigham Young manages to match his voice with his ecclesiastical leader the same way Nephi does for Laban, *Promised Valley* rhapsodizes on the idealism of collective singing, the Polynesian Cultural Center demonstrates how whiteness might resound through American song and dance, and *Saturday's Warrior* celebrates the capacity to listen for voices that predate the foundations of the world. Mormons and Mormon leaders today busily practice modeling a righteous-sounding voice in an effort to recapture the voice of God, a voice seemingly gone silent. So much energy is spent in Mormonism on disciplining the sounds of assenting bodies that it makes sense that disciplinary actions against dissenters might likewise be concerned with the voice. Excommunicated Mormons are not allowed to pray or bear testimony publicly, or participate in temple ordinances; essentially, excommunication prevents Mormons from practicing vocal vicariousness in the significant ways particular to Mormonism. This ensures that the incongruent vibrations of dissenting bodies won't disrupt the status quo. Galloway, Thacker, and Wark write that "excommunication is the fantasy of an absolute end to all communication."[18] This may be a fantasy, but the practice has real effects. With the excommunicated in Mormonism denied the capacity to practice vocal vicariousness in the most sacred and consequential theaters within Mormonism, dissenters effectively embody the complete fulfillment of sonic and communicatory estrangement.

These various concerns about excommunication as a concept rattle the cages of centuries-old feelings concerning religious boundary maintenance and clerics keeping at bay the rising tide of modernity. Those principles have been a part of Mormonism too, and increasingly so in the last few decades, when satirical representations of the Church on the musical stage have erupted. But I want to unravel the concept of excommunication as a punitive religious practice and place it in dialogue with the changing vocal

152 · CHAPTER 5

patterns and messaging within the Mormon Church. As I suggest, excommunication—the conditional antimessage that states there will be no more messages—may be a fitting qualifier of Mormonism in light of how the modern Mormon Church itself has ceased to communicate in vital ways. In fact, Correlated Mormonism presents a study for how standardized models of communication fail to impart a message that carries compassionate or ethical ideals, but instead maintain a purposeful rhetorical balance designed to make certain that change cannot happen.

In some ways, it seems as though the ex-communicated have always found voice in Mormonism. Joseph and his prophetic descendants forged a sonic path to vicariously speak for a God who, for centuries, had remained either contently silent or unable to speak for Himself. Joseph's translation of The Book of Mormon effectively recovered the whispering voices of ancient times, allowing them to speak again from the dust. Even the Mormon practice of performing saving ordinances on behalf of the dead gives perhaps the most excommunicated—the dead—a means of communicating again, at least in principle.

In other ways, the Church has gradually seized control over prophetic communication, raising questions about the nature of communication in the Church today. Some argue that the Mormon Church has fallen into a nonrevelatory period, beginning perhaps as far back as the late nineteenth century but certainly since the mid-twentieth century.[19] The absence of new revelation (a redundancy in terminology, yet pertinent nonetheless under the governance of Correlation) may have to do with the imposition of institutional, as opposed to spiritual, policies of the Correlated Mormon Church.

In other words, the Church cannot receive revelation because, for all intents and purposes, it is no longer on God's wavelength. Believers thus are left to their own devices. Linguistic anthropologist Daymon Smith argues that readers of The Book of Mormon ought to become their own translators rather than rely on the Church's textual exegesis. Smith goes on to suggest that Correlated explanations of The Book of Mormon do little justice to the fundamental message: "That we have, over time, not only altered the Book of Mormon itself, but also imposed manuals, sermons, and extra-canonical texts upon it, all these vanities may have something to do with the dearth of new revelations over the last century."[20] Smith chooses to defend The Book of Mormon from the institutional reach of Correlated Mormonism which "dominat[es] the voices of the text."[21] Whether or not Smith is correct in his assessment of the Church is not as relevant as his observation that the Mormon Church's ability to communicate effectively is stifled by the machinery of Correlation. If true, then the Church has effectively excommunicated itself; if not, then we still wait for another explanation for why revelations have all but ceased.

If excommunication is a message that ends messages, as Galloway, Thacker, and Wark contend it is, then what can be said about the increasing cases of excommunication within the Mormon Church at a time when the Church has demonstrably limited *what* can be said and *how* it can be delivered? What about changes in public relations, where the Church's Public Relations Department speaks on behalf of the Church while the prophets and apostles remain silent? Have the prophets now become excommunicated from their role as vicarious carriers of God's message by the very system established to ensure consistency in God's message to the world? Are Mormons to believe that public relations professionals are the new prophets, now endowed with the power to speak vicariously for God? Likely not, but the question of communication persists. The prophets are silent, but the Church continues to speak for God with an uninterrupted messaging not unlike a looped recording of Woodruff's wax cylinder testimony. In fact, the entire practice of vocal vicariousness is threatened with bankruptcy when the communication flow is corrupted by Correlation. Most pressing of all, Correlation continues to ask of Mormons the burning acousmatic question: Who is speaking for whom?

I return to *Book of Mormon* in the remainder of this chapter to discuss how the musical rather unsuspectingly captures this communication crisis within Mormonism. It seems prudent to examine how *Book of Mormon* intercepts and redirects the message of Mormonism through satire. In the context of vocal vicariousness, *Book of Mormon* shows how, through interruption, the message of Mormonism can be made different—maybe even improved.

The Mormon Moment

When Mormons first cast their lot with musical theater in 1947 with *Promised Valley*, they did so in part to cash in on whiteness. Their successful integration into American sensibilities came in part through this appropriation of musical theater as wholesome, white, American, assimilationist entertainment. From The Osmonds to the Mormon Tabernacle Choir, Mormon ideals of virtue and (white) propriety were reinforced through the workings of American musical theater. By the millennium, however, Mormons began receiving flak for being too white, too wholesome, too happy. In effect, for many Americans, Mormons just didn't seem real. In 2008 and again in 2012,

154 · CHAPTER 5

presidential hopeful Mitt Romney fulfilled the stereotype many outsiders had of Mormons; his life was so perfect, his offshore accounts so well-stocked, and his hair so perfectly coiffed that people had a hard time relating to him or trusting him. As Paul Reeve has written, Mormons tried so hard to overcome their ethnic branding as not white enough to become, by the late twentieth and early twenty-first centuries, *too* white.

The same might be said for Mormons and musicals. Mormons had patterned their lives and temperaments, their policies and doctrine, after the sensibilities of the musical theater stage a little too well. It became very easy under the spotlight of news media for Mormons to appear like characters cut from a book, or from a musical. As the creators of *Book of Mormon* have remarked, Mormons and musicals just seem to go hand in hand. In fact, *Book of Mormon* was not the first time creators Trey Parker and Matt Stone had tried their hand musically lampooning Mormonism. In 2003 their *South Park* television episode "All About the Mormons" musically dramatized Joseph Smith's First Vision, subsequent visits from the angel Moroni, and Joseph's methods of translating The Book of Mormon using seer stones tucked inside his hat. As off-camera voices narrate the story, the continuous trope "Dum, dum, dum, dum, dum" is eventually revealed to be a homonym for "dumb." The off-camera voices thus are conceptualized as a singing Greek chorus, moralizing the errancy of Smith's claims and the naivety of his early followers.[22] Parker and Stone were picking up on a cultural trait in Mormonism that had by then become prominent and used musical theater to critique Mormon beliefs. In an ongoing effort to use musicals to fit in, Mormons became too good at their own game and now they had to pay for it.

Book of Mormon appeared on Broadway in 2011 and traveled a path eerily similar to the one Mormons charted in the nineteenth century—the show springs up in New York (Broadway), moved to Illinois (Chicago) for an extended run, and then opened the first national tour in the intermountain west (Denver, Colorado). But the bigger story begins several years earlier. The 2008 debacle surrounding Proposition 8 in California—which held in balance the definition of marriage as a union between a man and a woman—catapulted the Mormon Church into the national spotlight when Church leaders encouraged its members to contribute time and resources to the campaign in order to protect traditional conceptions of marriage. The Church reeled from the public outcry against its role in the campaign, and its members suddenly became contestants in a fierce debate over the consequences of unpopular political involvement. When Broadway veteran Marc Shaiman (*Hairspray* [2002] and *Catch Me If You Can* [2009]) heard that Scott Eckern, the artistic director of the nonprofit California Musical Theatre and also a Mormon, had contributed $1,000 to support the campaign against gay marriage, he immediately set to work on a musical portrait of advocacy called *Prop 8: The Musical*. The musical theater community—heavily reliant on gay creators and performers—was infuriated by Eckern's contribution, seeing it as an act of betrayal. Jeffrey Seller, a Broadway producer, was among those who felt outrage: "That a man who makes his living exclusively through the musical theater could do something so hurtful to the community that forms his livelihood is a punch in the stomach."[23] For his part, Eckern eventually resigned from his position at California Musical Theatre and, as a sign of good faith toward the gay community, contributed $1,000 to a gay-rights group. Still, the association between Mormons and Proposition 8 was thick, and Eckern's position thrust musical theater into the mix in a satirical representation of religious infringement on civil rights.

Shaiman wrote *Prop 8: The Musical* in one day, filmed it with a cast of Hollywood regulars, including Jack Black, Neil Patrick Harris, and John C. Reilly, and, through the site funnyordie.com, the video became an instant hit—what Shaiman later called a "viral picket sign." Although the musical is barely over three minutes long, it characterizes the gay community as complacent and naive in the wake of Barack Obama's 2008 presidential election;[24] it also colors religious figures—who are dressed in loosely identifiable religious clothes, the prominent dark suit, white shirt, and tie of Mormon men chief among them—as hateful and scripturally selective in their condemnation of homosexuality. When Jesus appears to the gathered multitude, he condemns the religious zealot's selectivity, telling them that if they are going to pick and choose, they should choose love instead of hate. Finally, Neil Patrick Harris enters the stage and reminds everyone that there is money to be made in lavish gay weddings, which finally unites the two divided groups in a common goal of using the surplus money from gay marriages to bolster the limping American economy.

The drama surrounding Proposition 8 and the Mormon Church did not wane easily. After the ruling on Proposition 8 was overturned in the Ninth Court of Appeals, a new drama unfurled, though this time a staged one. Titled *8*, the play was a direct reenactment of the court proceedings in the case *Perry v. Schwarzenegger*.[25] A Los Angeles performance of the play took place on March 3, 2012, and, as with *Prop 8: The Musical*, featured a lineup of some of the most prominent stars in Hollywood, including George Clooney, Kevin Bacon, Brad Pitt, Jamie Lee Curtis, and John C. Reilly, but also the Tony-nominated actor from *Book of Mormon*, Rory O'Malley. Well known for

156 · CHAPTER 5

his role as Elder McKinley, the closeted missionary who sings of suppressing "gay thoughts" in order to remain worthy in the eyes of the Church, O'Malley provides just one strand connecting the vitriol surrounding Proposition 8 and the crass jocularity of *Book of Mormon*. In fact, given the opening of *Book of Mormon* on Broadway happened precisely three years after Proposition 8 was up for vote, one could consider the parodying of Mormons on stage by a host of gay or gay-allied performers a form of cultural retribution. If the Mormon Church had enough power to sway legislation against the gay community, then the musical theater community could go one better by putting on stage a version of Mormonism where openly gay men could don the label of Mormon missionary, preach a particularly queer gospel of inclusion, and through the magic of musical theater interrupt the message of one of the fastest-growing religions in the country.

The queerness of *Book of Mormon* and its proximity to Proposition 8 points to incongruent values held within Mormonism. It is not without some irony that the Mormon Church found itself defending the ideal of a traditional family given its relationship with polygamy. For that matter, Mormons likewise embody a paradox of performing musical theater for theological purposes while also rejecting out of principle the gay community arguably responsible for much of musical theater's performance and repertoire. This kind of selective absorption of musical theater culture is reflective of how Mormons have responded to and re-appropriated other parts of America culture. The synthesis project that undergirds Mormonism allows members to take what it wants while leaving the rest. This explains how Mormons have been able to leverage the "family-friendly" nature of the musical while minimizing or erasing the "queer" piece of it—even as their own history admits Mormons closer to queerness than to convention. In the hands of Mormons, the musical gets transposed to a distant, sometimes unrecognizable key, which allows Mormons to be *in* but not *of* the musical theater world.

As a result, Mormons themselves may not have been aware of how far their Pollyannaish perceptions of musicals had drifted from the current state of Broadway, which is why when *Book of Mormon* opened on Broadway, Mormons likely were unprepared for the kind of attention the show gave them. The musical is crass, its characters foul mouthed, and its depictions of religious piety irreverent—all qualities Mormons eschew. Mormons immediately distanced themselves from the production yet also found ways to benefit from the attention. The Church bought space in the *Playbill* ("The book is always better," reads one ad). Actual missionaries stood outside the theaters of Times Square and handed out copies of the actual Book of Mormon. The

BOOK OF MORMON AND CORRELATED MORMONISM · 157

Church publicized at least one conversion connected directly to the show.[26] The Church's official response to the musical also comes off as underplaying the jokes being waged at its expense: "The production may attempt to entertain audiences for an evening, but the Book of Mormon as a volume of scripture will change people's lives forever by bringing them closer to Christ."[27] As with their selective appropriation of American culture broadly, Mormons took advantage of the opportunity to spin the unexpected attention in their favor while downplaying or ignoring much of the reason they earned the attention in the first place.

Book of Mormon

In *Book of Mormon*, two dynamic and seemingly incompatible worlds are brought together in resolution. Mormonism—in this show an only somewhat-exaggerated white-bread religion with absurd beliefs and practices, replete with an uncompromising system of rules, conventions, and routines—is the world the principal characters Elder Kevin Price and Elder Arnold Cunningham represent and promote. This oddball missionary duo gets transplanted from suburban America to a remote village in Uganda, where they find themselves in a ludicrously challenging environment. A warlord runs the village they are assigned to evangelize, a severe AIDS epidemic has led villagers to take unmentionable measures for cure, and female genital mutilation is commonplace. These atrocities—hardly conventional fodder for a successful comedy—are yet so pervasive and outlandish they become the primary jokes for the show, discomfiting the dumbfounded Mormon missionaries while also framing life in Africa as a lesson in grit and hard luck. Elders Price and Cunningham, along with other Mormon missionaries in the area, enter Uganda with a naively optimistic proselytizing and colonizing agenda; the story becomes a musical, however, in the ways the missionaries are themselves changed in the process and the Ugandans are converted to American musical theater—a clever but suitable stand-in for Mormonism.

As I have argued throughout this book, the Mormon faith is distinctly a performative one, a characteristic the non-Mormon creators clued in to when structuring the show. In fact, part of what makes the otherwise screwball *Book of Mormon* characters so engaging, and even compelling, is that, like the actors on stage, actual Mormon missionaries are also performing a role, wearing a costume and often sporting a larger-than-life optimism with carefully scripted lines. Real Mormons are also quite fond of musical theater which, along with *Star Wars*, *Lord of the Rings*, and other vanguards of popular culture, also informs the worldview of Elders Price and Cunningham. Given the unique Mormon preoccupation with musicals, I would even argue that musical theater *is* the language of Mormonism. Therefore it seems reasonable that *Book of Mormon* features moments when the characters are compelled to actually vocalize not as characters in a show but as real Mormons might do.

One example of this last point is Elder Price's eleventh-hour song of renewed faith, "I Believe." Inasmuch as Mormonism is a pastiche of religious tenets, the *Book of Mormon* is a pastiche of several iconic musical theater tropes and tunes. "I Believe" is no exception. First of all, the five-note motif on the lyric "I am a Mormon" is lifted directly from the opening fanfare of Crawford Gates's music for the Hill Cumorah Pageant (example 7). The moment of Elder Price's great testament is framed by a familiar motif of Mormon musical and theatrical tradition, placing his testimony squarely within the realm of sincere, authentic Mormon conviction.

The amount of musical allusion in *Book of Mormon* also hints at a different kind of vicariousness. By alluding to other musical theater characters well known to theater enthusiasts, *Book of Mormon* creators create a space where new character identities are constructed using older material, in a way consistent with the metamusical strategies of other postmillennial shows. Just prior to that line, the orchestra pulsates with the same energy of Rodgers and Hammerstein's musical as Elder Price sings:

> It was s'pposed to be all so exciting,
> to be teaching of Christ 'cross the sea.
> But I allowed my faith to be shaken.
> Oh, what's the matter with me?

This verse and its musical language are obviously modeled on *The Sound of Music* (see examples 8 and 9). This allusion places Elder Price in dramatic

Example 7: Five-note motif in "I Believe" (top), from *Book of Mormon* (2011). Music and lyrics by Trey Parker, Robert Lopez, and Matt Stone, quoting the introductory brass fanfare (transposed and reduced) from the Hill Cumorah Pageant (bottom). Music by Crawford Gates.

Example 8: Excerpt of "I Believe," from *Book of Mormon* (2011). Music and lyrics by Trey Parker, Robert Lopez, and Matt Stone.

Example 9: Excerpt of "I Have Confidence," from the 20th Century Fox film *The Sound of Music* (1965). Music and lyrics by Richard Rodgers.

proximity to Maria and insists on a similarity between mounting courage to leave the sheltering comforts of convent life to govern a full house of children and the bravery necessary to reclaim one's faith. Both Maria and Price are in essence earnestly seeking a real, lived experience of their faith by stepping outside the borders of religious doxy and into the realm of religious praxy.

These moments from *The Sound of Music* and *Book of Mormon* also offer a realistic glimpse into the characters' actual practice. It is not difficult to

160 · CHAPTER 5

imagine a gifted singer like the real Maria von Trapp singing, even to her-self, in moments of anxiety as she "seeks the courage [she] lacks." Likewise, the rest of "I Believe" is built around the formulations Mormons regularly attend to when bearing testimony. The frequency of the words "I believe," followed by a series of what seems to be an increasingly bizarre and humor-ous litany of dogma, is in truth a real matter of practice an actual Mormon missionary would engage, in this case as a buffer against encroaching doubt. This wording is also directly related to the "Credo" of the Catholic Mass and the Catholic and Protestant recitation of the Apostles Creed, further link-ing the vocal practices of both Elder Price and Maria. Therefore, the act of singing "I Believe," just like the act of singing "I Have Confidence," should be understood as a moment when the character steps through the conven-tions of the musical stage and "sings for himself," as it may be—singing not only as a musical character, but also as a real expression built from necessity and experience in that moment. It is here that the singing-as-community of *Promised Valley* Mormonism moves to singing-as-practice of modern Mor-monism.

As this example illustrates, the creators of *Book of Mormon* build pastiche through frequent allusion. These moments point to other musicals, but in doing so they also suggest connections between *Book of Mormon* charac-ters and characters elsewhere in the musical theater canon. Deciphering the coded language of pastiche and allusion has always required a nuanced knowledge of the source material. Musicologists such as Charles Rosen, Ray-mond Knapp, Peter Burkholder, and Christopher Alan Reynolds have done important work in understanding musical allusions, especially in music of the nineteenth century.[28] Their work demonstrates that breaking the code of musical allusion requires less the mechanistic mind of a Turing machine than a careful and considered understanding of the rich expressive vocabu-lary of which such allusions were a part. Musical and motivic resemblances are not quite the same thing as a musical allusion; Charles Rosen warns that it is "only too easy to produce uninteresting triviality by finding similar or identical motifs in unrelated passages, particularly in tonal music."[29] Christo-pher Alan Reynolds makes clear the difference between allusion and resem-blances in his definition of allusion as "an intentional reference to another work made by means of a resemblance that affects the meaning conveyed to those who recognize it."[30] It is not enough for a work or phrase or motive to sound like something else; such compositional bumping-of-elbows is an inevitability within a tightly controlled and finite harmonic and melodic vocabulary, as Rosen points out. Rather, musicologists are more interested

BOOK OF MORMON AND CORRELATED MORMONISM · 161

in the intentionality behind allusions—the conventions and expectations for allusions held by nineteenth-century composers and audiences that continue to charm, delight, frustrate, mystify, and stupefy listeners still today—and how uncovering those intentions can open up new possibilities for listening to music from this era.

The same motive can be applied to *Book of Mormon*. Reynolds demarcates various functions of musical allusions into two broad groups—*assimilative* and *contrastive*, the difference being either "an allusion can accept the meaning of the earlier text or use it to create another meaning."[31] He chooses a dual theoretical skeleton on which to flesh out these two groups of musical allusions. Bakhtin's theories of double-voicedness prove a useful ancillary for Reynolds's grouping, as he takes a clever reading of Bakhtin's "unidirectional" and "varidirectional" discourse to underline the functions of assimilative and contrastive allusions. Inasmuch as "unidirectional" discourse supports the original meaning of a text and "varidirectional" discourse parodies or ironizes the original meaning, so too does Reynolds argue that composers used these two forms of allusion to work either with or against the original source material. Second, and less pervasively than Bakhtin, Reynolds keeps in hand Johan Huizinga's theories of play to capitalize on how composers and audiences perhaps understood musical metaphor as a form of play. Etymologically, "allude" means "to play on," and Reynolds's reading of Huizinga's playfulness acts as a convenient drop cloth to collect musical moments that otherwise fall off the page unnoticed and undeciphered.

As seen in examples 10 and 11, the piano motif in the opening bars of "Sal Tlay Ka Siti," sung by Ugandan dreamer Nabulungi, allude to the introduction of Audrey's song "Somewhere That's Green" from *Little Shop of Horrors* (1982, Off-Broadway). Nabulungi sings of a place where she can live a life of dignity; having now met the Mormon missionaries, she understands that place to be Salt Lake City, Utah. Similarly, Audrey feels trapped in the slums of Skid Row and fantasizes in her song about leading an idyllic life someplace else. Both songs share a sentiment about hoping for a better life in the suburbs, and both characters are humorously naive and somewhat misinformed about the prospects of life elsewhere.

The musical allusion, however, offers listeners the opportunity to hear the specificity of Audrey in Nabulungi. We are to understand that the dreams of an Audrey are not all that dissimilar from those of a Nabulungi, though they are oceans and worlds apart. Not only that, but Nabulungi's allusive singing places her within the narrative and musical structures of musical theater. Until this point, Nabulungi has only been heard singing as an African and

Example 10: Piano introduction to "Sal Tlay Ka Siti," from *Book of Mormon* (2011). Music and lyrics by Trey Parker, Robert Lopez, and Matt Stone.

Example 11: Piano Introduction to "Somewhere That's Green," from *Little Shop of Horrors* (1982, Off-Broadway). Music by Alan Menken and lyrics by Howard Ashman.

like an African ("Hasa Diga Eebowai"); it is after she learns about the Mormon prophet Joseph Smith from the missionaries that she reveals hints of assimilation and conversion by singing the language of musical theater. "I Believe" and "Sal Tlay Ka Siti" thus help frame Elder Price and Nabulungi as representative members of these opposing worlds.

The climax of the show, however, demonstrates musically how the Mormons and Africans can be united through the unique way Elder Cunningham miscommunicates the message he is sent to deliver. Using a grab bag of Mormon theology and popular culture references, Elder Cunningham manages to convert several of the villagers who are taken in by his evocative, nonsensical stories. In true Mormon fashion, Nabulungi organizes a musical pageant that visiting Mormon leaders will attend. Like the Hill Cumorah Pageant that was quoted in "I Believe," the villager's pageant also dramatizes the story of Joseph Smith's encounter with God. Yet in "Joseph Smith American Moses" the Africans perform not the standardized history of those events but rather the absurdity of Elder Cunningham's religious teachings, which now include a wizard angel Moroni, a visit from the Starship Enterprise, and a magical "fuck frog" that Smith uses to cure AIDS. The ridiculous pageant serves as a catalyst for the final reconciliation of the show and demonstrates how the act of singing and performing can bridge the world of Africa with that of America via Mormonism.

"Joseph Smith American Moses" shares some characteristics with another pageant within a musical, "Small House of Uncle Thomas" from *The King and I*. These two scenes are both narrated by a female character in broken English (with mispronunciations of American geography such as Tuptim's "Oheeo" and Nabulungi's "Oopstate New York"), and their eagerness to engage an unfamiliar language is second only to a desire to perform in the styles of American musical theater. Indeed, Anna gives Tuptim a copy of *Uncle Tom's Cabin* as part of her sustained effort to civilize her Siamese hosts, and Nabulungi is being taught Mormonism for similar reasons. And because both women show signs of their assimilation by modeling American practices of the theater, Tuptim and Nabulungi are similarly motivated to put on a show. In *The King and I*, Tuptim sees within the story of *Uncle Tom's Cabin* a metaphor for her oppression and uses the performance to stage a performative coup against the king. She misunderstands, or perhaps takes too literally, Harriet Beecher Stowe's title, leaving her audience instead with the droll phrase, "Small House of Uncle Thomas."

Raymond Knapp relates "Small House of Uncle Thomas" to the story of Moses, arguing that, fundamentally, both stories are about escaping slavery.[32] Similarly, Nabulungi's pageant title "Joseph Smith American Moses" mixes up the Mormon honorifics (it is Brigham Young, not Joseph Smith, who is commonly referred to as "the American Moses") but in doing so makes obvious how her story connects to that of Tuptim.[33] Nabulungi is attempting a different kind of escape—from a village terrorized by warlords and overrun with an AIDS epidemic—but the stakes for her are just as high. Nabulungi seems sincerely arrested by the message of the pageant and, along with the other villagers, is very much enjoying the performance. In fact, both Tuptim and Nabulungi latch onto the escapist quality of musical drama, playing out through the pageant a brazen political critique and tying up loose ends with musical theater's typical happy ending. "Joseph Smith American Moses" therefore takes on the musical qualities of what the show has heretofore designated as "African"—drum-inflected and upbeat rhythms with prominent call-and-response sections, also allusions to another musical repeatedly spoofed in the show, *The Lion King* (1997)—with the lyrics supporting a version of Mormonism steeped in folklore, Western cultural idioms, and unseemly superstition.

When the appalled Mormon leaders disband the missionaries and revoke the villager's memberships as punishment—likely for not "performing" Mormonism correctly—Elder Price realizes the potency of this new eclectic Mormonism and applauds Elder Cunningham's unique ability to mix up his religion. Thus the pageant acts as a "marriage" not only between Mormons and Africans, musically uniting the sounds of Africa with the sentiments of

164 · CHAPTER 5

bastardized Mormonism, but also the worlds of orthodoxy and modernity—the takeaway message at the end of the musical being that the opportunity to self-fashion the religion's myths to meet the needs of the Africans will provide the villagers a system of grace and benevolence from which they may be able to improve their livelihoods, and that traditional religious communities like Mormonism must embrace change and flexibility in order to survive.

As Matt Stone relates, *Book of Mormon* prods the necessarily ridiculous aspects of faith that, by definition, do not assume plausibility. "There's a catharsis in being able to really laugh at some of the goofier ideas of religion, without necessarily laughing at the people practicing them," says Stone. "I think it feels good to in some ways acknowledge that certain aspects of religion are just silly. But whatever anybody's religion is, we should be able to laugh at it and at the same time understand that we should accept people who believe and have faith, without dismissing their lives as unserious." Stone later adds that he and Parker "never wanted the musical to pretend it had any answers." "We wanted to be funny," he said, "and put on great numbers and get some of our ideas out there."[34] Stone and Parker's satire, in other words, derives easily from the subject matter provided by Mormonism, its truthfulness self-evident and readily apparent. In a grand act of cultural vicariousness, the show speaks on behalf of Mormonism, showing Mormons and non-Mormons alike an example of what happens when Mormonism gets synthesized with other ideologies—a practice similar to how Mormonism itself arose, but which has been absent from Mormonism since the mid-twentieth century. The same attributes that once made the Church easy fodder for faith-promoting Mormon musicals have become digested by popular culture and excreted as a foul-mouthed inversion of itself. How else could Michael Hicks have written that "even without the words, the show would feel like a Mormon musical"?[35]

Voice Interrupted

The Mormonism that *Book of Mormon* moralizes with and against is one that exists today only in principle. The process of Correlation ensures that Mormonism cannot expand beyond its current scope. The prophets may continue to speak, but they cannot speak beyond the dictates of a Correlation committee. Joseph Smith envisioned a religion that could synthesize all the world's truths into "one great whole" as part of what became known as "the fulness of the gospel." The only way to sort truth from untruth in this great mixture of affirmations was sensual, meaning the receiver of truths must attune himself to how his body resonates with the message. When Oliver

Cowdery attempted to translate The Book of Mormon himself, Joseph received a revelation that established the method for sensing specks of truth awash in a great sea of philosophical musings.

> But, behold, I say unto you, that you must study it out in your mind; then you must ask me if it be right, and if it is right I will cause that your bosom shall burn within you; therefore, you shall feel that it is right. But if it be not right you shall have no feelings, but you shall have a stupor of thought that shall cause you to forget the thing which is wrong; therefore, you cannot write that which is sacred save it be given you from me.[36]

The takeaway from Cowdery's lesson (other than his failure to translate a single word of the manuscript) is that the body can detect truth as it *senses* it. This theory suggests a seamless, unvaried reception of truth from person to person and, significantly, it is a stupor of thought—an *interruption*—that shows the receiver there are errors in his thinking.

Nonetheless, Correlated Mormonism presumes all hearers of the Mormon message will listen and feel the message in more or less the same way. An increasingly persistent message within Mormonism is that universality of perception is baked into The Book of Mormon itself, even as the prophets and Mormon laity alike model universality of voice. The final pages of The Book of Mormon feature what has been dubbed "Moroni's promise," a tribute to the perceptive power given to all people. The prophet Moroni asks future hearers and readers of The Book of Mormon to "ask God, the Eternal Father, in the name of Christ, if these things are not true; and if ye shall ask with a sincere heart, with real intent, having faith in Christ, he will manifest the truth of it unto you, by the power of the Holy Ghost. And by the power of the Holy Ghost ye may know the truth of all things."[37]

The Mormon Church has instructed missionaries to use these verses as a litmus test for investigators to gain a testimony of the literal truthfulness *of the book itself.* The differences between the medium and message in this case are slight but important. Accepting the *message* as true does not mean the receiver must accept the stories surrounding the book's inception as true, nor does it mean readers must necessarily accept every word of the book as infallible. On the other hand, if those verses are meant to confirm the truthfulness of The Book of Mormon as a *medium* for that message, then the book and its surrounding genesis story are what make the message meaningful and true.

I suggest that Correlated Mormonism has made the former belief nearly impossible to sustain in the light of the latter. The assumptions of universality

166 · CHAPTER 5

that have been read into Moroni's promise suggest that Mormonism is a singular, streamlined, and unfaltering message preserved from the beginning of humanity. Under this ideology humans are presumably hard-wired with the perceptive ability to sense truth in black-and-white terms: Moroni's *promise*, by definition, insists that all people can know its truthfulness. Therefore, The Book of Mormon is either true or it is not. A more nuanced understanding or appreciation of The Book of Mormon or its message is made suspect under these provisions. Mormons who find comfort in the message of redemption, love, and tranquility within The Book of Mormon but who are skeptical of it being an ancient script hewn from the hillside by a frontier prophet have found it difficult to navigate within a Correlated sociality that has made message and medium one and the same. Moreover, Mormons who are willing to accept the message of Mormonism as true but who distance themselves from the Church and its policies also find themselves in an almost indefensible position.

The multivalent message of Joseph Smith's Mormonism, then, has lost stock over the last several decades to a more powerful expression of Mormonism, one that recognizes only exact replications of itself. In all things, from ideology to voice to dress to behavior, Mormons find themselves replicating a standard established through Correlation. This exacting standard insists that Mormonism isn't Mormonism unless practiced the ways verified through the Correlation committee. And, as I have argued here, the message of Mormonism must necessarily be communicated the exact same way in all settings, or else it loses its standing as "official." For all the clamor of Correlation's homogenized message, Mormons today may have difficulty sensing the promised stupor of thought, the interrupting gesture signaling wildly that something is amok.

Book of Mormon makes an intriguing claim about contemporary Mormonism—that only through such disruption can the Mormon message become meaningful again. From the opening number of the show, Elder Cunningham is obvious in his departures from the Mormon norm. During Elder Cunningham's missionary training, officials must repeatedly correct him, admonishing him to stop "making things up." Elder Cunningham later admits that he is a pathological liar and has never read The Book of Mormon. This certainly goes a long way in explaining why and how the Ugandans present a confused version of the conventional Mormon narrative during the pageant.

Although humorously out of step, Elder Cunningham's fusion of mythologies is in truth a modern version of Joseph's synthesis project to unite all truths from all corners. This is all the more convincing when Elder

Cunningham's efforts pay off: the Ugandans discover through his synthesis of Mormonism and popular culture a meaningful narrative for constructively dealing with their reality in less harmful or demeaning ways. In providing the villagers with a powerful new mythology, and along the way upsetting the Mormon narrative through a combination of ignorance and ingenuity (hence his *cunning* nature), Elder Cunningham actually highlights the limitations of the singular, seamless message within Correlated Mormonism. Like Joseph Smith before him, Elder Cunningham is the American antihero who is able to take a narrative perceived as broken and reconstitute it in a synthesized form with broader appeal. Arguably, at the end of the show Elder Cunningham takes over the "role" originally played by Joseph; like Joseph, he is an unlikely understudy who becomes the star. In the end it matters little that Elder Cunningham is peddling the Ugandans an unauthorized version of Mormon mythology. As John Updike reminds us about myths and beliefs, "The crucial question isn't Can you prove it? but Does it give us a handle on the reality that otherwise would overwhelm us?"[38]

* * *

In effect, Elder Cunningham's version of Mormonism interrupts the flow of Correlated Mormonism. It is possible that such an interruption, the stupor of thought, is exactly what Mormonism needs to remain relevant. This essentially upholds Kierkegaard's point that only through *indirect* communication with the divine can a person come to have faith in God. In an innovative reading of Levinas's study of ethics, Amit Pinchevski argues that *lapses* in communication, not successful transmission, actually create a space for an ethical system of communication. He suggests that what is typically understood as effective communication, when ideas are translated from one person to another without interruption or misunderstanding, withholds the possibility for the speaker and listener to understand the Other. Instead, interruption "is an intrinsic and positive condition of communication, indeed of ethical communication, and this marks the beginning rather than the end of generosity and compassion."[39] In his Levinasian retelling of the story of Babel, for example, Pinchevski sees Babel as an example of God's benevolence rather than His vengeance; the collapsing tower "caused the people of Babel to retract their gazes from the tower to one another's faces, acknowledging, maybe for the first time, that they were different, finite, separate—a dialogue of baffled faces."[40]

Thus Elder Cunningham's interruption of Mormonism's singular narrative creates a space where a true "dialogue of baffled faces" can take place,

168 · CHAPTER 5

where multiple voices and concerns can be made known, and where various ways of sounding can strengthen the message, rather than being perceived as weakening it. He makes Mormonism relevant to the Ugandans by unknowingly bastardizing its core doctrines. As much as this might seem perverse to many Mormons, "Joseph Smith American Moses" also serves as an example of how vocal perversity can sometimes be just what is needed to enliven a religious message—in fact, such was the project of Joseph Smith.

It could even be said that *Book of Mormon* does Mormonism better than Mormons can do Mormonism. The faith today is dominated by a machinery that recognizes interruption as dissent—and dissent as intolerable—and is therefore bound to constantly repeat itself, like the ghostly echoes of Woodruff's recorded testimony. Ironically, interrupting and mixing up Correlated messaging may make the message Mormonism intends much clearer and more meaningful to both Mormons and non-Mormons alike. Interruption or misunderstanding allows words to get stuck and forces the speaker to take a different approach with the receiver's complex identity in mind. It makes sacred the gently cocked head of confusion, the translator's thick tongue; through such communicative lapses Mormonism can reclaim compassionate speech and intentional language, what Charles Hirschkind calls an "ethical soundscape."[41] As it did with Elder Cunningham in *Book of Mormon*, it may well be that the interrupted voice speaks louder and farther than the ceaseless message Correlation espouses.

Epilogue

Musical theater has thrived in Mormon culture for generations and will likely continue to do so. What effects the impervious satire of musical theater exacts upon Mormonism remains a matter unresolved. As Mormonism confronts its satirical attackers, it does so at a serious disadvantage given that the medium of musical theater seems so expertly chosen to cause the most damage. Inasmuch as musical theater has been for Mormons a balm and entertainment, a means of self-expression as well as identity, it has lately taken the shape of the legendary horse left outside the gates of Troy. The horse was the emblem of the city, Odysseus remembered, and could easily deceive with its flattery. If Mormon culture had an emblem, then perhaps it would be the theater and, like the horse of the Trojans, a reflection of its pride. Destruction need not ensue, of course. It is the favorable environment for satire that chokes true discourse—discourse not left awash in a sea of falsely dichotomized conceptions of belief and doubt. "There was belief before there was doubt," Jennifer Michael Hecht has eloquently argued, "but only after there was a culture of doubt could there be the kind of active believing that is at the center of modern faiths."[1]

Mormons have come full circle with musical theater, it seems. Once serving as a venue of oppression and cruelty toward Mormons, musicals became a source of control over the discourse surrounding whiteness and American acceptance, only to again mock the religion and its adherents. The story of Mormons and musical theater might well be a fitting encapsulation of the American interception of modernity. Musicals and Mormons have come a long way since their rootedness in Jacksonian principles; their regional genesis quickly fanned out to become immense global expressions of American values. In the meantime, America changed. What was once ideal and reputable has become goofy and outmoded, and Broadway and Mormonism have been forced to pay for their naive pasts with cynicism and guffaws. The musical theater industry opted to change its image by aggressively appropriating popular music genres, such as rock (*Jesus Christ Superstar*), hip hop (*Hamilton*), and country (*Hands on a Hard Body*). Mormon leaders have chosen a more passive response, having faith that stasis will eventually reveal the radical qualities of Mormon ideals. As a result, musical theater has begun to escape Mormonism as its once-familiar venue for practicing its theology of voice. *Book of Mormon* is one example of this fallout—its message both a condemnation and an invitation to become something better. In the end, the tale of Mormons and musicals is another story about how new ways of *sounding* create opportunities for other ways of *living*.

Mark Twain's short story from 1876, "A Literary Nightmare" (later published as "Punch, Brothers, Punch"), humorously depicts a situation where a persistent message—in his case, a rhyme: "Punch, brothers! punch with care! / Punch in the presence of the passenjare!"—haunts the narrator's thoughts until passed on to another unsuspecting victim within earshot. The troubling ear worm infects the minds of other travelers and friends. Finally rid of the problem himself, the narrator takes his friend (who is now beset with the malady) to a university and "made him discharge the burden of his persecuting rhymes into the eager ears of the poor, unthinking students. How is it with them, now? The result is too sad to tell." Only through regurgitating the offending material could the troubled mind find rest from the incessant message. Twain concludes with a warning to his readers: "If you should come across those merciless rhymes, to avoid them—avoid them as you would a pestilence."

Such a ludicrous, yet sympathetic, story seems fitting for our conclusion. The persistent, troubling narrative espoused by the Mormon Church since Correlation has prevented the possibilities for parallel or competing narratives in Mormonism to survive in the open. The theological underpinnings that guided vocal vicariousness from Mormonism's inception have been put asunder by a domineering policy machine that suggests seamless messaging will ensure relevance.

As I have been suggesting in this book, however, that ideology of communication undermines the vitality of a religion built upon a foundation of dusty voices speaking on behalf of a people long forgotten.

Their quiet whispers invite us to listen with greater care.

Notes

Prologue

1. A few notes about wording. Throughout this book, I refer to Joseph Smith by his first name only. This is in keeping with common Mormon practice of speaking of the founding prophet as "Joseph" or "Brother Joseph" and in order to distinguish between him and the many other Smiths in Church leadership. I use "Mormon" in reference to members of the Church of Jesus Christ of Latter-day Saints in order to be as inclusive of various Mormon beliefs and practices as possible, including those that predate the establishment of the LDS Church and those that the mainstream Church does not condone. Finally, for clarity, any reference to *Book of Mormon* the musical will be italicized, and any reference to the sacred text The Book of Mormon will not.

2. Qtd. in Brodie, *No Man Knows*, 211.

3. Staker, *Waiting for World's End*, 305.

4. *Juvenile Instructor*, November 15, 1895, 700.

5. *Journal of Discourses*, 102.

6. Lewis, *American Adam*, 5.

7. Ibid.

8. Hawthorne, *House of the Seven Gables*, 220.

9. See D. Michael Quinn, "Brigham Young: Man of the Spirit," *Ensign*, August 1977.

10. Joseph spoke these words in May 1843, almost one year before his death: "I am like a huge, rough stone rolling down from a high mountain; and the only polishing I get is when some corner gets rubbed off by coming in contact with something else, striking with accelerated force against religious bigotry, priestcraft, lawyer-craft, doctor-craft, lying editors, suborned judges and jurors, and the authority of perjured executives, backed by mobs, blasphemers, licentious and corrupt men and

women—all hell knocking off a corner here and a corner there. Thus I will become a smooth and polished shaft in the quiver of the Almighty, who will give me dominion over all and every one of them, when their refuge of lies shall fail, and their hiding place shall be destroyed, while these smooth-polished stones with which I come in contact become marred." See *Discourse to Saints*, May 1843; *Documentary History of the Church* 5:401.

11. Marx, *Machine in the Garden*, 43.

12. Steinberg, *Lost Book of Mormon*, 8.

13. Smith, *Listening*, 7.

Introduction

1. Although often attributed to Twain, this phrase has an unclear provenance. For a more historical examination of the quotation, see Garson O'Toole's investigative work on *Quote Investigator*, http://quoteinvestigator.com/2015/06/13/we.

2. Genesis 1:3. All biblical references are taken from the King James translation, which is the official version used by the Mormon Church.

3. The concept of the acousmatic voice or sound originated with Pierre Schaeffer, who used it to describe how Pythagoras's disciples listened to his voice through a curtain. In Schaeffer's words, the acousmatic refers to "a sound that one hears without seeing the causes behind it." See Schaeffer, *Traité des Objets Musicaux*, 91. The field of voice studies is rapidly growing and interdisciplinary. Notable texts in voice and sound studies include Eidsheim, *Sensing Sound*; Kane, *Sound Unseen*; and Cavarero, *For More than One Voice*.

4. Carson, *Glass, Irony, and God*, 119.

5. Joseph Smith History 1:15–17.

6. Schmidt, *Hearing Things*, 11.

7. Ibid.

8. Doctrine and Covenants 1:38, italics added.

9. Ihde, *Listening and Voice*, 173.

10. Cavarero, *For More Than One Voice*, 21.

11. McMurray, "Voice Crying from the Dust," 16.

12. Matthew 7:20.

13. Steiner, *After Babel*, 45.

14. Mavrodes, *Revelation in Religious Belief*, 25.

15. Ibid., 33.

16. Woolf, *Death of the Moth*, 195.

17. See Bial, *Playing God*, and Bradley, *You've Got to Have a Dream*.

18. Stone and Parker interview.

19. Sontag, "Notes on Camp" in *Against Interpretation*, 275.

20. Ehat, "Who Shall Ascend?," 49.

21. McDannell, *Material Christianity*, 2.

22. Bradley, *You've Got to Have a Dream*, 3.

NOTES TO INTRODUCTION AND CHAPTER 1 · 173

23. Ibid., 108.

24. Sylvan, *Traces of the Spirit*, 3–4.

25. See Knapp, *Performance of Personal Identity*, 141–50; Stowe's chapter "Jesus on Broadway" in *No Sympathy for the Devil*; and Most, *Making Americans* and *Theatrical Liberalism*.

26. See Chapman, "Knowing Your Audience"; Bringardner, "Politics of Region and Nation," 228.

27. Wolf, "Theatre as Social Practice," 1.

28. Wollman, *Theater Will Rock*, 6.

29. Qtd. in *Teachings of Presidents of the Church: Brigham Young* (1997): 14–20.

30. Park, "Early Mormon Patriarchy," 185.

31. Saxton, "Blackface Minstrelsy," 4.

32. Durkheim, *Elementary Forms*, 225–26.

Chapter 1. "Come, Listen to a Prophet's Voice, and Hear the Word of God"

1. Cox, *Fire From Heaven*, 87.

2. Qtd. in Parley P. Pratt, *The Latter-Day Saints' Millennial Star* 18 (1856): 373. Following the apostasy of second counselor William Law in 1844 and Joseph's death a few months later, Rigdon was the only surviving member of the First Presidency and therefore arguably the Church's legal heir.

3. Mark 1:11.

4. According to D. Michael Quinn's history of folk magic in Mormonism, Joseph's whistling speech would have been a sign of his astrological vocal identity. Quinn writes, "Persons such as Smith, born in the sign of Capricorn, were also expected by astrologists to be 'whistling in their delivery and speech, though otherwise quick and voluble enough.' As a result of a chipped tooth during a mob attack in 1832, Smith indeed 'had a slight whistle in his speech' throughout the last decade of his life." Quinn, *Early Mormonism*, 64.

5. Connor, *Dumbstruck*, 23.

6. For an extensive record by witnesses to Young's transfiguration, see Jorgensen, "Mantle of the Prophet."

7. Qtd. in Van Wagoner, "Making of a Mormon Myth," 179n77.

8. Ibid., 178–79.

9. Wood, "Evangelical America," 369.

10. Ibid., 369.

11. Connor, *Dumbstruck*, 36.

12. Steinberg, *Lost Book of Mormon*, 7.

13. *Authentic History of Remarkable Persons*, 3.

14. The Aaronic Priesthood, so named for Moses's brother Aaron, is the first set of priesthood offices in Mormonism, preparatory to the Melchizedek Priesthood, as was held by Abraham's ecclesiastical leader, Melchizedek. In ancient times, the

174 · NOTES TO CHAPTER 1

Aaronic Priesthood attended to traditional priestly duties and were almost exclusively associated with the tribe of Levi. According to Joseph and Cowdery, John the Baptist—who was a descendent of the tribe of Levi—appeared to them both along the banks of the Susquehanna River and conferred the priesthood to Cowdery, who then gave it to Joseph. See Joseph Smith—History, 1:68–72.

15. E. D. Howe first put this theory forward in 1834. The Spalding-Rigdon theory suggests The Book of Mormon was plagiarized from an unpublished manuscript written by Soloman Spalding in the first decades of the nineteenth century. As the story goes, Rigdon stole the manuscript and worked with Joseph Smith and Oliver Cowdery to write The Book of Mormon.

16. Alva Amasa Tanner, "His Confession: The Overstreet Letter" [pamphlet]. Church History Library.

17. Kreiman and Sidtis, *Foundations of Voice Studies*, 247.

18. 1 Nephi 4:20, 21.

19. Steinberg, *Lost Book of Mormon*, 19.

20. LaBelle, *Lexicon of the Mouth*, 2.

21. Qtd. in *Teachings of Presidents of the Church: Joseph Smith* (2011), 468.

22. McMurray, "Voice Crying from the Dust," 10.

23. Qtd. in "The Wentworth Letter," *Ensign* (July 2002).

24. Esplin, "Church as Broadcaster," 30.

25. See Most, "Jews, Theatricality, and Modernity" in *Theatrical Liberalism*.

26. 2 Corinthians 11:13, 14.

27. Ephesians 6:11.

28. Bagley, *Blood of the Prophets*, 42.

29. See Mason, *Mormon Menace*, 38–44.

30. Peters, *Speaking into the Air*, 71.

31. Qtd. in ibid., 71.

32. Kempis, *Imitation of Christ*, 1.

33. Lewis, *Mere Christianity*, 196.

34. Luhrmann, *When God Talks Back*.

35. Shlovsky, "Art as Technique," 12.

36. Matthew 18:3.

37. Matthew 5:48.

38. 3 Nephi 27:27.

39. John Durham Peters relates Jesus's "wasteful act" of sacrificing himself for the entire planet with the dissemination style Jesus used to communicate his gospel. See Peters, *Speaking into the Air*, 55.

40. As qtd. in "I Have a Question," *Ensign* (February 1982).

41. *Theatre Manual* (1983), 97.

42. Bell, *Road Show*, 110.

43. Ibid., 112.

44. Frost uses "oversound" in his poem "Never Again Would Bird's Song Be the Same" to refer to Eve's "tone of meaning but without the words."

NOTES TO CHAPTERS 1 AND 2 · 175

45. Qtd. in Walker, "Dust-Covered Testimonies," 2.

46. Qtd. in Kittler, *Gramophone, Film, Typewriter*, 72.

47. See Wilkinson, "A Voice From the Past: How a Physicist Resurrected the Earliest Recordings." *New Yorker*, May 19, 2014.

48. *The Twilight Zone*. "Long Distance Call." Directed by James Sheldon. Written by Charles Beaumont and William Idelson. March 31, 1961. *The Twilight Zone*. "Night Call." Directed by Jacques Tourneur. Written by Richard Matheson. February 7, 1964.

49. Kittler, *Gramophone, Film, Typewriter*, 36.

50. Pascoe, *Sarah Siddons Audio Files*, 14.

51. Ibid., 101.

52. Connor, *Dumbstruck*, 411.

53. Qtd. in Holzapfel and Smoot, "Wilford Woodruff's 1897 Testimony," 114. Woodruff's testimony regarding Joseph Smith also mirrors the way Joseph translated The Book of Mormon. Joseph used scribes rather than a phonograph, but the method was the same—a recitation of words and syllables captured from the air and inscribed onto pliable material.

54. Harkness, *Songs of Seoul*, 162.

55. Webb, *Divine Voice*, 15.

56. Knowlton, "Belief, Metaphor, and Rhetoric," 26–27.

57. Connor, *Dumbstruck*, 14.

58. Brown, "Sacred Code," 190.

59. Knowlton, "Belief, Metaphor, and Rhetoric," 27.

60. Practicing vocal delivery in public is a double-edged sword, however. As Tom Mould writes, "Frequent revelation signals a righteous person; frequent narration of revelation signals a self-righteous person." Mould, *Still, the Small Voice: Narrative, Personal Revelation, and the Mormon Folk Tradition* (Logan: Utah State University Press, 2011), 68.

61. It goes without saying that this hierarchical ascent is available almost never to nonnative English speakers. This is not to say that Mormons in other parts of the world can't or don't have leadership positions; they do, but not in the top echelons. Dieter F. Uchtdorf, the first nonnative speaker to become an apostle in over one hundred years, makes for a good counterexample. Although he is fluent in English, Uchtdorf reveals his German heritage when he speaks—because of his accent he literally cannot voice Mormonism the "proper" way and thus cannot sound like a Mormon prophet. Uchtdorf's accent may seem benign, but he speaks like no other Mormon prophet alive today. It may be Uchtdorf's inability to sound the prophetic voice that has made him attractive to unorthodox or progressive Mormons.

Chapter 2. *Promised Valley*, Integration, and the Singing Voice

1. Dolar, *Voice and Nothing More*, 30.

2. Qtd. in the *New York Daily Tribune*, December 5, 1865.

3. Ibid.

176 · NOTES TO CHAPTER 2

4. Hansen, "History and Influence," 50.

5. Whitney, *Drama in Utah*, 4.

6. *New York Daily Tribune*, December 5, 1865.

7. Lindsay, *Mormons and the Theatre*, 6–7.

8. Mumford, "Inca Priest."

9. Qtd. in Howard, *Life of Henry Ward Beecher*, 88.

10. Margetts, "Early Theatricals in Utah," 290–91.

11. Mason, *Mormon Menace*.

12. Boyd K. Packer, "The Mantle Is Far, Far Greater than the Intellect," CES Symposium on the Doctrine and Covenants and Church History, August 22, 1981, Brigham Young University.

13. Qtd. in "Lying for the Lord: An Essay," in B. Carmon Hardy, *Solemn Covenant: The Mormon Polygamous Passage* (Urbana: University of Illinois Press, 1992), 368.

14. Doctrine and Covenants 84:52.

15. Hardy, *Solemn Covenant*, 380.

16. Lamar, *Theater in Mormon Life*, 22.

17. "'His Little Widows' An Amusing Show," *New York Times*, May 1, 1917 http://query.nytimes.com/mem/archive-free/pdf?res=990CE7D6153AE433A25752C0A96 39C946696D6CF.

18. Bordman, *Jerome Kern*, 97–98.

19. Knapp and Morris, "Tin Pan Alley Songs," 83.

20. Reeve, *Religion of a Different Color*, 3.

21. Ibid., 262. Original emphasis.

22. Hicks, "Ministering Minstrels," 63.

23. Toni Morrison, "On the Backs of Blacks," *Time*, December 2, 1993.

24. Mauss, *Angel and the Beehive*, 5. This paradoxical sentiment bears resemblance to literary historian Stephen Greenblatt's notion that culture "gestures toward what appear to be opposite things: *constraint* and *mobility*." Paradox also describes what Mormon scholar Terryl Givens has most adamantly defended within the Mormon faith. See Greenblatt, "Culture," 225; Givens, *People of Paradox*.

25. Mauss, *Angel and the Beehive*, 8.

26. Most, *Making Americans*, 1.

27. Ibid., 7.

28. Ibid., 25.

29. Hicks, "Ministering Minstrels," 62.

30. Albert Goldberg, "'Deseret'—A Good Start for Any Year." *Los Angeles Times*, January 2, 1961.

31. Bloom, *American Religion*.

32. Rodgers, *Musical Stages*, 227.

33. The state's legislation charged the Commission "to commemorate the advent of the pioneers into Salt Lake Valley, to portray fittingly the natural resources and scenic wonders of Utah, the prehistoric culture of the west, the development of ir-

NOTES TO CHAPTER 2 · 177

rigation, farming, mining forestry, transportation, culture and the arts." Qtd. from "Utah Centennial Commission (1947)," Utah Department of Administrative Services Division of Archives and Records Service, http://archives.utah.gov/research/agencyhistories/180.html.

34. Correspondence from Utah Centennial Commission production manager Lorin F. Wheelwright to Crawford Gates, May 16, 1947. Crawford Gates Papers, L. Tom Perry Special Collections, Brigham Young University.

35. Jack Goodman, "Colorful Region History Lives Again at Stadium," *Salt Lake Tribune*, July 26, 1947.

36. "Promised Valley," *Salt Lake Tribune*, July 27, 1947.

37. Lowell M. Durham, "Impetus to Culture," *Salt Lake Tribune*, August 3, 1947.

38. *Promised Valley* has maintained a lasting legacy within Mormondom. In 1961 the Mormon Church commissioned "a simplified version of the choral parts, resulting in worldwide performances of both versions in six languages on five continents." CD liner notes for *Promised Valley*, Pacific Publications, 2006.

39. See Glassberg, *American Historical Pageantry*.

40. Correspondence from Arnold Sundgaard to Crawford Gates, April 17, 1947. Crawford Gates Papers, L. Tom Perry Special Collection, Brigham Young University.

41. Gates evidently attempted to write the lyrics to a state song on his own, which Sundgaard rejected out of principle. "My feeling was that it would be confusing to say that it came out of the play. The melody does but the words don't and if people got familiar with those words in advance i[t] would puzzle them to [hear] that melody sung to different words in the play. . . . If your words would fit into the play it would be different but I'm quite sure they won't." Arnold Sundgaard to Crawford Gates, April 17, 1947. Crawford Gates Paper, L. Tom Perry Special Collections, Brigham Young University.

42. O'Leary, "*Oklahoma!*," 144. See also Carter, *Oklahoma!*.

43. Qtd. in Lowell M. Durham, "Musical Notes," *Salt Lake Tribune*, May 25, 1947.

44. "Pioneer Play Stars Arrive," *Deseret News*, July 28, 1947.

45. Jack Goodman, "Colorful Region History Lives Again at Stadium," *Salt Lake Tribune*, July 26, 1947. Lynn Riggs's play *Green Grow the Lilacs* (1930) was also called a "folk-opera," and, as the source for Rodgers and Hammerstein's *Oklahoma!*, may in fact be where Goodman and others saw the comparison.

46. Bitton, *Ritualization of Mormon History*, 181.

47. See Naomi Graber, "Found in Translation: Kurt Weill on Broadway and in Hollywood, 1935–1939," PhD diss., University of North Carolina, Chapel Hill, 2013.

48. *Songs of the Mormons and Songs of the West*, Archive of Folk Song, ed. Duncan Emrich, Library of Congress, 1952.

49. Hicks, "Poetic Borrowing."

50. Doctrine and Covenants 25:11,12.

51. Hicks, *Mormon Tabernacle Choir*, 3. See also Hicks, "Music and Heaven."

52. Hicks, *Mormon Tabernacle Choir*, 121.

178 · NOTES TO CHAPTERS 2 AND 3

53. Carter, "Forging a Sound Citizenry," 12.

54. Ibid., 13.

55. See Pisani, *Imagining Native America*.

56. Celestial marriage is also referred to as "the new and everlasting covenant" in Doctrine and Covenants, 132.

57. There is also an argument to be made that all marriages performed inside Mormon temples are celestial, so that celestial marriages do not necessarily mean plural marriages, but it also does not preclude plural marriages from being sanctioned.

58. Isaiah 52:8.

59. Knapp, *National Identity*, 9.

60. Qtd. in Bradley, *You've Got to Have a Dream*, 73.

61. In an interview with Terry Gross, Parker and Stone reflected on the creative association between Mormons and other forms of whiteness: "We would always say when we're working on either the sets or the costumes or whatever, we'd say: No, make it more Rodgers and Hammerstein. Or make it more Disney. Or make it more Mormon. And they're like: Well, which one is it? And we're like: No, it's all the same word for the same thing." Stone and Parker interview.

Chapter 3. Exoticized Voices, Racialized Bodies

1. Alma 63:5–8.

2. Hokulani Aikau makes this point clear when she writes, "It is within the binary racial logic of *The Book of Mormon* that whiteness comes to be associated with people who possess higher intelligences, who were chosen by God to be leaders, and who were given the responsibility to save souls of the lesser intelligent, non-white peoples of the world." *Chosen People*, 43.

3. Qtd. in ibid., 24.

4. Ibid., 16. She continues on p. 43, "The category of nonwhite—read as black—was thus delineated along a ranking of lineages that distinguished between those who were chosen or were of a 'favored Israelite lineage,' such as American Indians and Polynesians, and those who were beyond salvation, such as people of African descent."

5. Ibid., 43.

6. As I will discuss later, the city of Zion was to be the gathering place for the ten tribes of Israel, while the tribe of Judah was to assemble in Jerusalem. This bi-located power structure during Christ's millennial reign fulfills the prophecy in Isaiah that "out of Zion shall go forth the law, and the word of the Lord from Jerusalem." (Isaiah 2:3). The Book of Mormon offers additional scriptural validation on this point. The prophet Jacob foresaw the destruction of Jerusalem by the Babylonians, noting that "they who shall not be destroyed shall be scattered among all nations. But behold, thus saith the Lord God: When the day cometh that they shall believe in me, that I am Christ, then have I covenanted with their fathers that they shall be restored in the flesh, upon the earth, unto the lands of their inheritance. And it shall come to

NOTES TO CHAPTER 3 · 179

pass that they shall be gathered in from their long dispersion, from the isles of the sea, and from the four parts of the earth." (2 Nephi 10:6–8)

7. Aikau, *Chosen People*, 117.

8. Ibid., 116.

9. Polynesian Cultural Center, http://www.polynesia.com/purpose-and-history.html#.VQiOBEtH3lI.

10. http://www.polynesia.com/evening-show.html#.VQiOTotH3lJ.

11. Ibid.

12. Stack, "Tattoo Dilemma."

13. Trask, *From a Native Daughter*, 192.

14. Aikau, *Chosen People*, 127.

15. Qtd. in McConachie, "Oriental Musicals," 389. Many scholars have pointed out how musicals treat race haphazardly, and not just during the so-called Golden Age. For a small but representative sampling of scholarship on this issue, see Pisani, "'I'm an Indian Too': Playing Indian in Song and on Stage, 1900–1946," in *Imagining Native America in Music*; Warren Hoffman, *The Great White Way: Race and the Broadway Musical* (New Brunswick, N.J.: Rutgers University Press, 2014); Knapp, *National Identity*; and Todd Decker, "'Do You Want to Hear a Mammy Song?' A Historiography of *Show Boat*," *Contemporary Theatre Review* 19, no. 1 (2009): 8–21.

16. See Knapp's discussion of Hammerstein and Stephen Sondheim's differing relationships with America in "Sondheim's America, America's Sondheim," *The Oxford Handbook of Sondheim Studies* (New York: Oxford University Press, 2015).

17. McConachie, "Oriental Musicals," 397.

18. Malcolm Barr, "Choreographer Gives Up Hollywood for Hawaii," *Free Lance-Star* (Fredericksburg, Va.), December 8, 1964.

19. Ibid.

20. 2 Nephi 30:6. This is the original text in The Book of Mormon. In 1981 the wording was changed from "white" to "pure."

21. Eidsheim, "Marian Anderson," 665.

22. For a discussion of Native American depictions in Mormon music, see P. Jane Hafen, "'Great Spirit Listen': The American Indian in Mormon Music," *Dialogue: A Journal of Mormon Thought* 18 (Winter 1985): 133–42.

23. Arrington, *Brigham Young*, 288.

24. Most, *Making Americans*, 3.

25. Articles of Faith 1:10.

26. Ezekiel 37:16–19.

27. Mauss, *All Abraham's Children*, 9.

28. The Mormon construct of Jews as Gentiles does not carry full support in modern Mormonism. Still, scholars both within and outside the Church, as well as Church leaders, have made concessions that, if not today, such perceptions must have existed in some form throughout the history of the Church. Prominent non-Mormon scholar Jan Shipps discusses her introduction to the "Saints-Gentile dichotomy," in

180 · NOTES TO CHAPTER 3

which Mormon labels of inclusion or exclusion—which includes the derogatory term "Jack Mormon" to designate members who distance themselves from the Church through violation of the Word of Wisdom, for example—suggest that "everyone else was Gentile. Everyone . . . Even Jews were Gentiles." See Shipps, *Sojourner in the Promised Land*, 2. Likewise, Mormon scholar Terryl Givens writes, "To insist that Mormons are Christians, but in a sense peculiar to them, is to appropriate the term to their private meaning and to impudently asserts that heresy is orthodoxy, and orthodoxy heresy. Such a move is not difficult for a religion that has long persisted in referring to the Jews as Gentiles." See "'This Great Modern Abomination': Orthodoxy and Heresy in American Religion," in *Mormons and Mormonism: An Introduction to a World Religion*, edited by Eric A. Eliason (Urbana: University of Illinois Press, 2001), 105. Furthermore, Mormon apostle Bruce R. McConkie made the note that "even Jews are Gentiles when they believe not the truth." *Mortal Messiah*, 93.

29. Qtd. in Isenberg, *Tradition!*, 56.

30. Thomas S. Monson, "The Women's Movement: Liberation or Deception?" *Ensign* (January 1971).

31. Monson, "Women's Movement."

32. L. Tom Perry, "The Tradition of a Balanced, Righteous Life," *Ensign* (August 2011). See also Thomas S. Monson, "If Ye Are Prepared Ye Shall Not Fear," October 2004 General Conference; Neal A. Maxwell, "The Tugs and Pulls of the World," October 2000 General Conference; Ardeth G. Knapp, "A Mighty Force for Righteousness," April 1992 General Conference; Elaine S. Dalton, "Arise and Shine Forth," Women's Conference, April 30, 2004; Thomas S. Monson, "Decisions Determine Destiny," CES Fireside, November 6, 2005; Thomas S. Monson, "Faces and Attitudes," *New Era* (September 1977).

33. Jeffrey R. Holland, "Who We Are and What God Expects Us to Do," BYU Devotional, September 15, 1987.

34. Article of Faith 1:13.

35. This line is taken from the Mormon temple endowment ceremony.

36. Email communication with author, April 22, 2015.

37. The anti-Semitic German music critic Rudolph Louis heard strains of Mahler's Jewishness in his scores, writing that Mahler's music "speaks German, but with an accent, with an inflection, and above all, with the gestures of an Eastern, all too Eastern Jew." Francesca Draughon and Raymond Knapp interpret this sentiment to mean that Mahler may have resisted assimilation by preserving some Jewish identity, even if subconsciously, in his music. See Francesca Draughon and Raymond Knapp, "Gustav Mahler and the Crisis of Jewish Identity," *Echo: A Music-Centered Journal* 3, no. 2 (Fall 2001).

38. Qtd. in Bradley, *You've Got to Have a Dream*, 72. Cole Porter learned how to emulate what he heard as Jewish themes in his musical theater songs. Porter is often presumed to have been Jewish, and Rodgers once said that Porter wrote "the most enduring 'Jewish' music," despite the fact that he was an Episcopalian from Indiana. See Rodgers, *Musical Stages*, 88.

NOTES TO CHAPTERS 3 AND 4 · 181

39. Locke, "Broader View," 483.

40. This same trope of conversion and assimilation has been operative for countless "Ethnic Jews" in the United States and abroad, and it played a significant role in the lives of Felix Mendelssohn and, as discussed earlier, Gustav Mahler. For an excellent overview of the Mendelssohns and assimilation, see Sposato, *Price of Assimilation*.

41. Sholom Aleichem is a pseudonym for Sholem Rabinowitz.

42. Doctrine and Covenants 110:11.

43. Doctrine and Covenants 133: 6–8, 12–13.

44. Qtd. in Aikau, *Chosen People*, 7.

45. Qtd. in David B. Galbraith, "Orson Hyde's 1841 Mission to the Holy Land," *Ensign* (October 1991).

46. Ibid.

47. The Book of Moses in The Pearl of Great Price provides a background on this mysterious city that will return from above. The scriptures state that Zion was an actual city on earth, led by a righteous man named Enoch. Enoch and the rest of the city's inhabitants were so righteous, according to the scriptures, that the entire city was taken from the earth and will return in the last days. See Moses 7.

48. Description found on home page of the BYU Jerusalem Center, http://ce.byu.edu/jc/.

49. Taken from Ronald Staheli's speech at BYU, "The Comprehending Soul: Open Minds and Hearts," June 18, 1996.

50. *Kol Ha'Ir*, 8 June 1984.

51. "B.Y.U. in Zion: Trouble for a Mormon Center." *Time* 127, no. 3 (1986): 73.

52. Olsen and Guelke, "Spatial Transgression," 512.

53. Ibid., 513.

54. Ibid., 504.

55. "Mormon Church Apologizes for Jewish Baptisms for the Dead," *Deseret News* February 15, 2012, http://www.deseretnews.com/article/765550827/LDS-Church-apologizes-for-Jewish-baptisms-for-the-dead.html?pg=all.

56. "Mormons Still Baptizing Dead Jews Despite Agreements to End Practice," *Daily Beast*, February 15, 2012, http://www.thedailybeast.com/articles/2012/02/15/mormons-still-baptizing-dead-jews-despite-agreements-to-end-practice.html.

57. John 3:5.

58. Ta-Nehisi Coates, "The First White President," *Atlantic*, October 2017, https://www.theatlantic.com/magazine/archive/2017/10/the-first-white-president-ta-nehisi-coates/537909.

Chapter 4. "I've Heard That Voice Before"

1. Sterne, *Audible Past*, 292.

2. Stanyek and Piekut, "Deadness," 18.

3. Gordon B. Hinckley, "The Marvelous Foundation of Our Faith," General Conference, October 2002.

182 · NOTES TO CHAPTER 4

4. See Brown, *In Heaven as It Is on Earth*. With no archaeological evidence in support of large Book of Mormon–era civilizations on the American continents, and with recent DNA testing that suggests Native Americans share few genetic traits with people in the Middle East, the Mormon Church has gradually downplayed its position that The Book of Mormon is a historical document.

5. 1 Nephi 13:12.

6. Shipps, *Mormonism*, 122.

7. Ibid., 114.

8. Ibid., 115.

9. Ibid., 128. Mormon prophet Joseph F. Smith received a vision in 1918 where he saw "the hosts of the dead" who were faithful in life in a state of celebration as they awaited resurrection. The wicked were kept separate from the righteous, but nonetheless were continually preached to and taught the tenets of God's truth by missionaries in this spirit world. Smith concluded that temple ordinances for the dead would offer the ignorant or wicked another opportunity to choose redemption over bondage. See Doctrine and Covenants 138.

10. Deeb, "Emulating," 243.

11. Ibid., 244.

12. Nora, "Between Memory and History," 21.

13. Bitton, *Ritualization of Mormon History*, 183.

14. Ibid., 180.

15. Magelssen, "This Is a Drama," 20.

16. *Big Love*. "Come, Ye Saints." Directed by Daniel Attias. Written by Melanie Marnich. HBO, February 22, 2009.

17. Card, "Pageant Wagon," from *Folk on the Fringe*, 138–39.

18. *Theatre Manual* (1980)

19. Card, "Pageant Wagon," 168.

20. See Özkirimli, *Theories of Nationalism*, 10–30.

21. Eliade, *Cosmos and History*, 90.

22. Jones, "(Re)living the Pioneer Past," 120.

23. Doctrine and Covenants 128:8.

24. Doctrine and Covenants 62:3.

25. 2 Nephi 29:11.

26. Spencer W. Kimball, "The True Way of Life and Salvation," April 1978 General Conference.

27. Eliot, "Tradition," 37.

28. Ibid., 37.

29. Wilford Woodruff quoting Brigham Young. Davies, "Reflections on the Mormon 'Canon,'" 59. Original emphasis.

30. Ibid., 58.

31. Connor, *Dumbstruck*, 252.

32. Lotman and Uspensky, "Semiotic Mechanism of Culture," 216.

NOTES TO CHAPTER 4 · 183

33. Ibid.

34. Flake, "Not to be Riten," 6.

35. Ibid., 8.

36. Hugh Nibley, qtd. in ibid., 4.

37. Ibid., 5.

38. Ibid., 9.

39. Ibid., 14–15.

40. Bowman, "Progressive Roots," 15.

41. Matthew Bowman, "Saturday's Warriors: How Mormons Went from Beard-Wearing Radicals to Clean-Cut Conformists," slate.com, April 25, 2012, http://www.slate.com/articles/life/faithbased/2012/04/mormon_correlation_the_bureaucratic_reform_policy_that_redefined_mormon_culture.html.

42. Smith, "LDS Anthropologist."

43. Paul H. Dunn, interview from October 6, 1995, qtd. in Prince and Wright, *David O. McKay*, 158.

44. Smith, *Book of Mammon*.

45. See https://genconpreview.wordpress.com for examples of these conference "previews."

46. Smith, "Source Over Content."

47. For more on Correlation, see Smith, "The Last Shall be First and the First Shall be Last: Discourse and Mormon History" (PhD diss., University of Pennsylvania, 2007).

48. See www.ziontheatricals.com/alpha-listings-musicals for descriptions of many of the musicals.

49. C. Michael Perry, "The Theatre as a Temple," July 21, 2014, www.ziontheatricals.com/the-theatre-as-a-temple.

50. Ibid.

51. Ibid.

52. Qtd. in Ibid.

53. Bial, *Playing God*, 150.

54. Ezra Taft Benson, "Satan's Thrust—Youth," *Ensign* (December 1971).

55. Lennon's full interview was printed in the London *Evening Standard* on March 4, 1966.

56. Sullivan, "More Popular than Jesus," 320.

57. Bryson, *Winning the Testimony War*, 11.

58. Ibid. Bryson puts forth an elaborate analogy around his connection between rock music and an ax: "With that picture in your mind . . . of the music represented merely as an ax . . . now picture the entertainer as a woodsman. Picture the youth of today as trees . . . about to be hewn down . . . or about to be fashioned into beautiful tabernacles of truth. The overwhelming majority of today's 'woodsmen' are voracious 'beatles' destroying every tree in sight. I wanted to send into the forest 'woodsmen' who were true 'carpenters' for the Lord. . . . To take the analogy one step further,

184 · NOTES TO CHAPTERS 4 AND 5

some entertainers are so unlike the 'carpenters' that they can fittingly be described as 'rolling stones!' They crush everything in their pathway . . . masticating the poor timbers that have barely been left standing by the disease-bearing 'beatles' that have preceded them." See Bryson, *Winning the Testimony War*, 11–12.

59. See, for example, Todd Decker's discussion of Paul Robeson in *Show Boat: Performing Race in an American Musical* and Dan Dinero's exploration of black women in musicals in "A Big Black Lady Stops the Show."

60. Most, *Making Americans*, 24.

61. Luke 21:18.

62. Alma 40:23.

63. Robert Wadsworth Lowry wrote this hymn in 1868.

64. Luke 21:33.

65. Thompson, "Language Planning," 47.

66. Hobsbawm and Ranger, *Invention of Tradition*, 1.

67. Morris, *Persistence of Sentiment*, 2. Morris intends this as a critique against scholars wary of divulging conceits that may be suspected of being "sentimental," although those same worries undoubtedly help determine behaviors and practices of many music lovers outside the academy. He writes, "I have often noted a disparity between the songs and styles many people seem to love to listen to—those they play in the privacy of their own homes, the ones that send them into paroxysms of delighted recollection, those they remember in remarkably detailed fashion—and the songs and styles that tend to get written about in vigorous, critically engaged terms."

68. Ibid., 3.

69. Bowman, *Mormon People*, 208.

70. Franklin D. Richards, "Be a Peacemaker," *Ensign* (October 1983).

Chapter 5. Voice Interrupted

1. Eidsheim, *Sensing Sound*, 157.

2. Email correspondence with the author, March 5, 2015.

3. Elkin, *Augustan Defence of Satire*, 201.

4. Griffin, *Satire*, 60.

5. Ibid., 139.

6. See link to pdf of the letter in "Ordain Women Releases LDS Bishop's Letter Giving Reasons for Kelly's Excommunication," *Deseret News*, June 23, 2014, http://www.deseretnews.com/article/865605659/Ordain-Women-releases-LDS-bishops-letter-giving-reasons-for-Kellys-excommunication.html?pg=all.

7. A stake president oversees a geographic subdivision called a "stake," which is similar to a Catholic diocese.

8. See pdf link to full letter in "Mormon Stories Founder Dehlin's Spread of 'False Concepts' Results in Excommunication from LDS Church," *Deseret News*, February 11, 2015,

NOTES TO CHAPTER 5 · 185

http://www.deseretnews.com/article/865621576/Mormon-Stories-founder-Dehlins
-spread-of-false-concepts-results-in-excommunication-from-LDS.html?pg=all.

9. Gaustad, *Dissent in American Religion*, 2.

10. Ibid., 7.

11. Robertson, *Characteristics*, 1:50–51.

12. In fact, in 1993 Apostle Boyd K. Packer listed these three groups as "dangers" to the Church.

13. Constantinou et al., "Communications/Excommunications," 34.

14. Ibid.

15. See Couldry, *Why Voice Matters*.

16. Galloway, Thacker, and Wark, *Excommunication*, 15.

17. Ibid., 16.

18. Ibid., 16.

19. Joseph F. Smith penned the last entry in the Doctrine and Covenants in 1918. Some Mormons believe the semiannual conference addresses are of the same stature as the canonized revelations in the Doctrine and Covenants, though these addresses are vetted by comparing them to previous, canonized passages in the scriptures themselves, which negates any sense of equality among the scriptures and contemporary speeches.

20. Smith, "On Translation," 530.

21. Ibid.

22. *South Park,* "All about the Mormons." Episode 12: directed by Trey Parker, written by Trey Parker, *Comedy Central*, November 19, 2003.

23. Qtd. in Jesse McKinley, "Theater Director Resigns amid Gay-Rights Ire," *New York Times*, November 12, 200,. http://www.nytimes.com/2008/11/13/theater/13thea .html.

24. Shaiman originally toyed with the idea of basing the musical around the poppy field scene in *The Wizard of Oz*: "I said, 'Well, maybe that first section should be all of us on a hill, with poppies, and it snows and we're put to sleep, and then the Proposition 8 people are looking through the crystal ball, like the Wicked Witch of the West in 'The Wizard of Oz.' Because that's what happened. We stupidly allowed ourselves to be lulled into a sense of, everything's fantastic now, look—everything's changing. And this couldn't possibly be voted into law. This is just like some little pesky thing that we're swatting at, and it will go away immediately." Qtd. in Dave Itzkoff, "Marc Shaiman on 'Prop 8—The Musical,'" *New York Times*, December 4, 2008, http://artsbeat .blogs.nytimes.com/2008/12/04/marc-shaiman-on-prop-8-the-musical/?_r=0.

25. *Perry v. Schwarzenegger* (later changed to *Hollingsworth v. Perry*) was the federal case that resulted in Proposition 8 being ruled unconstitutional. The plaintiffs were same-sex couple Kristin Perry and Sandra Stier, who in 2009 were denied a marriage license in Alameda County, California, because they were gay.

26. *Deseret News* published an account of musical theater student Liza Morong eventually converting to the Church after seeing *Book of Mormon* in New York City

and communicating with actual Church missionaries. See Emmilie Buchanan-Whitlock, "From 'Book of Mormon' musical to Mormon convert," *Deseret News*, May 3, 2013, http://www.deseretnews.com/article/865579364/From-Book-of-Mormon -musical-to-Mormon-convert.html?pg=all.

27. Lyman Kirkland, "Book of Mormon Musical: Church's Official Statement," The Church of Jesus Christ of Latter-Day Saints Newsroom, February 7, 2011, http://www .mormonnewsroom.org/article/church-statement-regarding-the-book-of-mormon -broadway-musical.

28. See for example Rosen, *Frontiers of Meaning*; Knapp, "Brahms and the Anxiety of Allusion"; Burkholder, *All Made of Tunes*; and Reynolds, *Motives for Allusion*.

29. Rosen, *Frontiers of Meaning*, 92.

30. Reynolds, *Motives for Allusion*, 6.

31. Ibid., 16.

32. Knapp, *National Identity*, 263.

33. See most notably Leonard J. Arrington's biography *Brigham Young: American Moses*.

34. Suskin, *Book of Mormon*, 55.

35. Hicks, "Elder Price Superstar," 228.

36. Doctrine and Covenants 9:8–9.

37. Moroni 10: 4–5.

38. Updike, *The Coup*, 143.

39. Pinchevski, *By Way of Interruption*, 7.

40. Ibid., 126.

41. Hirschkind, *Ethical Soundscape*.

Epilogue

1. Hecht, *Doubt*, xxi.

Bibliography

Aikau, Hokulani. *A Chosen People, a Promised Land: Mormonism and Race in Hawai'i.* Minneapolis: University of Minnesota Press, 2012.

An Authentic History of Remarkable Persons, Who Have Attracted Public Attention in Various Parts of the World; Including a Full Exposure of the Iniquities of the Pretended Prophet Joe Smith, and of the Seven Degrees of the Mormon Temple; Also an Account of the Frauds Practised by Matthias the Prophet, and Other Religious Impostors. New York: Wilson; Brother Jonathan, 1849.

Arrington, Leonard J. *Brigham Young: American Moses.* Urbana: University of Illinois Press, 1986.

Bagley, Will. *Blood of the Prophets: Brigham Young and the Massacre at Mountain Meadows.* Norman: University of Oklahoma Press, 2002.

Bell, Braden. *The Road Show: A Novel.* Springville, Utah: Bonneville, 2010.

Bial, Henry. *Playing God: The Bible on the Broadway Stage.* Ann Arbor: University of Michigan Press, 2015.

Bitton, Davis. *The Ritualization of Mormon History and Other Essays.* Urbana: University of Illinois Press, 1994.

Bloom, Harold. *The American Religion: The Emergence of the Post-Christian Nation.* New York: Simon and Schuster, 1993.

Bordman, Gerald. *Jerome Kern: His Life and Music.* New York: Oxford University Press, 1990.

Bowman, Matthew. *The Mormon People: The Making of an American Faith.* London: Routledge, 2012.

———. "The Progressive Roots of Mormon Correlation." In *Directions for Mormon Studies in the Twenty-First Century,* edited by Patrick Mason. Salt Lake City: University of Utah Press, 2016.

Bradley, Ian. *You've Got to Have a Dream: The Message of the Musical.* London: SCM, 2004.

188 · BIBLIOGRAPHY

Bringardner, Chase A. "The Politics of Region and Nation in American Musicals." In *Oxford Handbook of the American Musical*, edited by Raymond Knapp, Mitchell Morris, and Stacy Wolf. New York: Oxford University Press, 2011.

Brodie, Fawn. *No Man Knows My History*. New York: Knopf, 1945.

Brown, Samuel. "A Sacred Code: Mormon Temple Dedication Prayers, 1836–2000." *Journal of Mormon History* 32, no. 2 (2006): 173–96.

———. *In Heaven as It Is on Earth: Joseph Smith and the Early Mormon Conquest of Death*. New York: Oxford University Press, 2012.

Bryson, Lynn A. *Winning the Testimony War*. Lynn A. Bryson, 1982.

Burkholder, Peter. *All Made of Tunes: Charles Ives and the Uses of Musical Borrowing*. New Haven, Conn.: Yale University Press, 2004.

Card, Orson Scott. *The Folk on the Fringe*. Bloomfield, Mich.: Phantasia, 1989.

Carson, Anne. *Glass, Irony, and God*. New York: New Dimensions, 1995.

Carter, Scott A. "Forging a Sound Citizenry: Voice Culture and the Embodiment of the Nation, 1880–1920." *American Music Research Center Journal* 22 (2013).

Carter, Tim. *Oklahoma!: The Making of an American Musical*. New Haven, Conn.: Yale University Press, 2007.

Cavarero, Adriana. *For More than One Voice: Toward a Philosophy of Vocal Expression*. Palo Alto, Calif.: Stanford University Press, 2005.

Chapman, Jennifer. "Knowing Your Audience." In *Oxford Handbook of the American Musical*, edited by Raymond Knapp, Mitchell Morris, and Stacy Wolf. New York: Oxford University Press, 2011.

Connor, Steven. *Dumbstruck: A Cultural History of Ventriloquism*. New York: Oxford University Press, 2000.

Constantinou, Constas M., Armand Mattelart, Amandine Bled, and Jacques Guyout. "Communications/Excommunications: An Interview with Armand Mattelart." *Review of International Studies* 34 (2008): 21–42.

Couldry, Nick. *Why Voice Matters: Culture and Politics After Neoliberalism*. London: SAGE, 2010.

Cox, Harvey. *Fire from Heaven: The Rise of Pentecostal Spirituality and the Reshaping of Religion in the Twenty-First Century*. New York: Addison-Wesley, 1995.

Davies, W. D. 1986. "Reflections on the Mormon Canon." *Harvard Theological Review* 79, no. 1/3 (1986): 44–66.

Decker, Todd. *Show Boat: Performing Race in an American Musical*. New York: Oxford University Press, 2012.

Deeb, Lara. "Emulating and/or Embodying the Ideal: The Gendering of Temporal Frameworks and Islamic Role Models in Shi'i Lebanon." *American Ethnologist* 36, no. 2 (2009): 242–57.

Dinero, Dan. "A Big Black Lady Stops the Show: Black Women, Performances of Excess and the Power of Saying No." *Studies in Musical Theatre* 6, no. 1 (2012): 29–41.

Dolar, Mladen. *A Voice and Nothing More*. Cambridge, Mass.: MIT Press, 2006.

Durkheim, Émile. *The Elementary Forms of the Religious Life*. London: Allen and Unwin, 1915.

Ebat, Andrew. "'Who Shall Ascend into the Hill of the Lord?' Sesquicentennial Reflections of a Sacred Day: 4 May 1842." In *Temples of the Ancient World*, edited by Donald W. Parry. Salt Lake City: Deseret, 1994.

Eidsheim, Nina. "Marian Anderson and 'Sonic Blackness' in American Opera." *American Quarterly* 63, no. 3 (2011): 641–71.

———. *Sensing Sound: Singing and Listening as Vibrational Practice*. Durham, N.C.: Duke University Press, 2015.

Eliade, Mircea. 1954. *Cosmos and History: The Myth of the Eternal Return*. New York: Harper Torchbooks.

Eliot, T. S. "Tradition and the Individual Talent." *Perspecta* 19 (1982):36–42.

Elkin, P. K. *Augustan Defence of Satire*. New York: Oxford University Press, 1973.

Emrich, Duncan, ed. *Songs of the Mormons and Songs of the West*. From the Archive of Folk Song, Library of Congress, 1952.

Esplin, Fred C. "The Church as Broadcaster." *Dialogue: A Journal of Mormon Thought* 10 (1977): 25–45.

Flake, Kathleen. "'Not to be Riten': The Mormon Temple Rite as Oral Canon." *Journal of Ritual Studies* 9, no. 2 (1995): 1–21.

Galloway, Alexander R., Eugene Thacker, and McKenzie Wark. *Excommunication: Three Inquiries in Media and Mediation*. Chicago: University of Chicago Press, 2014.

Gaustad, Edwin Scott. *Dissent in American Religion*. 1973. Chicago: University of Chicago Press, 2006.

Givens, Terryl. *People of Paradox: A History of Mormon Culture*. New York: Oxford University Press, 2007.

Glassberg, David. *American Historical Pageantry: The Uses of Tradition in the Early Twentieth Century*. Chapel Hill: University of North Carolina Press, 1990.

Greenblatt, Stephen. "Culture." In *Critical Terms for Literary Study*, edited by Frank Lentricchia and Thomas McLaughlin. 2nd ed. Chicago: University of Chicago, 1995.

Griffin, Dustin. *Satire: A Critical Reintroduction*. Lexington: University Press of Kentucky, 1994.

Hansen, Harold I. "A History and Influence of the Mormon Theatre from 1839–1869." PhD diss., Brigham Young University, 1967.

Harkness, Nicolas. *Songs of Seoul: An Ethnography of Voice and Voicing in Christian South Korea*. Berkeley: University of California Press, 2014.

Hawthorne, Nathaniel. *The House of The Seven Gables and The Snow Image and Other Twice-Told Tales*. Boston: Houghton, Mifflin, 1882.

Hecht, Jennifer Michael. *Doubt: A History; The Great Doubters and Their Legacy of Innovation from Socrates and Jesus to Thomas Jefferson and Emily Dickinson*. New York: Harper Collins, 2003.

Hicks, Michael. "Elder Price Superstar. *Dialogue: A Journal of Mormon Thought* 44, no. 4 (2011): 226–36.

———. "Ministering Minstrels: Blackface Entertainment in Pioneer Utah." *Utah Historical Quarterly* 58, no. 1 (1990): 49–63.

———. *The Mormon Tabernacle Choir: A Biography*. Urbana: University of Illinois Press, 2015.

———. "Music and Heaven in Mormon Thought." In *The Oxford Handbook of Mormonism*, edited by Terryl L. Givens and Philip L. Barlow, 498–512. New York: Oxford University Press, 2015.

———. "Poetic Borrowing in Early Mormonism." *Dialogue: A Journal of Mormon Thought* 18, no. 1 (Spring 1985): 132–42.

Hirschkind, Charles. *The Ethical Soundscape: Cassette Sermons and Islamic Counterpublics*. New York: Columbia University Press, 2006.

Hobsbawm, Eric, and Terence Ranger, eds. *The Invention of Tradition*. New York: Cambridge University Press, 1983.

Holzapfel, Richard Neitzel, and Stephen H. Smoot. "Wilford Woodruff's 1897 Testimony." In *Banner of the Gospel: Wilford Woodruff*, edited by Alexander L. Baugh and Susan Easton Black. Brigham Young University. Provo, Utah: Brigham Young University, Religious Studies Center, 2010.

Howard, Joseph, Jr. *Life of Henry Ward Beecher: The Eminent Pulpit and Platform Orator*. Philadelphia: Hubbard, 1887.

Ihde, Don. *Listening and Voice: Phenomenologies of Sound*. 2nd ed. Albany: SUNY Press, 2007.

Isenberg, Barbara. 2014. *Tradition!: The Highly Improbable, Ultimately Triumphant Broadway-to-Hollywood Story of* Fiddler on the Roof, *the World's Most Beloved Musical*. New York: St. Martin's.

Johnson, Jake. "Building the Broadway Voice." In *Oxford Handbook of Voice Studies*, edited by Nina Sun Eidsheim and Katherine Meizel. New York: Oxford University Press, forthcoming.

———. "'That's Where They Knew Me When': Oklahoma Senior Follies and the Narrative of Decline." *American Music* 3, no. 2 (2016): 243–62.

Jones, Megan Sanborn. "(Re)living the Pioneer Past: Mormon Youth Handcart Trek Reenactments." *Theatre Topics* 16 (2006): 113–30.

Jorgensen, Lynne Watkins. "The Mantle of the Prophet Joseph Passes to Brother Brigham: One Hundred Twenty-One Testimonies of a Collective Spiritual Witness." In *Opening the Heavens: Accounts of Divine Manifestations, 1820–1844*, edited by John W. Welch. Provo, Utah: Brigham Young University, 2005.

Kane, Brian. *Sound Unseen: Acousmatic Sound in Theory and Practice*. New York: Oxford University Press, 2014.

Kempis, Thomas À. *The Imitation of Christ*. Translated by Alysius Croft and Harold Bolton. Peabody, Mass.: Hendrickson, 2004.

Kittler, Friedrich. *Gramophone, Film, Typewriter*. Palo Alto, Calif.: Stanford University Press, 1999.

Knapp, Raymond. *The American Musical and the Formation of National Identity*. Princeton, N.J.: Princeton University Press, 2004.

———. *The American Musical and the Performance of Personal Identity*. Princeton, N.J.: Princeton University Press, 2006.

———. "Brahms and the Anxiety of Allusion." *Journal of Musicological Research* 18, no. (1998): 1–30.

Knapp, Raymond, and Francesca Draughon. "Gustav Mahler and the Crisis of Jewish Identity." *Echo: A Music-Centered Journal* 3, no. 2 (2011).

Knapp, Raymond, and Mitchell Morris. "Tin Pan Alley Songs on Stage and Screen before World War II." In *Oxford Handbook of the American Musical*, edited by Raymond Knapp, Mitchell Morris, and Stacy Wolf. New York: Oxford University Press, 2011.

Knowlton, David. "Belief, Metaphor, and Rhetoric: The Mormon Practice of Testimony Bearing." *Sunstone* (April 1991): 20–27.

Kreiman, Jody, and Diana Sidtis. *Foundations of Voice Studies: An Interdisciplinary Approach to Voice Production and Perception*. Malden, Mass.: Wiley Blackwell, 2011.

LaBelle, Brandon. *Lexicon of the Mouth: Poetics and Politics of Voice and the Oral Imaginary*. New York: Bloomsbury, 2014.

Lamar, Howard R. *The Theater in Mormon Life and Culture*. Leonard J. Arrington Mormon History Lecture Series No. 4. Logan: Utah State University Press, 1999.

Lewis, C. S. *Mere Christianity*. New York: Harper Collins, 2009.

Lewis, R. W. B. *The American Adam: Innocence, Tragedy, and Tradition in the Nineteenth Century*. Chicago: University of Chicago Press, 1955.

Lindsay, John S. *The Mormons and the Theatre; or, The History of Theatricals in Utah*. Salt Lake City, Utah: Century, 1905.

Locke, Ralph. "A Broader View of Musical Exoticism." *Journal of Musicology* 24, no. 4 (2007): 477–521.

Lotman, Yu M., and George Uspensky. "On the Semiotic Mechanism of Culture." *New Literary History* 9, no. 2 (1978): 211–32.

Luhrmann, Tanya. *When God Talks Back: Understanding the American Evangelical Relationship with God*. New York: Knopf, 2012.

Magelssen, Scott. "'This Is a Drama. You Are Characters': The Tourist as Fugitive Slave in Conner Prairie's 'Follow the North Star.'" *Theatre Topics* 16, no. 1 (2006): 19–34.

Margetts, Philip. "Early Theatricals in Utah." *Juvenile Instructor* 38 (1903).

Marx, Leo. *The Machine in the Garden: Technology and the Pastoral Ideal in America*. New York: Oxford University Press, 1964.

Mason, Patrick Q. *The Mormon Menace: Violence and Anti-Mormonism in the Postbellum South*. New York: Oxford University Press, 2011.

Mauss, Armand. *All Abraham's Children: Changing Mormon Conceptions of Race and Lineage*. Urbana: University of Illinois Press, 2003.

———. *The Angel and the Beehive: The Mormon Struggle with Assimilation*. Urbana: University of Illinois Press, 1994.

Mavrodes, George. *Revelation in Religious Belief*. Philadelphia: Temple University Press, 1988.

McConachie, Bruce. "The Oriental Musicals of Rodgers and Hammerstein and the U.S. War in Southeast Asia." *Theatre Journal* 64, no 3 (1994): 385–98.

192 · BIBLIOGRAPHY

McConkie, Bruce R. *The Mortal Messiah: From Bethlehem to Calvary*. Salt Lake City: Deseret, 1979.

McDannell, Colleen. *Material Christianity: Religion and Popular Culture in America*. New Haven, Conn.: Yale University Press, 1995.

McMurray, Peter. "A Voice Crying from the Dust: The Book of Mormon as Sound." *Dialogue: A Journal of Mormon Thought* 48, no. 4 (2015): 3–44.

Morris, Mitchell. *The Persistence of Sentiment: Display and Feeling in Popular Music of the 1970s*. Berkeley: University of California Press, 2013.

Most, Andrea. *Making Americans: Jews and the Broadway Musical*. Cambridge, Mass.: Harvard University Press, 2004.

———. *Theatrical Liberalism: Jews and Popular Entertainment in America*. New York: New York University Press, 2013.

Mumford, Jeremy Ravi. "The Inca Priest on the Mormon Stage." *Common-Place: The Journal of Early American Life* 5, no. 4 (2005).

Nora, Pierre. "Between Memory and History: *Les Lieux de Memoire*." Translated by Marc Roudebush. *Representations* 26 (1989): 7–24.

O'Leary, James. "*Oklahoma!*, 'Lousy Publicity,' and the Politics of Formal Integration in the American Musical Theater." *Journal of Musicology* 31, no. 1 (2014): 139–82.

Olsen, Daniel H., and Jeanne Kay Guelke. "Spatial Transgression and the BYU Jerusalem Center Controversy." *Professional Geographer* 56, no. 4 (2008): 503–15.

Özkirimli, Umut. *Theories of Nationalism: A Critical Introduction*. 2nd ed. New York: Palgrave Macmillan, 2010.

Park, Benjamin E. "Early Mormon Patriarchy and the Paradoxes of Democratic Religiosity in Jacksonian America." *American Nineteenth Century History* 14, no. 2 (2013): 183–208.

Pascoe, Judith. *The Sarah Siddons Audio Files: Romanticism and the Lost Voice*. Ann Arbor: University of Michigan Press, 2011.

Perry, C. Michael. "The Theatre as a Temple." ZionTheatricals.com, 2014.

Peters, John Durham. *Speaking into the Air: A History of the Idea of Communication*. Chicago: University of Chicago Press, 1999.

Pinchevski, Amit. *By Way of Interruption: Levinas and the Ethics of Communication*. Pittsburgh: Duquesne University Press, 2005.

Pisani, Michael. *Imagining Native America in Music*. New Haven, Conn.: Yale University Press, 2006.

Prince, Gregory A., and William Robert Wright. *David O. McKay and the Rise of Modern Mormonism*. Salt Lake City: University of Utah Press, 2005.

Quinn, D. Michael. *Early Mormonism and the Magic World View*. Salt Lake City: Signature,1987.

Reeve, Paul. *Religion of a Different Color: Race and the Mormon Struggle for Whiteness*. New York: Oxford University Press, 2015.

Reynolds, Christopher Alan. *Motives for Allusion: Context and Content in Nineteenth-Century Music*. Cambridge, Mass.: Harvard University Press, 2003.

Robertson, J. M. *Characteristics: Men, Manners, Opinions, Times, Etc.* London: Grant Richards, 1900.

Rodgers, Richard. *Musical Stages.* New York: Da Capo, 1975.

Rosen, Charles. *The Frontiers of Meaning: Three Informal Lectures on Music.* New York: Farrar, Straus, and Giroux, 1994.

Saxton, Alexander. "Blackface Minstrelsy and Jacksonian Ideology." *American Quarterly* 27, no. 1 (1975): 3–28.

Schaeffer, Pierre. *Traité des Objets Musicaux.* Paris: Éditions du Seuil, 1966.

Schmidt, Leigh Eric. *Hearing Things: Religion, Illusion, and the American Enlightenment.* Cambridge, Mass.: Harvard University Press, 2000.

Shipps, Jan. *Mormonism: The Story of a New Religious Tradition.* Urbana: University of Illinois Press, 1985.

———. *Sojourner in the Promised Land: Forty Years among the Mormons.* Urbana: University of Illinois Press, 2007.

Shlovsky, Viktor. "Art as Technique." In *Russia Formalist Criticism: Four Essays,* translated and with an introduction by Lee T. Lemon and Marion J. Reis. Lincoln: University of Nebraska Press, 1965.

Signorello, Rosario. "Voice in Charismatic Leadership." In *Oxford Handbook of Voice Studies,* edited by Nina Sun Eidsheim and Katherine Meizel. New York: Oxford University Press, forthcoming.

Smith, Daymon. *Book of Mammon: A Book about a Book about the Corporation That Owns the Mormons.* CreateSpace Independent Publishing Platform, 2010.

———. "LDS Anthropologist Daymon Smith on Post-Manifesto Polygamy, Correlation, the Corporate LDS Church, and Mammon." Mormon Stories Podcast, May 13, 2010.

———. "On Translation." In *The Abridging Works: The Epic and Historic Book of Mormon Arranged in Sequence of Composition by Ancient Authors, as Translated by Joseph Smith, Jr.* CreateSpace Independent Publishing Platform, 2011.

———. "Source Over Content: General, Generic, and General Conferences." *Mormonism Uncorrelated,* October 10, 2013.

Smith, Mark M. *Listening to Nineteenth-Century America.* Chapel Hill: University of North Carolina Press, 2001.

Sontag, Susan. *Against Interpretation and Other Essays.* New York: Delta, 1966.

Sposato, Jeffrey S. *The Price of Assimilation: Felix Mendelssohn and the Nineteenth-Century Anti-Semitic Tradition.* New York: Oxford University Press, 2008.

Stack, Peggy Fletcher. "Tattoo Dilemma Leaves Its Marks on BYU-Hawaii Students Who Work at Mormon-Owned Polynesian Cultural Center." *Salt Lake Tribune,* June 23, 2016.

Staker, Susan, ed. *Waiting for World's End: The Diaries of Wilford Woodruff.* Salt Lake City: Signature,1993.

Stanyek, Jason, and Benjamin Piekut. "Deadness: Technologies of the Intermundane." *TDR: The Drama Review* 54, no. 1 (2010): 14–38.

194 · BIBLIOGRAPHY

Steinberg, Avi. *The Lost Book of Mormon: A Journey Through the Mythic Lands of Nephi, Zarahemla, and Kansas City, Missouri*. New York: Doubleday, 2014.

Steiner, George. *After Babel: Aspects of Language and Translation*. New York: Oxford University Press, 1975.

Sterne, Jonathan. *The Audible Past: Cultural Origins of Sound Reproduction*. Durham, N.C.: Duke University Press, 2003.

Stone, Matt, and Trey Parker. 2011. "'Book of Mormon' Creators on Their Broadway Smash." *Fresh Air* with Terry Gross. May 9, 2011. http://www.npr.org/2011/05/19/136142322/book-of-mormon-creators-on-their-broadway-smash.

Stowe, David. *No Sympathy for the Devil: Christian Pop Music and the Transformation of American Evangelicalism*. Chapel Hill: University of North Carolina Press, 2011.

Sullivan, Mark. "'More Popular than Jesus': The Beatles and the Religious Far Right." *Popular Music* 6, no. 3 (1987): 313–26.

Suskin, Steven. 2012. *The Book of Mormon: The Testament of a Broadway Musical*. New York: Newmarket.

Sylvan, Robin. *Traces of the Spirit: The Religious Dimensions of Popular Music*. New York: New York University Press, 2002.

Thompson, Roger M. "Language Planning in Frontier America: The Case of the Deseret Alphabet." *Language Problems and Language Planning* 6, no. 1 (1982): 45–62.

Trask, Haunani-Kay. *From a Native Daughter: Colonialism and Sovereignty in Hawai'i*. Rev. ed. Honolulu: University of Hawaii Press, 1999.

Updike, John. *The Coup: A Novel*. New York: Random House, 2012.

Van Wagoner, Richard S. "The Making of a Mormon Myth: The 1844 Transfiguration of Brigham Young." *Dialogue: A Journal of Mormon Thought* 28, no. 4 (1995): 159–82.

Walker, Alice. *Meridian*. Orlando: Harcourt, 1976.

Walker, Philip Lyon. "Dust-Covered Testimonies: The Phonograph and Its Role in the L.D.S. Church Prior to April, 1939." May 23, 1968. Unpublished document, LDS Church History Library.

Webb, Stephen H. *The Divine Voice: Christian Proclamation and the Theology of Sound*. Eugene, Ore.: Wipf and Stock, 2004.

Whitney, Horace G. *The Drama in Utah: The Story of the Salt Lake Theatre*. Salt Lake City: Deseret News, 1915.

Wolf, Stacy. "Theatre as Social Practice: Local Ethnographies of Audience Reception." PhD diss., University of Wisconsin, Madison, 1994.

Wollman, Elizabeth. "The Economic Development of the 'New' Times Square and Its Impact on the Broadway Musical." *American Music* 20, no. 4 (2002): 445–65.

———. *The Theater Will Rock: A History of the Rock Musical, from Hair to Hedwig*. Ann Arbor: University of Michigan Press, 2006.

Wood, Gordon S. 1980. "Evangelical America and Early Mormonism." *New York History* 61, no. 4 (1980): 358–86.

Woolf, Virginia. *The Death of the Moth and Other Essays*. New York: Harcourt, Brace, 1942.

Index

Adam: in Adam-ondi-Ahman, 3–4; and
  Correlation, 139; language of, 5; in literature, 4–5; and original religion, 25, 97, 124;
  pretending to be, 20
Aikau, Hokulani, 86–88
allusion: in *Book of Mormon* (musical),
  158–63; to Judaism, 105
American musical theater: as assimilation,
  56, 67–68, 81–82, 93, 133; conventions of
  the genre, 101–5, 118–20, 132, 134–36, 154,
  160–63; as critique of Mormonism, 140,
  145–49, 154–56; ethnicity in, 64, 87, 89,
  92–93, 98; historiography, 21–26, 73; and
  Mormon history, 1–2, 7–8, 18–20, 26–27,
  28–31, 169–70; and the performance of
  whiteness, 82–84, 90–92, 112, 153, 157; religiosity of, 18, 21, 128; voice, 54–55, 158. *See
  also* blackface minstrelsy; operetta
Annie Get Your Gun, 70, 71
Augustine, Saint, 43–45
de Azevedo, Lex. See *Saturday's Warrior*

Babes in Arms, 136
baptism for the dead. *See* temple
Bell, Brandon, 47
Benson, Ezra Taft, 129–30
Bernstein, Leonard, 40, 67
Bitton, Davis, 74, 117
blackface minstrelsy: in early musical theater, 25–26; in Mormonism, 43, 65–68,
  125; part of Jacksonian ideology, 26. *See
  also* Jolson, Al; Rice, Thomas "Daddy"

Blackton, Jay, 71
Bloom, Harold, 5, 29, 68
Book of Mormon (musical): allusions in,
  157–64; Correlation, 142–45; mentions, 1,
  19–20, 30, 82, 131, 134; and Mormon messaging, 164–68, 170; queerness in, 153,
  155–57
Book of Mormon, The (scripture): and
  American history, 114–15, 182n4; and
  American literature, 7; and *Book of
  Mormon* (musical), 156–57; examples of
  voice, 13, 15, 28, 137, 152; and Jesus, 46;
  and Judaism, 94, 109, 178n6; mentions,
  79, 121, 122; and mimicry, 39–41, 42; and
  the Mormon Church, 152, 165–66; origins
  of, 6–7, 24–25, 37, 154, 165, 174n15, 175n53;
  race and lineage, 84–85, 90, 97, 178n2; and
  sound, 41–42
book musical. *See* integrated musical
Bowman, Matthew, 125
Boyé, Alex, 132
Brigham Young University (BYU), 70, 91,
  97, 136
Brigham Young University—Hawaii, 86–87
Brigham Young University—Jerusalem
  Center, 109–11
Brother Jake, 145–49
Bryson, Lynn, 130
Buck, Dudley, 63

camp, 19–20, 92, 136
Cannon, George Q., 84–86

196 · INDEX

Card, Orson Scott, 117
Carousel, 89, 133–34
Carson, Anne, 11
Church of Jesus Christ of Latter-day Saints,
  The (LDS). *See* Mormon Church, The
Coates, Ta-Nehisi, 112
Community of Christ. *See* Reorganized
  Church of Jesus Christ of Latter-day
  Saints (RLDS)
Connor, Stephen, 34–35, 36, 50, 52, 123
Correlation: and dissent, 143–147, 170; as
  machine, 126; origins of, 114, 125–26; and
  revelation, 152–53, 164–66; and voice, 30,
  114, 127, 138–41, 168
Cowdery, Oliver, 37–38, 165

Davis, Pat. See *Life . . . More Sweet than Bit-
  ter*
Dayley, K. Newell. See *Life . . . More Sweet
  than Bitter*
Deeb, Lara, 115–16
Dehlin, John, 147–49
Deseret (opera), 68
Deseret (Utah), 79
Deseret Alphabet, 138
Deseret Musical and Dramatic Society, 57
Dinah Shore Show, The, 90
Disney, 19–20, 82
Dolar, Mladen, 11, 55
Down in the Valley, 70
Drake, Alfred, 71, 90
Durkheim, Emile, 16, 31, 51, 115

Eckern, Scott, 154–55
Edison, Thomas, 48–49
Eidsheim, Nina, 11, 91, 143–44
Eliade, Mircea, 119, 124
excommunication: and messaging, 149–153;
  in the Mormon Church, 143–44, 148–49
exoticism: and Judaism, 29, 98–99, 103–6; in
  polygamy, 25; in *Promised Valley*, 79; and
  race, 84, 88–89

Fiddler on the Roof, 29, 92, 93; and *Life . . .
  More Sweet than Bitter*, 97–98, 103–5; in
  Mormonism, 95–96, 112
Flake, Kathleen, 124
Flower Drum Song, 88, 89

Gates, Crawford: Hill Cumorah Pageant, 117,
  158; *Promised Valley*, 70–71, 74–75

Gershwin, George, 63, 67, 101
Gilbert and Sullivan, 25–26, 105, 145–46
glossolalia, 32–33, 51
Godspell, 128
"Golden Age" musicals. *See* Rodgers and
  Hammerstein
Green Grow the Lilacs, 76

Hagoth, 84–85
Hahn's Mill Massacre, 59
Hair, 128
Hammerstein, Oscar, 40, 67, 82, 89. *See also*
  Rodgers and Hammerstein
Harkness, Nicolas, 51
Harline, Leigh, 19
Hart, Lorenz, 67, 136
Hawthorne, Nathaniel, 4–5
Herbert, Victor, 61, 63
Hicks, Michael, 66–67, 77–78, 164
Hill Cumorah Pageant. *See* pageants
Hinckley, Gordon B., 114, 149
Hobsbawm, Eric, 138–39
Hyde, Orson, 35, 38, 108–9

impersonation. *See* mimicry
Indians. *See* Native Americans
integrated musical, 26, 69–70, 73–74, 99, 119
Isaiah, 13, 80
Islam. *See* Muslims

Jack Benny Program, The, 90
Jacksonian ideology, 26–27, 58, 66, 112, 169
Jacob and Esau, 40, 43
Jazz Singer, The, 100, 132
Jesus Christ: as a character, 155; baptism of,
  34; bearing testimony of, 122; and The
  Beatles, 129; Correlation, 125; Joseph
  Smith revelation, 6, 12, 14, 37, 38; teach-
  ings of, 50, 110, 111, 128; theatricality,
  44–46, 47, 115; voice of, 49, 51, 137
Jesus Christ Superstar, 128, 170
John Birch Society, 129, 130
John the Baptist, 13, 14, 37, 174n14
Jolson, Al, 100
Judaism: Holocaust, 110–11, 132; House of Is-
  rael, 29, 84–85, 93–94, 106–8; Lost Tribes
  of Israel, 7; Zionism, 108

Kastle, Leonard, 68
Kelly, Kate, 147–49
Kern, Jerome, 63, 70

INDEX · 197

King and I, The, 22, 88–89, 133, 162–63
Knapp, Raymond: allusion, 160; "marriage trope," 81, 102; musical theater historiography, 23–24; race in musicals, 64, 89, 163; religion in musicals, 21
Knowlton, David, 52–53

Laban, 28, 39–41, 42, 60, 151
Lady in the Dark, 74–75
Lamanites. *See* Native Americans; Polynesians
Laugh In, 90
Lehi, 39–40, 85, 94
Levinas, Emmanuel, 30, 167–68
Lewis, C.S., 44–46
Life . . . More Sweet than Bitter: conventions of musical theater, 119; and exoticism, 84, 98–106, 112; and Mormon weddings, 102–3; as sequel to *Fiddler on the Roof,* 29, 97–98, 111
Little Night Music, A, 93
Little Shop of Horrors, 161–62
Lloyd Webber, Andrew, 21
Locke, Ralph, 99–106
Luhrmann, Tanya, 45
"lying for the Lord," 59–60, 137. *See also* mimicry; vicarious voice

Mahler, Gustav, 98, 180n37
Marconi, Guglielmo, 49–50
Mason, Patrick Q., 43, 59
Mauss, Armand, 66, 94–95
Mavrodes, George, 16–17
McKay, David O., 70, 107
McMurray, Peter, 15, 41
Melville, Herman, 4–5, 7
Mendelssohn, Felix, 98
mimicry: Brigham Young, 33–36, 38–39, 41, 59–60; in Christianity, 43–46, 51; drawing closer to godliness, 47, 52; and exoticism, 98; foundational to Mormonism, 15, 20, 38, 41, 53, 127; and Joseph Smith, 37; Nephi and Laban, 28, 39–41; Oliver Overstreet, 38. *See also* ventriloquism; vicarious voice
minstrelsy. *See* blackface minstrelsy
Monson, Thomas S., 95–97
Mormon Church, The: in American history, 114–15, 118, 130; assimilation of, 26, 43, 78, 83, 87, 106; Correlation, 30, 95, 114, 120–21, 125–27; critiques against, 30, 38,

145–49, 151, 157; and dress, 87; and excommunication, 141, 144–49, 150, 153, 170; and *Fiddler on the Roof,* 95–97, 112; forms of communication, 28–29, 42, 50–51, 138, 152; General Conference, 120–23, 125; and Jews, 107–11; organization of, 33–35, 48, 108, 165–66; origins, 24–25, 26, 50, 86; and polygamy, 60, 80, 82, 141, 156; and race, 84, 85, 91, 94, 141; and theater, 45, 47, 56, 68, 71, 82; and Utah Centennial Commission, 29, 70. *See also* Polynesian Cultural Center; Proposition 8; temple
Mormon Priesthood: as authority, 47, 114, 122; origins, 37, 173n14; and the racial ban, 84, 85, 141; women and, 147, 148
Mormon Tabernacle Choir, 77–78, 153
Moroni, 6, 154, 162, 165–66
Morris, Mitchell, 64, 140
Morrison, Toni, 66
Moses: Brigham Young as, 115, 163; and Joseph Smith, 32, 37, 162–63, 168; "Small House of Uncle Thomas," 163
Most, Andrea, 21–23, 40, 42–43, 67, 93, 133
Mountain Meadows Massacre, 43, 59
Music and the Spoken Word, 78
Muslims, 64–65, 115–16

Native Americans: as characters, 43, 59; and history, 3, 114, 182n4; and the House of Israel, 7, 29, 84–86, 97, 107; Lamanite Generation, 91; Mormon representations of, 179n22; and white supremacy, 26, 43, 58
Nephi and Laban, 28, 39–41, 42, 60, 151
Nephites, 6, 46, 84
New Jerusalem. *See* Zion

Obama, Barack, 112, 155
Offenbach, Jacques, 25, 62
Oklahoma!: and Correlation, 146; integration, 26, 69–70, 72–73; and Jewish representation, 67, 93; and musical theater conventions, 119–20, 133–34; and progressive politics, 88–89; and *Promised Valley,* 29, 71, 73–81, 89; and regional productions, 23
operetta: anti-Mormon, 61–64, 89; *Barbe-bleue,* 25, 62–63; *Deseret, or a Saint's Afflictions,* 63; *Girl From Utah,* 63; *His Little Widows,* 61; *The Mormons,* 63; *Naughty Marietta,* 61; overview, 23, 25–26, 28
Osmonds, The, 92, 112, 130, 132, 153

198 · INDEX

pageants: Hill Cumorah, 128, 158; history, 71; "Joseph Smith American Moses," 162–64, 166; memory and, 116–17, 119; "Pageant Wagon," 117–18; Polynesian Cultural Center as, 87

Paint Your Wagon, 67–68

Parade, 93

Parker, Trey, 1, 19, 82, 154, 158–62, 164

Pascoe, Judith, 49–50

Pentecost. *See* glossolalia

performing whiteness: through minstrelsy, 65–66; musical theater as a means of, 82–84, 86, 91, 153, 169; at Polynesian Cultural Center, 89–92, 112, 151; power in, 29, 112

Perry, C. Michael, 98, 127–28

Peters, John Durham, 44

phonograph: God listening through, 49, 137; recording of Wilford Woodruff, 47, 49–50, 53, 137, 153; speaking on behalf of, 10, 113, 144–45

Pirates of Penzance, The, 25, 105

Pizarro, 58

polygamy: and ethnicity, 65; in media, 117, 145; on the musical stage, 25, 61–65, 67–68, 83, 89; opposition to, 59; post-Manifesto, 80, 106, 115, 120, 125, 141, 156; Woodruff Manifesto, 60,115

Polynesian Cultural Center: *Ha: Breath of Life*, 87; overview, 1, 29, 84, 86–92; Polynesian Panorama, 87

Polynesians, 29, 84–91, 97, 107

Promised Valley: and assimilation, 56, 68, 80–81, 82, 83; and integrated musical, 29, 71, 73–74; mentions, 103; and *Oklahoma!*, 29, 71, 73–81; origins, 70–71, 116, 117; Polynesian Cultural Center, 89–91; and singing, 74–81, 113, 133, 151, 160; whiteness, 153

Promised Valley Playhouse, 71

Prop 8: The Musical, 30, 155–56, 185n24

Proposition 8, 30, 154–56

recording technology. *See* phonograph

Reeve, Paul, 65–66, 154

Regas, Jack, 89–90

Reorganized Church of Jesus Christ of Latter-day Saints (RLDS), 2, 48

reprise: in *Promised Valley*, 72, 76; and sacred time, 119–20; in *Saturday's Warrior*, 132, 135; two types of, 119–20

Rice, Thomas "Daddy," 26

Rice, Tim, 26

Rigdon, Sidney, 33–34, 36, 37

road shows, 2, 19, 47

Rodgers, Richard, 40, 67, 70, 98, 136. *See also* Rodgers and Hammerstein

Rodgers and Hammerstein: comparison to Mormonism, 19–20, 82, 158–59; exoticism in works of, 88–89; integrated musical, 26, 69–76

Romney, Mitt, 125, 153–54

sacred time: in Islam, 115–16; in Mormonism, 115–17; and reprises in musical theater, 119–21; and voice, 131

Salt Lake City: as cosmopolitan site within Mormonism, 59, 71, 121, 145; place in musical theater, 19, 29, 63, 98, 161; and the Salt Lake Theatre, 35, 56–57

Salt Lake Theatre, 35, 56–58, 60

satire: and *Book of Mormon* (musical), 153, 164; in Brother Jake; 145–47, 149; as sign of repression, 148–49, 169

Saturday's Voyeur, 145

Saturday's Warrior: and Correlation, 30, 129, 136–40; and ethnicity, 132–33; Mormon culture, 1, 2, 131, 139–40; voice, 29–30, 113–14, 131, 135–37, 139, 151

Second Great Awakening, 14

Second Manifesto, 60

Shaiman, Marc, 154–55

Sheridan, Richard, 58

Shipps, Jan, 115

Show Boat, 70, 93

Siddons, Sarah, 49–50

Smith, Daymon, 125–27, 145, 152

Smith, Emma, 77

Smith, Hyrum, 33, 43

Smith, Joseph: as Adam, 3, 4; and The Book of Mormon, 7, 94, 114, 152, 165–66; death, 5, 33, 40, 43, 46, 58, 77; First Vision, 6, 12–18, 38, 154, 162; founding the Church, 24, 26; and minstrelsy, 26; and Moses, 162–63, 168; revelations, 107, 121, 164; in *South Park*, 154; theatricality, 36–37, 56; voice, 4, 32, 41, 48, 152. *See also under* Young, Brigham

Smith, Joseph III. *See* Reorganized Church of Jesus Christ of Latter-day Saints (RLDS)

INDEX · 199

Smith, Joseph F., 60, 182n9, 185n19. *See also* Second Manifesto
Sondheim, Stephen, 40, 67
Sontag, Susan, 20
Sound of Music, The, 83, 158–60
South Pacific, 67, 87–89, 93
South Park, 154
Spamalot, 93
speaking in tongues. *See* glossolalia
Steinberg, Avi, 7, 36, 39
Stone, Matt: *Book of Mormon* (musical), 1, 19, 82, 154, 158–59, 162; on mocking religion, 164
Street Scene, 70, 93
Sundgaard, Arnold, 70–75

Tamaris, Helen, 71
temple: enactments, 20, 37, 112, 116, 118; in Hawaii, 86; history of, 48, 56–57; and memory, 123–24; Mormon ceremony, 41, 57, 102, 110–11, 128; Mormon temple in Jerusalem, 108; and polygamy, 60, 80; saving ordinances in, 114–15, 120, 151, 182n9; theatre as, 57, 127–28
theology of voice: first use, 38 (*see also under* Young, Brigham); Mormonism as, 12–15, 33; practiced in musical theater, 170; vocal modeling, 41–42, 82. *See also* vicarious voice
Thoreau, Henry David, 7
Tommy, 128
Tower of Babel, 13, 32, 167
Trump, Donald, 112
Twain, Mark, 9–10, 170
Twilight Zone, The, 49

Uchtdorf, Dieter F., 175n61

University of Utah, 70
Utah Centennial Commission, 69–74

ventriloquism, 36, 52
vicarious voice: and *Book of Mormon* (musical), 164; and Correlation, 138, 144, 153, 170; excommunication from, 151–53; as form of godliness, 38–42, 45–46, 52, 55; as measure of conversion, 90, 117; overview, 9–20, 27, 31; and prophets, 47–50, 53, 127; and reprise, 120, 123; as theater, 32–33, 36, 45, 118

Warshaw, Maurice, 98–106, 119
Webb, Stephen, 51–52
Weill, Kurt, 70, 74
West Side Story, 67, 81, 93
Wicked, 146
Wizard of Oz, The, 146, 185n24
Woodruff, Wilford: Correlation, 144–45, 153, 168; manifesto, 60, 115; recording, 47–50, 53, 113, 137

Young, Brigham: and American history, 4, 118; Correlation 25, 125; mentions, 63; mimicry, 53, 151; as Moses, 115, 163; race, 85, 91; and the Salt Lake Theatre, 56–60; on scriptures, 122; on stage, 68, 128; successor to Joseph Smith, 48; transfiguration, 28, 33–39, 41, 50, 123; voice, 5, 138. *See also* Brigham Young University (BYU)
Young, Rida Johnson, 61

Zion: figurative language of Mormon temple ceremony, 41, 115; gathering place, 55, 80, 56, 93, 107
Zion Theatricals, 127–28

JAKE JOHNSON is an assistant professor of musicology in the Wanda L. Bass School of Music at Oklahoma City University.

MUSIC IN AMERICAN LIFE

Only a Miner: Studies in Recorded Coal-Mining Songs   *Archie Green*
Great Day Coming: Folk Music and the American Left   *R. Serge Denisoff*
John Philip Sousa: A Descriptive Catalog of His Works   *Paul E. Bierley*
The Hell-Bound Train: A Cowboy Songbook   *Glenn Ohrlin*
Oh, Didn't He Ramble: The Life Story of Lee Collins, as Told to Mary Collins
   Edited by Frank J. Gillis and John W. Miner
American Labor Songs of the Nineteenth Century   *Philip S. Foner*
Stars of Country Music: Uncle Dave Macon to Johnny Rodriguez
   Edited by Bill C. Malone and Judith McCulloh
Git Along, Little Dogies: Songs and Songmakers of the American West   *John I. White*
A Texas-Mexican *Cancionero*: Folksongs of the Lower Border   *Américo Paredes*
San Antonio Rose: The Life and Music of Bob Wills   *Charles R. Townsend*
Early Downhome Blues: A Musical and Cultural Analysis   *Jeff Todd Titon*
An Ives Celebration: Papers and Panels of the Charles Ives Centennial
   Festival-Conference   *Edited by H. Wiley Hitchcock and Vivian Perlis*
Sinful Tunes and Spirituals: Black Folk Music to the Civil War   *Dena J. Epstein*
Joe Scott, the Woodsman-Songmaker   *Edward D. Ives*
Jimmie Rodgers: The Life and Times of America's Blue Yodeler   *Nolan Porterfield*
Early American Music Engraving and Printing: A History of Music Publishing
   in America from 1787 to 1825, with Commentary on Earlier and Later
   Practices   *Richard J. Wolfe*
Sing a Sad Song: The Life of Hank Williams   *Roger M. Williams*
Long Steel Rail: The Railroad in American Folksong   *Norm Cohen*
Resources of American Music History: A Directory of Source Materials from
   Colonial Times to World War II   *D. W. Krummel, Jean Geil, Doris J. Dyen,
   and Deane L. Root*
Tenement Songs: The Popular Music of the Jewish Immigrants   *Mark Slobin*
Ozark Folksongs   *Vance Randolph; edited and abridged by Norm Cohen*
Oscar Sonneck and American Music   *Edited by William Lichtenwanger*
Bluegrass Breakdown: The Making of the Old Southern Sound   *Robert Cantwell*
Bluegrass: A History   *Neil V. Rosenberg*
Music at the White House: A History of the American Spirit   *Elise K. Kirk*
Red River Blues: The Blues Tradition in the Southeast   *Bruce Bastin*
Good Friends and Bad Enemies: Robert Winslow Gordon and the Study of American
   Folksong   *Debora Kodish*
Fiddlin' Georgia Crazy: Fiddlin' John Carson, His Real World, and the World of His
   Songs   *Gene Wiggins*
America's Music: From the Pilgrims to the Present (rev. 3d ed.)   *Gilbert Chase*
Secular Music in Colonial Annapolis: The Tuesday Club, 1745–56   *John Barry Talley*
Bibliographical Handbook of American Music   *D. W. Krummel*
Goin' to Kansas City   *Nathan W. Pearson Jr.*

"Susanna," "Jeanie," and "The Old Folks at Home": The Songs of Stephen C. Foster from His Time to Ours (2d ed.)   *William W. Austin*

Songprints: The Musical Experience of Five Shoshone Women   *Judith Vander*

"Happy in the Service of the Lord": Afro-American Gospel Quartets in Memphis   *Kip Lornell*

Paul Hindemith in the United States   *Luther Noss*

"My Song Is My Weapon": People's Songs, American Communism, and the Politics of Culture, 1930–50   *Robbie Lieberman*

Chosen Voices: The Story of the American Cantorate   *Mark Slobin*

Theodore Thomas: America's Conductor and Builder of Orchestras, 1835–1905   *Ezra Schabas*

"The Whorehouse Bells Were Ringing" and Other Songs Cowboys Sing   *Collected and Edited by Guy Logsdon*

Crazeology: The Autobiography of a Chicago Jazzman   *Bud Freeman, as Told to Robert Wolf*

Discoursing Sweet Music: Brass Bands and Community Life in Turn-of-the-Century Pennsylvania   *Kenneth Kreitner*

Mormonism and Music: A History   *Michael Hicks*

Voices of the Jazz Age: Profiles of Eight Vintage Jazzmen   *Chip Deffaa*

Pickin' on Peachtree: A History of Country Music in Atlanta, Georgia   *Wayne W. Daniel*

Bitter Music: Collected Journals, Essays, Introductions, and Librettos   *Harry Partch; edited by Thomas McGeary*

Ethnic Music on Records: A Discography of Ethnic Recordings Produced in the United States, 1893 to 1942   *Richard K. Spottswood*

Downhome Blues Lyrics: An Anthology from the Post–World War II Era   *Jeff Todd Titon*

Ellington: The Early Years   *Mark Tucker*

Chicago Soul   *Robert Pruter*

That Half-Barbaric Twang: The Banjo in American Popular Culture   *Karen Linn*

Hot Man: The Life of Art Hodes   *Art Hodes and Chadwick Hansen*

The Erotic Muse: American Bawdy Songs (2d ed.)   *Ed Cray*

Barrio Rhythm: Mexican American Music in Los Angeles   *Steven Loza*

The Creation of Jazz: Music, Race, and Culture in Urban America   *Burton W. Peretti*

Charles Martin Loeffler: A Life Apart in Music   *Ellen Knight*

Club Date Musicians: Playing the New York Party Circuit   *Bruce A. MacLeod*

Opera on the Road: Traveling Opera Troupes in the United States, 1825–60   *Katherine K. Preston*

The Stonemans: An Appalachian Family and the Music That Shaped Their Lives   *Ivan M. Tribe*

Transforming Tradition: Folk Music Revivals Examined   *Edited by Neil V. Rosenberg*

The Crooked Stovepipe: Athapaskan Fiddle Music and Square Dancing in Northeast Alaska and Northwest Canada   *Craig Mishler*

Traveling the High Way Home: Ralph Stanley and the World of Traditional Bluegrass Music   *John Wright*

Carl Ruggles: Composer, Painter, and Storyteller   *Marilyn Ziffrin*

Never without a Song: The Years and Songs of Jennie Devlin, 1865–1952   *Katharine D. Newman*

The Hank Snow Story   *Hank Snow, with Jack Ownbey and Bob Burris*

Milton Brown and the Founding of Western Swing   *Cary Ginell, with special assistance from Roy Lee Brown*

Santiago de Murcia's "Códice Saldívar No. 4": A Treasury of Secular Guitar Music from Baroque Mexico   *Craig H. Russell*

The Sound of the Dove: Singing in Appalachian Primitive Baptist Churches   *Beverly Bush Patterson*

Heartland Excursions: Ethnomusicological Reflections on Schools of Music   *Bruno Nettl*

Doowop: The Chicago Scene   *Robert Pruter*

Blue Rhythms: Six Lives in Rhythm and Blues   *Chip Deffaa*

Shoshone Ghost Dance Religion: Poetry Songs and Great Basin Context   *Judith Vander*

Go Cat Go! Rockabilly Music and Its Makers   *Craig Morrison*

'Twas Only an Irishman's Dream: The Image of Ireland and the Irish in American Popular Song Lyrics, 1800–1920   *William H. A. Williams*

Democracy at the Opera: Music, Theater, and Culture in New York City, 1815–60   *Karen Ahlquist*

Fred Waring and the Pennsylvanians   *Virginia Waring*

Woody, Cisco, and Me: Seamen Three in the Merchant Marine   *Jim Longhi*

Behind the Burnt Cork Mask: Early Blackface Minstrelsy and Antebellum American Popular Culture   *William J. Mahar*

Going to Cincinnati: A History of the Blues in the Queen City   *Steven C. Tracy*

Pistol Packin' Mama: Aunt Molly Jackson and the Politics of Folksong   *Shelly Romalis*

Sixties Rock: Garage, Psychedelic, and Other Satisfactions   *Michael Hicks*

The Late Great Johnny Ace and the Transition from R&B to Rock 'n' Roll   *James M. Salem*

Tito Puente and the Making of Latin Music   *Steven Loza*

Juilliard: A History   *Andrea Olmstead*

Understanding Charles Seeger, Pioneer in American Musicology   *Edited by Bell Yung and Helen Rees*

Mountains of Music: West Virginia Traditional Music from *Goldenseal*   *Edited by John Lilly*

Alice Tully: An Intimate Portrait   *Albert Fuller*

A Blues Life   *Henry Townsend, as told to Bill Greensmith*

Long Steel Rail: The Railroad in American Folksong (2d ed.)   *Norm Cohen*

The Golden Age of Gospel   *Text by Horace Clarence Boyer; photography by Lloyd Yearwood*

Aaron Copland: The Life and Work of an Uncommon Man   *Howard Pollack*

Louis Moreau Gottschalk   *S. Frederick Starr*
Race, Rock, and Elvis   *Michael T. Bertrand*
Theremin: Ether Music and Espionage   *Albert Glinsky*
Poetry and Violence: The Ballad Tradition of Mexico's Costa Chica
    John H. McDowell
The Bill Monroe Reader   *Edited by Tom Ewing*
Music in Lubavitcher Life   *Ellen Koskoff*
Zarzuela: Spanish Operetta, American Stage   *Janet L. Sturman*
Bluegrass Odyssey: A Documentary in Pictures and Words, 1966–86
    Carl Fleischhauer and Neil V. Rosenberg
That Old-Time Rock & Roll: A Chronicle of an Era, 1954–63   *Richard Aquila*
Labor's Troubadour   *Joe Glazer*
American Opera   *Elise K. Kirk*
Don't Get above Your Raisin': Country Music and the Southern Working Class
    Bill C. Malone
John Alden Carpenter: A Chicago Composer   *Howard Pollack*
Heartbeat of the People: Music and Dance of the Northern Pow-wow   *Tara Browner*
My Lord, What a Morning: An Autobiography   *Marian Anderson*
Marian Anderson: A Singer's Journey   *Allan Keiler*
Charles Ives Remembered: An Oral History   *Vivian Perlis*
Henry Cowell, Bohemian   *Michael Hicks*
Rap Music and Street Consciousness   *Cheryl L. Keyes*
Louis Prima   *Garry Boulard*
Marian McPartland's Jazz World: All in Good Time   *Marian McPartland*
Robert Johnson: Lost and Found   *Barry Lee Pearson and Bill McCulloch*
Bound for America: Three British Composers   *Nicholas Temperley*
Lost Sounds: Blacks and the Birth of the Recording Industry, 1890–1919   *Tim Brooks*
Burn, Baby! BURN! The Autobiography of Magnificent Montague
    Magnificent Montague with Bob Baker
Way Up North in Dixie: A Black Family's Claim to the Confederate Anthem
    Howard L. Sacks and Judith Rose Sacks
The Bluegrass Reader   *Edited by Thomas Goldsmith*
Colin McPhee: Composer in Two Worlds   *Carol J. Oja*
Robert Johnson, Mythmaking, and Contemporary American Culture
    Patricia R. Schroeder
Composing a World: Lou Harrison, Musical Wayfarer   *Leta E. Miller*
    and Fredric Lieberman
Fritz Reiner, Maestro and Martinet   *Kenneth Morgan*
That Toddlin' Town: Chicago's White Dance Bands and Orchestras,
    1900–1950   *Charles A. Sengstock Jr.*
Dewey and Elvis: The Life and Times of a Rock 'n' Roll Deejay   *Louis Cantor*
Come Hither to Go Yonder: Playing Bluegrass with Bill Monroe   *Bob Black*
Chicago Blues: Portraits and Stories   *David Whiteis*
The Incredible Band of John Philip Sousa   *Paul E. Bierley*

"Maximum Clarity" and Other Writings on Music   *Ben Johnston,*
   edited by Bob Gilmore
Staging Tradition: John Lair and Sarah Gertrude Knott   *Michael Ann Williams*
Homegrown Music: Discovering Bluegrass   *Stephanie P. Ledgin*
Tales of a Theatrical Guru   *Danny Newman*
The Music of Bill Monroe   *Neil V. Rosenberg and Charles K. Wolfe*
Pressing On: The Roni Stoneman Story   *Roni Stoneman, as told to Ellen Wright*
Together Let Us Sweetly Live   *Jonathan C. David,*
   with photographs by Richard Holloway
Live Fast, Love Hard: The Faron Young Story   *Diane Diekman*
Air Castle of the South: WSM Radio and the Making of Music City
   Craig P. Havighurst
Traveling Home: Sacred Harp Singing and American Pluralism   *Kiri Miller*
Where Did Our Love Go? The Rise and Fall of the Motown Sound   *Nelson George*
Lonesome Cowgirls and Honky-Tonk Angels: The Women of Barn Dance
   Radio   *Kristine M. McCusker*
California Polyphony: Ethnic Voices, Musical Crossroads   *Mina Yang*
The Never-Ending Revival: Rounder Records and the Folk Alliance   *Michael F. Scully*
Sing It Pretty: A Memoir   *Bess Lomax Hawes*
Working Girl Blues: The Life and Music of Hazel Dickens   *Hazel Dickens*
   and Bill C. Malone
Charles Ives Reconsidered   *Gayle Sherwood Magee*
The Hayloft Gang: The Story of the National Barn Dance   *Edited by Chad Berry*
Country Music Humorists and Comedians   *Loyal Jones*
Record Makers and Breakers: Voices of the Independent Rock 'n' Roll Pioneers
   John Broven
Music of the First Nations: Tradition and Innovation in Native North America
   Edited by Tara Browner
Cafe Society: The Wrong Place for the Right People   *Barney Josephson,*
   with Terry Trilling-Josephson
George Gershwin: An Intimate Portrait   *Walter Rimler*
Life Flows On in Endless Song: Folk Songs and American History   *Robert V. Wells*
I Feel a Song Coming On: The Life of Jimmy McHugh   *Alyn Shipton*
King of the Queen City: The Story of King Records   *Jon Hartley Fox*
Long Lost Blues: Popular Blues in America, 1850–1920   *Peter C. Muir*
Hard Luck Blues: Roots Music Photographs from the Great Depression
   Rich Remsberg
Restless Giant: The Life and Times of Jean Aberbach and Hill and Range Songs
   Bar Biszick-Lockwood
Champagne Charlie and Pretty Jemima: Variety Theater in the Nineteenth
   Century   *Gillian M. Rodger*
Sacred Steel: Inside an African American Steel Guitar Tradition   *Robert L. Stone*
Gone to the Country: The New Lost City Ramblers and the Folk Music Revival
   Ray Allen

The Makers of the Sacred Harp   *David Warren Steel with Richard H. Hulan*
Woody Guthrie, American Radical   *Will Kaufman*
George Szell: A Life of Music   *Michael Charry*
Bean Blossom: The Brown County Jamboree and Bill Monroe's Bluegrass
    Festivals   *Thomas A. Adler*
Crowe on the Banjo: The Music Life of J. D. Crowe   *Marty Godbey*
Twentieth Century Drifter: The Life of Marty Robbins   *Diane Diekman*
Henry Mancini: Reinventing Film Music   *John Caps*
The Beautiful Music All Around Us: Field Recordings and the American
    Experience   *Stephen Wade*
Then Sings My Soul: The Culture of Southern Gospel Music   *Douglas Harrison*
The Accordion in the Americas: Klezmer, Polka, Tango, Zydeco, and More!
    Edited by Helena Simonett
Bluegrass Bluesman: A Memoir   *Josh Graves, edited by Fred Bartenstein*
One Woman in a Hundred: Edna Phillips and the Philadelphia Orchestra
    Mary Sue Welsh
The Great Orchestrator: Arthur Judson and American Arts Management
    James M. Doering
Charles Ives in the Mirror: American Histories of an Iconic Composer   *David C. Paul*
Southern Soul-Blues   *David Whiteis*
Sweet Air: Modernism, Regionalism, and American Popular Song
    Edward P. Comentale
Pretty Good for a Girl: Women in Bluegrass   *Murphy Hicks Henry*
Sweet Dreams: The World of Patsy Cline   *Warren R. Hofstra*
William Sidney Mount and the Creolization of American Culture
    Christopher J. Smith
Bird: The Life and Music of Charlie Parker   *Chuck Haddix*
Making the March King: John Philip Sousa's Washington Years, 1854–1893
    Patrick Warfield
In It for the Long Run   *Jim Rooney*
Pioneers of the Blues Revival   *Steve Cushing*
Roots of the Revival: American and British Folk Music in the 1950s   *Ronald D. Cohen
    and Rachel Clare Donaldson*
Blues All Day Long: The Jimmy Rogers Story   *Wayne Everett Goins*
Yankee Twang: Country and Western Music in New England   *Clifford R. Murphy*
The Music of the Stanley Brothers   *Gary B. Reid*
Hawaiian Music in Motion: Mariners, Missionaries, and Minstrels   *James Revell Carr*
Sounds of the New Deal: The Federal Music Project in the West   *Peter Gough*
The Mormon Tabernacle Choir: A Biography   *Michael Hicks*
The Man That Got Away: The Life and Songs of Harold Arlen   *Walter Rimler*
A City Called Heaven: Chicago and the Birth of Gospel Music   *Robert M. Marovich*
Blues Unlimited: Essential Interviews from the Original Blues Magazine
    Edited by Bill Greensmith, Mike Rowe, and Mark Camarigg

Hoedowns, Reels, and Frolics: Roots and Branches of Southern Appalachian Dance *Phil Jamison*

Fannie Bloomfield-Zeisler: The Life and Times of a Piano Virtuoso *Beth Abelson Macleod*

Cybersonic Arts: Adventures in American New Music *Gordon Mumma, edited with commentary by Michelle Fillion*

The Magic of Beverly Sills *Nancy Guy*

Waiting for Buddy Guy *Alan Harper*

Harry T. Burleigh: From the Spiritual to the Harlem Renaissance *Jean E. Snyder*

Music in the Age of Anxiety: American Music in the Fifties *James Wierzbicki*

Jazzing: New York City's Unseen Scene *Thomas H. Greenland*

A Cole Porter Companion *Edited by Don M. Randel, Matthew Shaftel, and Susan Forscher Weiss*

Foggy Mountain Troubadour: The Life and Music of Curly Seckler *Penny Parsons*

Blue Rhythm Fantasy: Big Band Jazz Arranging in the Swing Era *John Wriggle*

Bill Clifton: America's Bluegrass Ambassador to the World *Bill C. Malone*

Chinatown Opera Theater in North America *Nancy Yunhwa Rao*

The Elocutionists: Women, Music, and the Spoken Word *Marian Wilson Kimber*

May Irwin: Singing, Shouting, and the Shadow of Minstrelsy *Sharon Ammen*

Peggy Seeger: A Life of Music, Love, and Politics *Jean R. Freedman*

Charles Ives's *Concord*: Essays after a Sonata *Kyle Gann*

Don't Give Your Heart to a Rambler: My Life with Jimmy Martin, the King of Bluegrass *Barbara Martin Stephens*

Libby Larsen: Composing an American Life *Denise Von Glahn*

George Szell's Reign: Behind the Scenes with the Cleveland Orchestra *Marcia Hansen Kraus*

Just One of the Boys: Female-to-Male Cross-Dressing on the American Variety Stage *Gillian M. Rodger*

Spirituals and the Birth of a Black Entertainment Industry *Sandra Jean Graham*

Right to the Juke Joint: A Personal History of American Music *Patrick B. Mullen*

Bluegrass Generation: A Memoir *Neil V. Rosenberg*

Pioneers of the Blues Revival, Expanded Second Edition *Steve Cushing*

Banjo Roots and Branches *Edited by Robert Winans*

Bill Monroe: The Life and Music of the Blue Grass Man *Tom Ewing*

Dixie Dewdrop: The Uncle Dave Macon Story *Michael D. Doubler*

Los Romeros: Royal Family of the Spanish Guitar *Walter Aaron Clark*

Transforming Women's Education: Liberal Arts and Music in Female Seminaries *Jewel A. Smith*

Rethinking American Music *Edited by Tara Browner and Thomas L. Riis*

Leonard Bernstein and the Language of Jazz *Katherine Baber*

Dancing Revolution: Bodies, Space, and Sound in American Cultural History *Christopher J. Smith*

Peggy Glanville-Hicks: Composer and Critic *Suzanne Robinson*

Mormons, Musical Theater, and Belonging in America *Jake Johnson*

The University of Illinois Press
is a founding member of the
Association of American University Presses.

Composed in 10.5/13 Minion Pro
with Optima LT Std display
by Lisa Connery
at the University of Illinois Press
Cover designed by Jim Proefrock
Cover illustration: ©iStock.com/luckyraccoon

University of Illinois Press
1325 South Oak Street
Champaign, IL 61820-6903
www.press.uillinois.edu